EGOISTS

A BOOK OF SUPERMEN

STENDHAL, BAUDELAIRE, FLAUBERT, ANATOLE FRANCE,
HUYSMANS, BARRÈS, NIETZSCHE, BLAKE, IBSEN,
STIRNER, AND ERNEST HELLO

BY

JAMES HUNEKER

WITH PORTRAIT OF STENDHAL; UNPUBLISHED LETTER OF
FLAUBERT; AND ORIGINAL PROOF PAGE OF MADAME BOVARY

Ormond Beach, Fl.

2017

NEW YORK
CHARLES SCRIBNER'S SONS
1909

Foreword

This new edition of Huneker's book that saw his first appearance in 1909, is wholly devoted to those modern poets, philosophers and prose masters whose writings embody the individualistic idea as opposed to altruistic and socialistic sentiments. Amply discussed are Stendhal, whose cult, recently revived on the Continent, is steadily growing; Maurice Barres, French Academician; Anatole France, blithe pagan and delicious ironist; Max Stimer, the forerunner of Nietzsche; The mystics, Ernest Hello new to American readers and William Blake. Much new historical material can be found in the studies of Charles Baudelaire and Gustave Flaubert. The hitherto unpublished letter of the novelist, along with an original page proof of "Madame Bovary," corrected by his own hand, will prove of interest to his admirers. That brilliant virtuoso of the French language, J. K. Huysmans, forms the subject of a chapter, while certain phases of Nietzsche, including his famous published biography, "Ecce Homo", and Ibsen dramas, are also subjects of discussion.

Altogether the book represents the most mature critical and analytical thought of the author applied to some of the most interesting literary characters in the modern Europe of 1909.
Ormond Beach,Fl. August 2017

F. Guzzardi

TO

DR. GEORG BRANDES

———

" Leb' ich, wenn andere leben ? "—GOETHE

CONTENTS

I

A SENTIMENTAL EDUCATION

HENRY BEYLE-STENDHAL

I

THE fanciful notion that psychical delicacy is accompanied by a corresponding physical exterior should have received a death-blow in the presence of Henry Beyle, better known as Stendhal. Chopin, Shelley, Byron and Cardinal Newman did not in personal appearance contradict their verse prose and music; but Stendhal, possessing an exquisite sensibility, was, as Hector Berlioz cruelly wrote in his Memoirs: "A little pot-bellied man with a spiteful smile, who tried to look grave." Sainte-Beuve is more explicit. "Physically his figure, though not short, soon grew thick-set and heavy, his neck short and full-blooded. His fleshy face was framed in dark curly hair and whiskers, which before his death were assisted by art. His forehead was fine: the nose turned up, and somewhat Calmuck in shape. His lower lip, which projected a little, betrayed his tendency to scoff. His eyes were rather small but very bright, deeply set in their cavities, and pleasing when he smiled. His hands, of which he was proud, were small and daintily shaped. In the last years of his life he grew heavy and apoplectic. But he always took great pains to conceal the symptoms of physical decay even from his own friends."

Henri Monnier, who caricatured him, apparently in a gross manner, denied that he had departed far from his model. Some one said that Stendhal looked like an apothecary — Homais, presumably, or M. Prudhomme. His maternal grandfather, Doctor Gagnon, assured him when a youth that he was ugly, but he consolingly added that no one would reproach him for his ugliness. The piercing and brilliant eye that like a mountain lake could be both still and stormy, his eloquent and ironical mouth, pugnacious bearing, Celtic profile, big shoulders, and well-modelled leg made an ensemble, if not alluring, at least striking. No man with a face capable of a hundred shades of expression can be ugly. Furthermore, Stendhal was a charming *causeur*, bold, copious, witty. With his conversation, he drolly remarked, he paid his way into society. And this demigod or monster, as he was alternately named by his admirers and enemies, could be the most impassioned of lovers. His life long he was in love; Prosper Mérimée declares he never encountered such furious devotion to love. It was his master passion. Not Napoleon, not his personal ambitions, not even Italy, were such factors in Stendhal's life as his attachments. His career was a sentimental education. This ugly man with

2

the undistinguished features was a haughty cav-
alier, an intellectual Don Juan, a tender, sigh-
ing swain, a sensualist, and ever lyric where the
feminine was concerned. But once seated, pen
in hand, the wise, worldly cynic was again master.
"My head is a magic-lantern," he said. And
his literary style is on the surface as unattractive
as were the features of the man; the inner ear for
the rhythms and sonorities of prose was missing.
That is the first paradox in the Beyle-Stendhal
case.

Few writers in the nineteenth century were
more neglected; yet, what a chain of great critics
his work begot. Commencing with Goethe in
1818, who, after reading Rome, Naples, and
Florence, wrote that the Frenchman attracted
and repulsed him, interested and annoyed him,
but it was impossible to separate himself from the
book until its last page. What makes the opinion
remarkable is that Goethe calmly noted Stendhal's plagiarism of his own Italian Journey.
About 1831 Goethe was given Le Rouge et le
Noir and told Eckermann of its worth in warm
terms. After Goethe another world-hero praised
Stendhal's La Chartreuse de Parme: Balzac literally exploded a bouquet of pyrotechnics, calling the novel a masterpiece of observation, and
extolling the Waterloo picture. Sainte-Beuve was
more cautious. He dubbed Stendhal a "romantic hussar," and said that he was devoid of
invention; a literary Uhlan, for men of letters,
not for the public. Shortly after his sudden

3

death, M. Bussière wrote in the *Revue des Deux Mondes* of Stendhal's "clandestine celebrity." Taine's trumpet-call in 1857 proclaimed him as the great psychologue of his century. And later, in his English Literature, Taine wrote: "His talents and ideas were premature, his admirable divinations not understood. Under the exterior of a conversationalist and a man of the world Stendhal explained the most esoteric mechanisms — a scientist who noted, decomposed, deduced; he first marked the fundamental causes of nationality, climate, temperament; he was the naturalist who classified and weighed forces and taught us to open our eyes." Taine was deeply influenced by Stendhal; read carefully his Italian Pilgrimage, and afterward Thomas Graindorge. He so persistently preached Stendhalism — *beylisme*, as its author preferred to term his vagrant philosophy — that Sainte-Beuve reproved him. Melchior de Vogüé said that Stendhal's heart had been fabricated under the Directory and from the same wood as Barras and Talleyrand. Brunetière saw in him the perfect expression of romantic and anti-social individualism. Caro spoke of his "serious blague," while Victor Hugo found him "somniferous." But Mérimée, though openly disavowing discipleship, acknowledged privately the abiding impression made upon him by the companionship of Beyle. Much of Mérimée is Stendhal better composed, better written.

About 1880 Zola, searching a literary pedigree for his newly-born Naturalism, pitched upon

4

Stendhal to head the movement. The first Romantic — he employed the term Romanticism before the rest — the first literary Impressionist, the initiator of Individualism, Stendhal forged many formulas, was a matrix of *genres*, literary and psychologic. Paul Bourget's Essays in Contemporary Psychology definitely placed Beyle in the niche he now occupies. This was in 1883. Since then the swelling chorus headed by Tolstoy, Georg Brandes, and the amiable fanatics who exhumed at Grenoble his posthumous work, have given to the study of Stendhal fresh life. We see how much Nietzsche owed to Stendhal; see in Dostoïevsky's Raskolnilikow — Crime and Punishment — a Russian Julien Sorel; note that Bourget, from Le Disciple to Sensations d'Italie, is compounded of his forerunner, the dilettante and cosmopolitan who wrote Promenades dans Rome and Lamiel. What would Maurice Barrès and his "culte du Moi" have been without Stendhal — who employed before him the famous phrase "deracination"? Amiel, sick-willed thinker, did not alone invent: "A landscape is a state of soul"; Stendhal had spoken of a landscape not alone sufficing; it needs a moral or historic interest. Before Schopenhauer he described Beauty as a promise of happiness; and he invented the romance of the petty European Principality. Meredith followed him, as Robert Louis Stevenson in his Prince Otto patterned after Meredith. The painter-novelist Fromentin mellowed Stendhal's procedure; and dare we con-

5

ceive of Meredith or Henry James composing
their work without having had a complete cog-
nizance of Beyle-Stendhal? The Egoist is *beylisme*
of a superior artistry; while in America Henry B.
Fuller shows sympathy for Beyle in his Chevalier
Pensieri-Vani and its sequel. Surely the Prorege
of Arcopia had read the Chartreuse. And with
Edith Wharton the Stendhal touch is not absent.
In England, after the dull essay by Hayward
(prefixed to E. P. Robbin's excellent translation
of Chartreuse), Maurice Hewlett contributed an
eloquent introduction to a new edition of the
Chartreuse and calls him "a man cloaked in ice
and fire." Anna Hampton Brewster was possibly
the first American essayist to introduce to us Stendhal in her St. Martin's Summer. Saintsbury,
Dowden, Benjamin Wells, Count Lützow have
since written of him; and in Germany the Stendhal cult is growing, thanks to Arthur Schurig,
L. Spach, and Friedrick von Oppeln-Bronikowski.

It has been mistaken criticism to range Beyle
as only a "literary" man. He despised the profession of literature, remarking that he wrote as
one smokes a cigar. His diaries and letters, the
testimony of his biographer, Colomb, and his
friend Mérimée, betray this pose — a greater
poser and *mystificateur* it would be difficult to
find. He laboured like a slave over his material,
and if he affected to take the Civil Code as his
model of style it nettled him, nevertheless, when
anyone decried his prose. His friend Jacque-
mont spoke of his detestable style of a grocer;

6

HENRY BEYLE-STENDHAL

Balzac called him to account for his carelessness. Flattered, astounded, as was Stendhal by the panegyric of Balzac, his letter of thanks shows that the reproof cut deeply. He abused Chateaubriand, Madame de Staël, and George Sand for their highly coloured imagery and flowing manner. He even jeered at Balzac, saying that if he—Beyle —had written "It snows in my heart," or some such romantic figure, Balzac would then have praised his style.

Thanks to the labours of Casimir Stryienski and his colleagues, we may study the different drafts Stendhal made of his novels. He seldom improved by recasting. The truth is that his dry, naked method of narration, despite its clumsiness, despite the absence of plan, is excellently adapted to the expression of his ideas. He is a psychologue. He deals with soul-stuff. An eighteenth-century man in his general ideas and feelings, he followed the seventeenth century and Montesquieu; he derives from Montaigne and Chamfort, and his philosophy is coloured by a study of Condillac, Hobbes, Helvétius, Cabanis, Destutt Tracy, and Machiavelli. He is a descendant of Diderot and the Encyclopædists, a *philosophe* of the *salons*, a *petit maître*, a materialist for whom nothing exists but his ideas and sensations. A French epicurean, his pendulum swings between love and war—the adoration of energy and the adoration of pleasure. What complicates his problem is the mixture of warrior and psychologist. That the man who fol-

7

lowed Napoleon through several of his campaigns, serving successfully as a practical commissary and fighter, should have been an adorer of women, was less strange than that he should have proved to be the possessor of such vibrating sensibility. Jules Lemaitre sees him as "a grand man of action paralysed little by little because of his incomparable analysis." Yet he never betrayed unreadiness when confronted by peril. He read Voltaire and Plato during the burning of Moscow — which he described as a beautiful spectacle — and he never failed to present himself before his kinsman and patron, Marshal Daru, with a clean-shaved face, even when the Grand Army was a mass of stragglers.

"You are a man of heart," said Daru, Frenchman in that phrase. When Napoleon demanded five millions of francs from a German province, Stendhal — who adopted this pen-name from the archæologist Winckelmann's birthplace, a Prussian town — raised seven millions and was in consequence execrated by the people. Napoleon asked on receiving the money the name of the agent, adding, *"c'est bien!"* We are constrained to believe Mérimée's assertion that Stendhal was the soul of honour, and incapable of baseness, after this proof. At a time when plunder was the order of the day's doings, the poor young aide-de-camp could have pocketed with ease at least a million of the excess tax. He did not do this, nor did he, in his letters or memoirs, betray any remorse for his honesty.

8

HENRY BEYLE-STENDHAL

Sainte-Beuve said that Beyle was the dupe of his fear of being duped. This was confirmed by Mérimée in the concise little study prefixed to the Correspondence. It is doubtful if these two men were drawn to each other save by a certain contemptuous way of viewing mankind. Stendhal was the more sentimental of the pair; he frequently reproached Mérimée for his cold heart. He had also a greater sense of humour. That each distrusted the other is not to be denied. Augustin Filon, in his *brochure* on Mérimée, said that "the influence exercised by Stendhal on Mérimée during the decisive years in which his literary eclecticism was formed, was considerable, even more than Mérimée himself was aware." But the author of Carmen was a much finer artist. The Danish critic, Georg Brandes, has described Beyle's relation to Balzac as "that of the reflective to the observant mind; of the thinker in art to the seer. We see into the hearts of Balzac's characters, into the 'dark-red mill of passion' which is the motive force of their action; Beyle's characters receive their impulse from the head, the 'open light-and-sound chamber'; the reason being that Beyle was a logician, and Balzac a man of an effusively rich animal nature. Beyle stands to Victor Hugo in much the same position as Leonardo da Vinci to Michaelangelo. Hugo's plastic imagination creates a supernaturally colossal and muscular humanity fixed in an eternal attitude of struggle and suffering; Beyle's mysterious, complicated, refined intellect produces a

9

small series of male and female portraits, which exercise an almost magic fascination on us with their far-away, enigmatic expressions, and their sweet, wicked smile. Beyle is the metaphysician among the French authors of his day, as Leonardo was the metaphysician among the great painters of the Renaissance."

According to Bourget, Beyle's advent into letters marked the "tragic dawn of pessimism." But is it precise to call him a pessimist? He was of too vigorous a temper, too healthy in body, to be classed with the decadents. His was the soul of a sixteenth-century Italian, one who had read and practised the cheerful scepticism of Montaigne. As he served bravely when a soldier, so, stout and subtle in after life, he waged war with the blue devils — his chief foe. Disease weakened his physique, weakened his mentality, yet he fought life to its dull end. He was pursued by the secret police, and this led him to all sorts of comical disguises and pseudonyms. And to the last he experienced a childish delight in the invention of odd names for himself.

Felix Fénéon, in speaking of Arthur Rimbaud, asserted that his work was, perhaps, "outside of literature." This, with some modification, may be said of Beyle. His stories are always interesting; they may ramble and halt, digress and wander into strange places; but the psychologic vision of the writer never weakens. His chief concern is the mind or soul of his characters. He hitches his kite to earth, yet there is the paper air-ship float-

10

ing above you, lending a touch of the ideal to his most matter-of-fact tales. He uses both the microscope and scalpel. He writes, as has been too often said, indifferently; his formal sense is nearly *nil;* much of his art criticism mere gossip; he has little feeling for colour; yet he describes a soul and its manifold movements in precise terms, and while he is at furthest remove from symbolism, he often has an irritating spiritual suggestiveness. The analogue here to plastic art — he, the least plastic of writers — is unescapable. Stendhal, whatever else he may be, is an incomparable etcher of character. His acid phrases "bite" his arbitrary lines deeply; the sharp contrasts of black and white enable him to portray, without the fiery-hued rhetoric of either Chateaubriand or Hugo, the finest split shades of thought and emotion. Never colour, only *nuance* — and the slash and sweep of a drastic imagination.

He was an inveterate illusionist in all that concerned himself; even with himself he was not always sincere — and he usually wrote of himself. His many books are a masquerade behind which one discerns the posture of the mocker, the sensibility of a reversed idealist, and the spirit of a bitter analyst. This sensibility must not be confounded with the *sensibilité* of a Maurice de Guérin. Rather it is the morbid sensitiveness of a Swift combined with an unusual receptivity to sentimental and artistic impressions. Professor Walter Raleigh thus describes the sensibility of those times: "The sensibility that came into vogue during the eighteenth century was of a finer grain than its modern counterpart. It studied delicacy, and sought a cultivated enjoyment in evanescent shades of feeling, and the fantasies of unsubstantial grief." Vanity ruled in Stendhal. Who shall say how much his unyielding spirit suffered because of his poverty, his enormous ambitions? His motto might have been: Blessed are the proud of spirit, for they shall inherit the Kingdom of Earth. He wrote in 1819: "I have had three passions in my life. Ambition — 1800–1811; love for a woman who deceived me, 1811–1818; and in 1818 a new passion." But then he was ever on the verge of a new passion, ever deceived — at least he believed himself to be — and he, the fearless theoretician of passion, often was, he has admitted, in practice the timid amateur. He planned the attack upon a woman's heart as a general plans the taking of an enemy's citadel. He wrote L'Amour for himself. He defined the rules of the game, but shivered when he saw the battle-field. Magnificent he was in precept, though not always in action. He was for this reason never *blasé*, despite continual grumblings over his *ennui*. In his later years at Cività Vecchia he yearned for companionship like a girl, and, a despiser of Paris and the Parisians, he suffered from the nostalgia of the boulevard. He adored Milan and the Milanese, yet Italy finally proved too much for his nerves; *J'ai tant vu le soleil*, he confessed. Contradictory and

12

fantastic, he hated all authority. Mérimée puts down to the account of the sour old *abbé* Raillane, who taught him, the distaste he entertained for the Church of Rome. Yet he enjoyed its æsthetic side. He was its admirer his life long, notwithstanding his gibes and irreligious jests, just as he was a Frenchman by reason of his capacity for reaction under depressing circumstances. But how account for his monstrous hatred for his father? The elder Beyle was penurious and as hard as flint. He nearly starved his son, for whom he had no affection. Henry could not see him salute his mother without loathing him. She read Dante in the original, and her son assured himself that there was Italian blood on her side of the house. The youth's hatred, too, of his aunt Séraphie almost became a mania. It has possibly enriched fiction by the portrait of Gina of the resilient temperament, the delicious Duchess of Sanseverina. All that she is, his aunt Séraphie was not, and with characteristic perversity he makes her enamoured of her nephew Fabrice del Dongo. Did he not say that parents are our first enemies when we enter the world?

His criticisms of music and painting are chiefly interesting for what they tell us of his temperament. He called himself "observer of the human heart," and was taken by a cautious listener for a police spy. He seldom signed the same name twice to his letters. He delighted to boast of various avocations; little wonder the Milanese police drove him out of the city. He said that to

13

be a good philosopher one must be *sec*, and without illusions. Perspicacious, romantic, delicate in his attitude toward women, he could be rough, violent, and suspicious. He scandalised George Sand, delighted Alfred de Musset; Madame Lamartine refused to receive him in her drawing-room at Rome. His intercourse with Byron was pleasant. He disliked Walter Scott and called him a hypocrite — possibly because there is no freedom in his love descriptions. Lord Byron in a long letter expostulated with Stendhal, defending his good friend, Scott; but Stendhal never quite believed in the poet's sincerity — indeed, suspecting himself, he suspected other men's motives. He had stage-fright when he first met Byron — whom he worshipped. A tremulous soul his, in a rude envelope. At Venice he might have made the acquaintance of young Arthur Schopenhauer and Leopardi, but he was too much interested in the place to care for new faces.

He said that without passion there is neither virtue nor vice. (Taine made a variation on this theme.) A dagger-thrust is a dignified gesture when prompted by passion. After the Napoleonic disaster, Stendhal had lost all his hopes of preferment; he kept his temper admirably, though occasionally calling his old chief bad names. It was a period of the flat, stale, platitudinous, and bourgeois. "In the nineteenth century one must be either a monster or a sheep," wrote Beyle to Byron. A patriot is either a dolt or a rogue! My country is where there are most people like me — Cosmopolis! The only excuse for God is that he does not exist! Verse was invented to aid the memory! A volume of maxims, witty and immoral, might be gathered from the writings of Stendhal that would equal Rivarol and Rochefoucauld. "I require three or four cubic feet of new ideas per day, as a steamboat requires coal," he told Romain Colomb. What energy, what lassitude this man possessed! He spoke English — though he wrote it imperfectly — and Italian; the latter excellently because of his long residence in Italy.

Nietzsche, in Beyond Good and Evil, described Stendhal as "that remarkable man who, with a Napoleonic *tempo*, traversed *his* Europe, in fact several centuries of the European soul, as a surveyor and discoverer thereof. It has required two generations to overtake him one way or other; to divine long afterward some of the riddles that perplexed and enraptured him — this strange Epicurean and man of interrogation, the last great psychologist of France." He also spoke of him as "Stendhal, who has, perhaps, had the most profound eyes and ears of any Frenchman of this century."

Stendhal said that Shakespeare knew the human heart better than Racine; yet despite his English preferences, Stendhal is a psychologist of the *Racinien* school. When an English company of players went to Paris in 1822, Stendhal defended them by pen and in person. He was chagrined that his fellow-countrymen should hiss

15

Othello or The School for Scandal. He despised *chauvinisme*, he the ideal globe-trotter. And he was contradictory enough to have understood Tennyson's "That man's the best cosmopolite who loves his native country best." He scornfully remarked that in 1819 Parisian literary logic could be summed up thus: "This man does not agree with me, therefore he is a fool; he criticises my book, he is my enemy; therefore a thief, an assassin, a brigand, and forger." Narrow-mindedness must never be imputed to Stendhal. Nor was he a modest man — modesty that virtue of the mediocre.

How much Tolstoy thought of the Frenchman may be found in his declaration that all he knew about war he learned first from Stendhal. "I will speak of him only as the author of the Chartreuse de Parme and Le Rouge et le Noir. These are two great, inimitable works of art. I am indebted for much to Stendhal. He taught me to understand war. Read once more in the Chartreuse de Parme his account of the battle of Waterloo. Who before him had so described war — that is, as it is in reality?" In 1854 they said Balzac and Hugo; in 1886, Balzac and Stendhal. Some day it may be Stendhal and Tolstoy. The Russian with his slow, patient amassing of little facts but follows Stendhal's chaplet of anecdotes. The latter said that the novel should be a mirror that moves along the highway; a novel, he writes elsewhere, is like a bow — the violin which gives out the sound is the soul of the reader. And Goncourt assimilated this method with surpri-

16

sing results. Stendhal first etched the soul of the new Superman, the exalted young man and woman — Julien Sorel and Matilde de la Môle. They are both immoralists. Exceptional souls, in real life they might have seen the inside of a prison. Stendhal is the original of the one; the other is the source of latter-day feminine souls in revolt, the souls of Ibsen and Strindberg. Laclos's Les Liaisons Dangereuses and Marivaux he has re-moulded —Valmont is a prototype of Julien Sorel.

J. J. Weiss has said that profound immorality is probably an attribute common to all great observers of human nature. It would require a devil's advocate of unusual acuity to prove Stendhal a moral man or writer. His philosophy is materialistic. He wrote for the "happy few" and longed for a hundred readers, and wished his readers to be those amiable, unhappy souls who are neither moral nor hypocritical. His egoism brought him no surcease from boredom. His diaries and letters and memoirs, so rich in general ideas, are valuable for the student of human nature. The publication of his correspondence was a revelation — a very sincere, human Stendhal came into view. His cosmopolitanism is unaffected; his chapters are mosaics of facts and sensations; his manner of narrative is, as Bourget says, a method of discovery as well as of exposition. His heroes and heroines delve into their motives, note their ideas and sensations. With a few exceptions, modern romancers, novelists, psychologists of fiction seem shallow after Stendhal. Taine

17

confesses to reading Le Rouge et le Noir between
thirty and forty times. Stendhal disliked America;
to him all things democratic were abhorrent.
He loathed the mass, upheld the class; an individualist and aristocrat like Ibsen, he would not
recognize the doctrine of equality. The French
Revolution was useful only because it evolved
a strong man — Napoleon. America, being democratic, would therefore never produce art, tragedy,
music, or romantic love.

It is the fate of some men to exist only as a source
of inspiration for their fellow-artists. Shelley is
the poet's poet, Meredith the novelist's novelist,
and Stendhal a storehouse for psychologues.
His virile spirit, in these times of vapid socialistic
theories, is a sparkling and sinister pool wherein
all may dip and be refreshed — perhaps poisoned.
He is not orthodox as thinker or artist; but it is
a truism that the wicked of a century ago may be
the saints of to-morrow. To read him is to in-
crease one's wisdom; he is dangerous only to fools.
Like Schopenhauer and Ibsen, he did not flatter
his public; now he has his own public. And
nothing· would have amused this charming and
cynical man more than the knowledge of his canon-
isation in the church of world literature. He
gayly predicted that he would be understood
about 1880–1900; but his impertinent shadow
projects far into the twentieth century. Will he
be read in 1935? he has asked. Why not? A
monument is to be erected to him in Paris.
Rodin has designed the medallion portrait.

18

II

The labours, during the past twenty years, of
Casimir Stryienski, François de Nion, L. Bélugon,
Arthur Chuquet, Henry Cordier, Pierre Brun,
Ricciotto Canudo, Octave Uzanne, Hugues Rebell
— to quote the names of a few devoted Sten-
dhalians — have enabled us to decipher Stendhal's troubled life. M. Stryienski unearthed
at Grenoble a mass of manuscript, journals, tales,
half-finished novels, and they have been published.
Was there any reason to doubt the existence of a
Stendhal Club after the appearance of those two
interesting books, Soirées du Stendhal Club, by
Stryienski? The compact little study in the series,
Les Grands Ecrivains Français, by Edouard Rod,
and Colomb's biographical notice at the head of
Armance, and Stryienski's Etude Biographique
are the principal references for Stendhal students.
And this, too, despite the evident lack of sympathy
in the case of M. Rod. It is a minute, painstaking *étude*, containing much fair criticism;
fervent Stendhalians need to be reminded of their
master's defects and of the danger of self-dupery.
If Stendhal were alive, he would be the first to
mock at his disciples' enthusiasm — the enthusiasm of the *parvenu*, as he puts it. (He ill concealed his own in the presence of pictorial masterpieces or the ballets of Viganò.) Rod, after admitting the wide influence of Stendhal upon the
generations that followed him, patronisingly

19

concludes by a quotation: "Les petits livres ont leurs destinées." What, then, does he call great, if Le Rouge et le Noir and La Chartreuse de Parme are "little books"?

Marie-Henry Beyle was born at Grenoble, Dauphiny, January 23, 1783. He died at Paris, March 23, 1842, stricken on the Rue Neuve des Capucines by apoplexy. Colomb had his dying friend carried to his lodgings. He was buried in Montmartre Cemetery, followed there by Mérimée, Colomb, and one other. Upon his monument is an epitaph composed a short time before he died. It is in Italian and reads: Arrigo Beyle, Milanese. *Scrisse, Amò, Visse.* Ann. 59. M.2. Mori 2. 23 Marzo. MDCCCXLII. (Harry Beyle, Milanese. Wrote, Loved, Lived. 59 years and 2 months. He died at 2 A.M. on the 23rd of March, 1842.) This bit of mystification was quite in line with Beyle's career. As he was baptised the English Henry, he preferred to be known in death as the Milanese Harry. Pierre Brun says that there was a transposition in the order of *Scrisse, Amò, Visse;* it should read the reverse. The sculptor David d'Angers made a medallion of the writer in 1825. It is reproduced in the Rod monograph, and his son designed another for the tomb. This singular epitaph of a singular man did not escape the eyes of his enemies. Charles Monselet called him a renegade to his family and country; which is uncritical tomfoolery. Stendhal was a citizen of the world — and to the last a Frenchman. And

20

not one of his cavilling contemporaries risked his life with such unconcern as did this same Beyle in the Napoleonic campaigns. Mérimée has drawn for us the best portrait of Stendhal, Colomb, his earliest companion, wrote the most gossipy life. Stryienski, however, has demonstrated that Colomb attenuated, even erased many expressions of Stendhal's, and that he also attempted to portray his hero in fairer colours. But deep-dyed Stendhalians will not have their master transformed into a tame cat of the Parisian salons. His wickedness is his chief attraction, they think. An oft-quoted saying of Stendhal's has been, Stryienski shows, tampered with: "A party of eight or ten agreeable persons," said Stendhal, "where the conversation is gay and anecdotic, and where weak punch is handed around at half past twelve, is the place where I enjoy myself the most. There, in my element, I infinitely prefer hearing others talk to talking myself. I readily sink back into the silence of happiness; and if I talk, it is only to pay my ticket of admission." What Stendhal wrote was this: "Un salon de huit ou dix personnes dont toutes les femmes ont eu les amants," etc. The touch is unmistakable.

Henry was educated at the Ecole Centrale of Grenoble. When he was ten years of age, Louis XVI was executed, and the precocious boy, to annoy his father, displayed undisguised glee at the news. He served the mass, an altar-boy at the Convent of the Propagation, and revealed unpleasant traits of character. His father he called by a shocking name, but the death of his mother, when he was seven, he never forgot. He loved her in true Stendhalian style. His maiden aunt Séraphie ruled the house of the elder Beyle, and Henry's two sisters, Pauline — the favourite of her brother — and Zenaïde, most tyrannically. His young existence was a cruel battle with his elders, excepting his worthy grandfather, Doctor Gagnon, an *esprit fort* of the approved eighteenth-century variety. On his book-shelves Henry found Voltaire, Rousseau, d'Holbach, and eagerly absorbed them. A great-aunt taught him that the pride of the Spaniard was the best quality of a man. When he heard of his aunt's death, he threw himself on his knees and passionately thanked the God in whom he had never believed. His father, Chérubin-Joseph Beyle, was chevalier of the Legion of Honor and his family of old though not noble stock. Its sympathies were aristocratic, royalist, while Henry — certainly not a radical in politics — loved to annoy his father by his Jacobin opinions. He in turn was ridiculed by the Dauphinois when he called himself *de* Stendhal. Not a lovable boy, certainly, and, it is said, scarcely a moral one. At school they nicknamed him "la Tour ambulante," because of his thick-set figure. He preferred mathematics to all other studies, as he contemplated entering l'École Polytechnique. November 10, 1799, found him in Paris with letters for his cousins Daru. They proved friendly. He was after-

22

ward, through the influence of Pierre Daru, minister of war, made lieutenant of cavalry, commissary and auditor of the Council of State. He served in the Italian campaign, following Napoleon through the Saint Bernard pass two days later. Aide-de-camp of General Michaud, he displayed *sang-froid* under fire. He was present at Jena and Wagram, and asked, during a day of fierce fighting, "Is that all?" War and love only provoked from this nonchalant person the same question. He was always disappointed by reality; and, as Rod adds, "Is that all?" might be the *leit motiv* of his life. Forced by sickness to retire to Vienna, he was at the top-notch of his life in Paris and Milan, 1810–1812. He left a brilliant position to rejoin the Emperor in Russia. In 1830 he was nominated consul at Trieste; but Metternich objected because of Stendhal's reputation as a political intrigant in Milan, ten years earlier— a reputation he never deserved. He was sent to Cività Vecchia, where he led a dull existence, punctuated by trips to Rome, and, at long intervals, to Paris. From 1814 to 1820 he lived in Milan, and in love, a friend of Manzoni, Silvio Pellico, Monti. The police drove him back to Paris, and he says it was the deadliest blow to his happiness. For a decade he remained here, leading the life of a man around town, a sublimated gossip, dilettante, surface idler; withal, a hard worker. A sybarite on an inadequate income, he was ever the man of action. Embroiled in feminine intrigues, sanguine, clairvoyant, and

23

a sentimentalist, he seldom contemplated marriage. Once, at Città Vecchia, a young woman of bourgeois extraction tempted him by her large *dot;* but inquiries made at Grenoble killed his chances. Indeed, he was not the stuff from which the ideal husband is moulded. He did not entertain a high opinion of matrimony. He said that the Germans had a mania for marriage, an institution which is servitude for men. On a trip down the Rhone, in 1833, he met George Sand and Alfred de Musset going to Italy — to that Venice which was the poet's Waterloo and Pagello's victory. Stendhal behaved so madly, so boisterously, and uttered such paradoxes that he offended Madame Dudevant-Sand, who openly expressed her distaste for him, though admiring his brilliancy. De Musset had a pretty talent for sketching and drew Stendhal dancing at the inn before a servant. It is full of verve. He also wrote some verse about the French consul at Città Vecchia:

> "Où Stendhal, cet esprit charmant,
> Remplissait si dévotement
> Sa sinécure."

Sinecure it was, though *ennui* ruled; but he had his memories, and Rome was not far away. In 1832, while at San Pietro in Montorio, he bethought himself of his age. Fifty years would soon arrive. He determined to write his memoirs. And we have the Vie de Henri Brulard, Souvenirs d'Egotisme, and the Journal (1801–1814). In

24

their numerous pages—for he was an indefatigable graphomaniac — may be found the thousand and one experiences in love, war, diplomacy that made up his life. His boasted impassibility, like Flaubert's, does not survive the test of these letters and intimate confessions. Mérimée, too, wrote to Jenny Dacquin without his accustomed mask. Stendhal is the most personal of writers; each novel is Henry Beyle in various situations, making various and familiar gestures.

His presence was welcome in a dozen salons of Paris. He preferred, however, a box at la Scala, listening to Rossini or watching a Viganò ballet, near his beloved Angela. But after seven years Milan was closed to him, and as he was known in a restricted circle at Paris as a writer of power, originality, and as an authority on music and painting, he returned there in 1821. He frequented the salon of Destutt de Tracy, whose ideology and philosophic writings he admired. There he saw General Lafayette and wrote maliciously of this hero, who, though seventy-five, was in love with a Portuguese girl of nineteen. The same desire to startle that animated Baudelaire kept Beyle in hot water. He was a visitor at the home of Madame Cabanis, of M. Cuvier, of Madame Ancelot, Baron Gérard, and Castellane, and on Sundays, at the salon of Etienne Délacluze, the art critic of the *Débats*, and a daily visitor at Madame Pasta's. He disliked, in his emphatic style, Victor Cousin, Thiers, and his host Délacluze. For Beyle to dislike a man was to

25

announce the fact to the four winds of heaven, and he usually did so with a brace of bon-mots that set all Paris laughing. Naturally, his enemies retaliated. Some disagreeable things were said of him, though none quite so sharp as the remark made by a certain Madame Céline: "Ah! I see M. Beyle is wearing a new coat. Madame Pasta must have had a benefit." This witticism was believed, because of the long friendship between the Italian *cantatrice* and the young Frenchman. He occupied a small apartment in the same building, though it is said the attachment was platonic.

In 1800 he met, at Milan, Signora Angela Pietragrua. He loved her. Eleven years later, when he returned to Italy, this love was revived. He burst into tears when he saw her again. *Quello è il chinese!* explained the massive Angela to her father. Even that lovetap did not disconcert the furnace-like affection of Henry. This Angela made him miserable by her coquetries. The feminine characters in his novels and tales are drawn from life. His essay on Love is a *centaine* of experiences crystallised into maxims and epigrams. This man of too expansive heart, who confessed to trepidation in the presence of a woman he loved, displayed surprising delicacy. Where he could not respect, he could not love. His sensibility was easily hurt; he abhorred the absence of taste. Love was for him a mixture of moonshine, *esprit*, and physical beauty. A very human man, Henry Beyle, though he never viewed woman exactly from the same

26

angle as did Dante; or, perhaps, his many Beatrices proved geese.

Stryienski relates that, on their return from Italy in 1860, Napoleon III and the Empress Eugénie visited Grenoble and, in the municipal library, saw a portrait of Stendhal. "But that is M. Beyle, is it not?" cried the Empress. "How comes his portrait here?" "He was born at Grenoble," responded Gariel, the librarian. She remembered him, this amusing mature friend of her girlhood. The daughters of Madame de Montijo, Eugénie and Paca, met Beyle through Mérimée, who was intimate with their mother. The two girls liked him; he spun for them his best yarns, he initiated them into new games; in a word, he was a welcome guest in the household, and there are two letters in the possession of Auguste Cordier, one addressed to Beyle by E. Guzman y Palafox dated December, 1839, when the future Empress of the French was thirteen; the other from her sister Paca, both affectionate and of a charm. The episode was a pleasant one in the life of Beyle.

Mérimée also arranged a meeting between Victor Hugo and Beyle in 1829 or 1830. Sainte-Beuve was present, and in a letter to Albert Collignon, published in *Vie littéraire*, 1874, he writes of the pair as two savage cats, their hair bristling, both on the defensive. Hugo knew that Beyle was an enemy of poetry, of the lyric, of the "ideal." The ice was not broken during the evening. Beyle had an antipathy for Hugo, Hugo thoroughly

27

disliked Beyle. And if we had the choice to-day between talking with Hugo or Beyle, is there any doubt as to the selection? — Beyle the *raconteur* of his day. He was too clear-sighted to harbour any illusions concerning literary folk. Praise from one's colleagues is a brevet of resemblance, he has written. Doesn't this sound like old Dr. Johnson's "The reciprocal civility of authors is one of the most risible scenes in the farce of life"?

III

Prosper Mérimée has told us that his friend and master, Henry Stendhal-Beyle, was wedded to the old-fashioned theory: a man should not be in a woman's company longer than five minutes without making love; granting, of course, that the woman is pretty and pleasing. This idea Stendhal had imbibed when a soldier in the Napoleonic campaign. It was hussar tactics of the First Empire. "Attack, attack, attack," he cries. His book De l'Amour practically sets forth the theory; but like most theoreticians, Stendhal was timid in action. He was a sentimentalist—he the pretended cynic and *blasé* man of the world. Mérimée acknowledges that much of his own and Stendhal's impassibility was pure posing. Nevertheless, with the exceptions of Goethe and Byron, no writer of eminence in the last century enjoyed such a sentimental education as Stendhal. At Weimar the passionate pilgrim may see a small

28

plaque which contains portraits of the women beloved by Goethe — omitting Frederike Brion. True to the compass of Teutonic sentimentality, Goethe's mother heads the list. Then follow the names of Cornelia, Kätchen Schönkopf, Lotte Buff, Lili Schönemann, Corona Schröter, Frau von Stein, Christiane Vulpius — later Frau von Goethe — Bettina von Arnim, Minna Herzlieb, and Marianne v. Willemer; with their respective birth and death dates. Several other names might have been added, notably that of the Polish *pianiste* Goethe encountered at Marienbad. The collection is fair-sized, even for a poet who lived as long as Goethe and one who reproached Balzac with digging from a woman's heart each of his novels. To both Goethe and Stendhal the epigram of George Meredith might be applied: "Men may have rounded Seraglio Point. They have not yet doubled Cape Turk."

The wonder is that thus far no devoted Stendhalian has prepared a similar *carton* with the names and pictures of their master's — dare we say? — victims. Stendhal loved many women, and like Goethe his first love was his mother. For him she was the most precious image of all, and he was jealous of his father. This was at the age of seven; but the precocity of the boy and his exaggerated sensibility must be remembered— which later brought him so much unhappiness and so little joy. A casual examination of the list of his loves, reciprocated or spurned, would make a companion to that of Weimar. Their names are

29

EGOISTS

Mélanie Guilbert-Louason, Angela Pietragrua, Mlle. Beretter, the Countess Palffy, Menta, Elisa, Livia B., Madame Azur, Mina de Grisheim, Mme. Jules, and *la petite P.* The number he loved without consolation was still larger. Despite his hussar manœuvres, Stendhal was easily rebuffed. It is odd that Goethe's and Stendhal's fair ones, upon whom they poured poems and novels, did not die — that is, immediately — on being deserted. Goethe relieved the pain of many partings by writing a poem or a play and seeking fresh faces. Stendhal did the same — substituting a novel or a study or innumerable letters for poems and plays. He believed that one nail drove out another; which is very soothing to masculine vanity. But did any woman break her heart because of his fickleness? Frau von Stein of all the women loved by Goethe probably took his defection seriously. She didn't kill herself, however. He wounded many a heart, yet the majority of his loves married, and apparently happily. Stendhal, ugly as he was, slew his hundreds; they recovered after he had passed on to fresh conquests; a fact that he, with his accustomed sincerity, did not fail to note. Yet this same gallant was among the few in the early years of the nineteenth century to declare for the enfranchisement, physical and spiritual, of woman. He was a *féministe*. But, in reality, his theory of love resembled that of the writer who said that "it was simple and brief, like a pressure of the hand between sympathetic persons,

30

or a gay luncheon between two friends of which a pleasant memory remains, if not also a gentle gratitude toward the companion." I quote from memory.

It was at Rome that he first resolved to tell the story of his life. In the dust he traced the initials of the beloved ones. In his book he omitted no details. His motto was: *la vérité toute nue.* If he·has not spared himself, he has not spared others. What can the critics, who recently blamed George Moore for his plain speech in his memoirs, say to Stendhal's journals and La Vie de Henri Brulard? Many of the names were at first given with initials or asterisks; Mérimée burned the letters Stendhal sent him, and regretted the act. But the Stendhalians, the young enthusiasts of the Stendhal Club, have supplied the missing names—those of men and women who have been dead half a century and more.

De l'Amour, Stendhal's remarkable study of the love-passion, is marred by the attempt to imprison a sentiment behind the bars of a mathe-matical formula. He had inherited from his study of Condillac, Helvétius, Tracy, Chamfort the desire for a rigid schematology, for geometrical demonstration. The word "logic" was always on the tip of his tongue, and he probably would have come to blows with Professor Jowett for his dictum, uttered at the close of a lecture: "Logic is neither an art nor a science, but a dodge." Love for Stendhal was without a Beyond. It was a matter of the senses entirely.

3ɪ

The soul counted for little, manners for much. A sentimental epicurean, he is the artistic descendant of Benjamin Constant's Adolphe, both by tradition and temperament. Stendhal fell into the mistake of the metaphysician in setting up numerous categorical traps to snare his subject. They are artificial, and yet bear a resemblance to certain Schopenhauerian theories. Both men practised what they did not preach. "Beauty is a promise of happiness," wrote Stendhal, and it was so effective that Baudelaire rewrote it with a slight variation. The "crystallisation" formula of Stendhal occurred to him while down in a salt mine near Salzburg. He saw an elm twig covered with sparkling salt crystals, and he used it as an image to express the love that discerns in the beloved one all perfections. There are several crystallisations during the course of "true love." His book is more autobiographical than scientific; that the writer gleaned the facts from his own heart-experiences adds to the value and veracity of the work. As a catechism for lovers, it is unique; and it was so well received that from 1822 to 1833 there were exactly seventeen copies sold. But it has been plundered by other writers without acknowledgment. Stendhal and Schopenhauer could have shaken hands on the score of their unpopularity — and about 1880 on their sudden recrudescence.

With all his display of worldly wisdom Stendhal really loved but three times in his life; this statement may shock some of his disciples

32

who see in him a second Casanova, but a study
of his life will prove it. He had gone to Paris
with the established conviction that he must
become a Don Juan. That was — comical or
shocking as it may sound — his projected profession. Experience soon showed him other aspects. He was too refined, too tender-hearted,
to indulge in the conventional dissipations of adolescent mankind. The lunar ray of sentiment
was in his brain; if he couldn't idealise a woman,
he would leave her. It was his misfortune, the
lady's fortune — whoever she might have been
— and the world's good luck that he never was
married. As a husband he would have been
a glorious failure. Mélanie Guilbert-Louason
was an actress in Paris, who, after keeping him on
tenter-hooks of jealousy, accepted his addresses.
He couldn't marry her, because the allowance
made by his father did not suffice for himself;
besides, she had a daughter by a former marriage.
He confesses that lack of money was the chief
reason for his timidity with women; a millionaire,
he might have been a conquering and detestable
hero. Like Frédéric Moreau in L'Education
Sentimentale, Stendhal always feared interruption
from a stronger suitor, and his fears were usually
verified. But he went with Guilbert to Marseilles,
where she was acting, and to support himself took
a position in a commercial house. That for him
meant a grand passion; he loathed business. She
married a Russian, Baskow by name. Stendhal was inconsolable for weeks. How he would

33

have applauded the ironical cry of Jules Laforgue's Hamlet: "Stability! stability! thy name
is Woman." Although he passed his days em-
broidering upon the canvas of the Eternal Masculine portraits of the secular sex, Stendhal first
said, denying a certain French king, that women
never vary.

He fell into abysmal depths of love with Angela
Pietragrua at Milan. He was a dashing soldier,
and if Angela deceived him he was youthful
enough to stand the shock. Eleven years later
he revisited Milan and wept when he saw Angela
again. He often wept copiously, a relic possibly
of eighteenth-century sensibilities. Angela did not
weep. She, however, was sufficiently touched to
start a fresh affair with her faithful Frenchman.
He did not always enjoy smooth sailing. There
were a dozen women that either scorned him or
else remained unconscious of his sentiments.
One memory remained with him to the last
— recall his cry of loneliness to Romain Colomb
when languishing as a French consul at Cività
Vecchia: "I am perishing for want of love!"
He thought doubtless of Métilde, wife of General Dembowsky, who from 1818 to 1824 (let
us not concern ourselves if these dates coincide
with or overlap other love-affairs; Stendhal was
very versatile) neither encouraged nor discour-
aged at Milan the ardent exile. So infatuated was
he that he neglected his chances with the actress
Viganò, and also with the Countess Kassera.
Madame Dembowsky, who afterward did not

34

prove so cruel to the conspirator Ugo Foscolo, allowed Stendhal the inestimable privilege of kissing her hand. He sighed like a schoolboy and trailed after the heartless one from Milan to Florence, from Florence to Rome. The gossip that he was the lover in Paris of the singer Pasta caused the Dembowsky to deny him hope. He was sincerely attached to her. Had she said "Kill yourself," he would have done so. Yes, such a romantic he was. She was born Viscontini and separated from a brutal soldier of a husband. Her cousin, Madame Traversi, was an obstacle in this unhappy passion of Stendhal's. She hated him. Métilde died at the age of thirty-eight, in 1825. Because of her he had replied to Mlle. Viganò — when she asked him: "Beyle, they say that you are in love with me!" "They are fooling you." For this he was never forgiven. It is a characteristic note of Stendhalian frankness—Stendhal, who never deceived anyone but himself. Here is a brace of his amiable sayings on the subject of Woman:—

"La fidélité des femmes dans le mariage, lorsqu' il n'y a pas d'amour, est probablement une chose contre nature."

"La seule chose que je voie à blâmer dans la pudeur, c'est de conduire à l'habitude de mentir."

IV

A promenader of souls and cities, Stendhal
was a letter-writer of formidable patience; his
published correspondence is enormous. How
enormous may be seen in the three volumes published at Paris by Charles Bosse, the pages of
which number 1,386. These letters begin in
1800, when Stendhal was a precocious youth of
seventeen, and end 1842, a few days before his
death. There are more than 700 of them, and
he must have written more—probably several
thousand; for we know that Mérimée destroyed
nearly all his correspondence with Stendhal, and
we read of 300 written to a Milanese lady — his
one grand, because unsuccessful, passion. But
a few of these are included, the remainder doubtless having been burned for prudence' sake. The
earliest edition of the Stendhal letters appeared
in 1855, edited by Prosper Mérimée, with an introduction by the author of Carmen. The present
edition is edited by two devoted Stendhalians,
Ad. Paupe and P. A. Cheramy. It comprises all
the earlier correspondence, the letters printed in
the Souvenirs d'Egotisme (1892), some letters
never before published, Lettres Intimes (1892),
and letters published in the first series of Soirées
du Stendhal Club (1905). There are also letters
from the archives of the Ministers of the Interior,
of War, and of Foreign Affairs — altogether a
complete collection, though ugly in appearance,

36

resembling a volume of Congressional reports, but valuable to the Stendhal student.

For the first time the names of his correspondents appear in full. Mérimée suppressed most of them or gave only the initials. We learn who these correspondents were, and there is a general key for the deciphering of the curious names Stendhal bestowed upon them — he was a wag and a mystifier in this respect. His own signature was seldom twice alike. A list is given and reaches the number of one hundred and seventy-nine pseudonyms. Maurice Barrès has written a gentle preface rather in the air, which he entitled: Stendhal's Sentiment of Honour. One passage is worthy of quotation. Barrès asserts that Stendhal never asked whether a sentiment or an act was useful or fecund, but whether it testified to a thrilling energy. Since the pragmatists are claiming the Frenchman as one of their own, this statement may prove revelatory.

The first volume is devoted to his years of apprenticeship (1800–1806) and his active life (1808–1814). The majority of the letters are addressed to his sister, Pauline Beyle, at Grenoble, a sympathetic soul. With the gravity of a young, green philosopher, he addresses to her homilies by the yard. Sixty instructing twenty! He tells her what to read, principally the eighteenth century philosophers: Rousseau, Voltaire, Helvétius, Tracy, Locke — amusing and highly moral reading for a lass — and he never wearies of praising Shakespeare. "I am a Romantic," he says else-

37

where; "that is, I prefer Shakespeare to Racine, Byron to Boileau." This worldly-wise youth must have bored his sister. She understood him, however, and as her life at home with a disagreeable and avaricious father was not happy, her correspondence with brother Henry must have been a consolation. He does not scruple to call his father hard names, and recommends his sister not to marry for love but for a comfortable home. She actually did both. Edouard Mounier is another correspondent; also Félix Faure, born in Stendhal's city, Grenoble. We learn much of the Napoleonic campaigns in which Stendhal served, particularly of the burning of Moscow and the disastrous retreat of the French army. Related by an eye-witness whose style is concise, whose power of observation is extraordinary, these letters possess historic value.

All Paris and Milan are in the second volume, The Man of the World and the Dilettante (1815–1830); while The Public Functionary and Novelist are the themes of volume three (1830–1842). The friends with whom Stendhal corresponded were Guizot, Thiers, Balzac, Byron, Walter Scott, Sainte-Beuve, and many distinguished noblemen and men of affairs. He had friends in London, Thomas Moore and Sutton-Sharp among the rest; and he visited England several times. Baron Mareste and Romain Colomb were confidants. Stendhal, with an irony that never deserted him, wrote obituary notices of himself because Jules Janin had jestingly remarked that when Stendhal

38

died he would furnish plenty of good material for the necrologists. The articles in guise of letters sent to M. Stritch of the *German Review*, London, are tedious reading; besides, there are too many of them.

As a man whose ears and eyes were very close to the whirring of contemporary events, his descriptions of Napoleon and Byron are peculiarly interesting. At first Napoleon had been a demigod, then he was reviled because with the Corsican's downfall he lost his chances for the future. He had witnessed the coronation and did not forget that Talma had given the young Bonaparte free tickets to the Comédie Française; also that Pope Pius VII. pronounced Latin Italian fashion, thus: *Spiritous sanctous*. As the Emperor passed by on horseback, cheered by the mobs, "he smiled his smile of the theatre, in which one shows the teeth, but with eyes that smile not." Stendhal tells us that the Emperor had forehead and nose in an unbroken line, a common trait in certain parts of France, he adds.

He first encountered Byron in the year 1812, at Milan. It was in a box of the Scala. He was overcome by the beauty of the poet, by his graciousness. Here we see Stendhal, no longer a soldier or a cynic, but a man of sensibility, almost a hero-worshipper. Byron was agreeable. They met often. When Byron's physician and secretary, Polidori, was arrested by the Milan secret police, Stendhal relates that the Englishman's rage was appalling. Byron resembled

39

Napoleon, declared Stendhal, in his marble wrath. Another time the French author advised Byron, who lived at a distance from the opera house, to take a carriage, as after midnight walking was dangerous in Milan. Coldly though politely Byron asked for some indication of his route and then, during a painful silence, he left poor Stendhal staring after him as he hobbled away in the darkness. Such human touches are worth more than the letters in which the literature of the day is discussed.

Ten years later, from Genoa (1823), Byron wrote Stendhal, whom he apparently liked, thanking him for a notice he had read of himself in the latter's book, Rome, Naples, et Florence. Supreme master of the anecdote, these letters may serve as an introduction to Stendhal's works, though we wish for more of the tender epistles. However, in The Diary, the Journal and the Life of Henri Brulard, one may find copious and frank confessions of Stendhal's love-life. So little of the literary man was in him that at the close of his career, when he had received the Legion of Honor, he was indignant because this was bestowed upon him not in his capacity of public functionary but as a man of letters. Adolphe Paupe, the editor of this bulky correspondence — and who knows how much more material there may be in the Grenoble archives! — fittingly closes his brief introduction with a quotation from a writer the antipodes of Stendhal, the parabolic Barbey d'Aurevilly, who, after calling

40

the correspondence "adorable," adds that it possesses the unheard-of charm of Stendhal's other books, a charm which is inexhaustible. Notwithstanding this eloquence, I prefer the old edition compiled by Mérimée. There is such a thing as too much Stendhal, although every scrap of his writing may be sacred to his disciples.

I am glad, therefore, to note in the second series of the Soirées du Stendhal Club, that the principal Stendhalian — or Beyliste, as some name themselves — Casimir Stryienski, shows a disposition to mock at the antics of over-heated Stendhalians. M. Stryienski, who has been called by Paul Bourget "the man of affairs of the Beyliste family," dislikes the idea of a Stendhal cult and wonders how the ironic and humorous Beyle would have treated the worshippers who wish to make of him a mystic god — which is the proper critical attitude. Beyle-Stendhal would have been the first man to overthrow any altar erected to his worship. The second series, collated by Stryienski and Paul Arbelet, is hardly as novel as the first. The most important article is devoted to the question whether Stendhal dedicated to Napoleon his History of Painting (mostly borrowed from Lanzi's book). The 1817 dedication is enigmatic; it might have meant Napoleon, or Louis XVIII., or the Czar Alexander of Russia. M. Arbelet holds to the latter, as Stendhal was so poor that he hoped for a position as preceptor in Russia and thought by the ambiguity of his dedication to catch the favourable eye of the Czar.

Napoleon was at Saint Helena and a hateful king was on the throne of France. Let all three be duped, said to himself the merry Stendhal. That is Arbelet's theory. When in 1854 a new edition of the history appeared, it was headed by a touching, almost tearful dedication to the exile at Saint Helena! Stendhal's executor, Romain Colomb, had found it among the papers of the dead author, and as Napoleon was dead he published it. Evidently Stendhal had written several, and for politic reasons had selected the misleading one of the 1817 edition. Recall Beethoven's magnificent rage when he tore into pieces the dedicatory page of his Eroica Symphony, on hearing that his hero, Napoleon, had crowned himself Emperor. Quite Stendhalian this, Machiavellian, and also time-serving. No doubt he smiled his wicked smile — with tongue in cheek — at the trick, and no doubt his true disciples applaud it. He was the Superman of his day, one who bothered little with moral obligations. His favourite device was a line of verse from an old opera bouffe: "*Vengo adesso di Cosmopoli*"; and what has a true cosmopolitan, a promenader of cities and prober of souls, in common with such a bourgeois virtue as truth-telling? If, as Metchnikoff asserts, a man is no older than his arteries, then a thinker is only as old as his curiosity. Beyle was ever curious, impertinently so — the Paul Pry of psychologists.

42

HENRY BEYLE-STENDHAL

V

His cult grows apace, and like all cults will be overdone. First France, then Italy, and now Germany has succumbed to the novels, memoirs, and delightful gossiping books of travel written by the Frenchman from Grenoble. But what a literary and artistic gold-mine his letters, papers, manuscripts of unfinished novels have proved to men like Casimir Stryienski and the rest. Even in 1909 the Stendhal excavators are busy with their pickers and stealers. Literary Paris becomes enthusiastic when a new batch of correspondence is unearthed at Grenoble or elsewhere. Recently a *cahier*—incomplete to be sure, but indubitably Stendhal's — was found and printed. It was a section of the famous journal exhumed in the library of Grenoble by Stryienski during 1888. Published in the *Mercure de France*, it bore the title of Fin du Tour d'Italie en 1811. It consists of brief, almost breathless notes upon Naples, its music, customs, streets, inhabitants. References to Ancona, to the author's second sojourn in Milan, and to his numerous lady-loves — each one of whom he lashed himself into believing unique — are therein. He placed Mozart and Cimarosa above all other composers, and Shakespeare above Racine. Naturally the man who loved Mozart was bound to adore Raphael and Correggio. Lombard and Florentine masters he rated higher than the Dutch. Indeed, he abhorred Rem-

43

brandt and Rubens almost as much as William Blake abhorred them, though not for the same reason. Despite his perverse and whimsical spirit, Stendhal was, in the larger sense, all of a piece. His likes and dislikes in art are so many witnesses to the unity of his character.

Maurice Barrès relates that at the age of twenty he was in Rome, where he met in the Villa Medici its director, M. Hébert, the painter (died 1908), who promptly asked the young Frenchman: "Do you admire Stendhal?" and proceeded to explain that the writer of La Chartreuse de Parme was his cousin, and once consul at Cività Vecchia, although he spent most of his time in Rome. Stendhal's Promenades had offended the Pope, so these visits were really stolen ones. Bored to death in the stuffy little town where he represented the French Government, Stendhal had been reproved more than once for the dilatory performance of his duties. Hébert, after warning Barrès not to study him too deeply, described him as an old gentleman of exceeding but capricious *esprit*. He roamed among the picture galleries, exclaiming joyously before some old Greek marble or knitting his brows in the Sistine Chapel. Raphael was more to his taste than Michaelangelo, as might have been expected from one who went wild over the ballets Viganò. Another anecdote is one that ·reveals the malicious, almost simian trickiness of Beyle-Stendhal. An English lady, a traveller bent on taking notes for a book about Paris, was shown around the city by Stendhal. Seriously, and with

44

his usual courtesy, he gave her an enormous amount of misinformation, misnaming public buildings, churches, the Louvre, its pictures, and nicknaming well-known personages. All this with the hope that she would reproduce it in print. Not very *spirituel*, this performance of M. Beyle. He was an admirer of English folk and their literature, and corresponded in a grotesque sort of English with several prominent men and women in London. We find him writing a congratulatory letter to Thomas Moore on his Lalla Rookh, complacently remarking that the ingrained Hebraism of English character and literature made the production of such an exotic poem all the more wonderful. Though he could praise the gewgaws and tinsel of Moore's mock Orientalism, he openly despised the limpidity of Lamartine's elegiac verse and the rhythmic illuminated thunder of Victor Hugo.

It is not generally known that Stendhal's friend and disciple, Prosper Mérimée, left an anonymous book, of which there are not many examples, though it has been partially reprinted. It is entitled "H. B. [Henry Beyle], par un des quarante, avec un frontispice stupéfiant dessiné et gravé. Eleutheropolis, l'an 1864 du mensonge Nazaréen." Now, there is a "stupefying" drawing, a project for a statue, by Félicien Rops, the etcher. It depicts the new world-city of Eleutheropolis — a Paris raised to the seventh heaven of cosmopolitanism — with Stendhal set in its midst. Rops was evidently contented to take the little pot-

45

bellied caricature of Henri Monnier, which Monnier declared was not exaggerated, and put it on a pedestal. In his familiar and amusing manner the illustrator shows us multitudes from every quarter of the globe travelling by every known method of conveyance. The idea of teeming nationalities is evoked. All sorts and conditions of men and women are hurrying to pay their homage to Stendhal, who, hat in hand, stomach advancing, legs absurdly curving, umbrella under his arm, and his ironical lips compressed, contemplates with his accustomed imperturbability these ardent idolators. He seems to say: "I predicted that I should be understood about 1880."

But if this cartoon of Rops is amusing, the contents of Mérimée's book are equally so, both amusing and blasphemous. Stendhal and Mérimée got on fairly well together. Mérimée tells what he thought of Stendhal. There are shocking passages and witty. An atheist, more because of political reasons than religious, Stendhal relates a story about the death of God from heart disease. Since that time the cosmical machine, he asserted, has been in the hands of his son, an inexperienced youth who, not being an engineer, reversed the levers; hence the disorder in matters mundane.

To prove how out of tune was Stendhal with his times, we have only to read his definitions of romanticism and classicism in his Racine et Shakespeare. He wrote: "Romanticism is the art of presenting to people literary works which

46

in the actual state of their habitudes and beliefs are capable of giving the greatest possible pleasure; classicism, on the contrary, is the art of presenting literature which gave the greatest possible pleasure to their great-grandfathers." He also proclaimed as a corollary to this that every dead classic had at one time been a live romantic. Yet he was far from sympathising, both romantic and realist as he was, with the 1830 romantic movement. Nor did he suspect its potential historical significance; or his own possible significance, despite his clairvoyant prediction. He disliked Hugo, ignored Berlioz, and had no opinion at all on the genius of Delacroix. The painters of 1830, that we knew half a century later as the Barbizon school, he never mentions. We may imagine him abusing the impressionists in his choleric vein. His appreciations of art, while sound — who dare flout Raphael and Correggio?— are narrow. The immense claims made continually by the Stendhalians for their master are balked by evidences of a provincial spirit. Yes; he, the first of the cosmopolitans, the indefatigable globe-trotter, keenest of observers of the human heart, man without a country — he has said, "My country is where there are most people like me" — was often as blindly prejudiced as a dweller in an obscure hamlet. And doesn't this epigram contradict his idea of the proud, lonely man of genius? It may seem to; in reality he was not like a Nietzschian, but a sociable, pleasure-loving man, seldom putting to the test his theories of individualism. He

47

always sought the human quality; the passions of humanity were the prime things of existence for him. A landscape, no matter how lovely, must have a human or a historic interest. The fiercest assassin in the Trastevere district was at least a man of action and not a sheep. "Without passion there is neither virtue nor vice," he preached. Therefore he greatly lauded Benvenuto Cellini. He loathed democracy and a democratic form of government. Brains, not votes, should rule a nation. He sneered at America as being hopelessly utilitarian.

In the preface to his History of Italian Painting he quoted Alfieri: "My only reason for writing was that my gloomy age afforded me no other occupation." From Città Vecchia he wrote: "It's awful: women here have only one idea, a new Parisian hat. No poetry here or tolerable company — except with prisoners; with whom, as French Consul, I cannot possibly seek friendship." To kill the ennui of his existence he either slipped into Rome for a week or else wrote reams of "copy," most of which he never saw in print. Among certain intellectual circles in Paris he was known and applauded as a man of taste, a dilettante of the seven arts, though his lack of original invention occasionally got him into scrapes. Stendhal might have echoed Molière's "Je prends mon bien où je le trouve"; but he would not have forgotten to remind the dramatic poet that the very witticism was borrowed from Cyrano.

Stryienski's Soirées du Stendhal Club actually

48

presents for the delectation of the Stendhalians parallel columns from Lanzi and Stendhal — so proud are the true believers of the fold that even such evidences of plagiarism do not disconcert them. The cribbing occurs in the general reflections devoted to the Renaissance. It is as plain as a pikestaff. Notwithstanding, we can · read Stendhal with more interest than the original. His lively spirit adorns Lanzi's laborious pages.

Beyle's joke about the "reversed engines of Christianity," quoted by Mérimée, and his implacable dislike of the Jesuits (as may be seen in his masterpiece, Le Rouge et le Noir — in those days the Yellow Peril was the Jesuits), did not dull his perception of what the papacy had done for art in Italy. He nearly approaches eloquence in his Philosophy of Art (which Taine appreciated and profited by) when writing of the popes of the Renaissance. He does not fail to note the vivifying and reforming influence of the Church at this period upon the brutality and lusts of the nobility and upon poets and painters. Adoring Raphael as much as he did Napoleon and Byron, he declared that Raphael failed in *chiaroscuro* and vaunted the superiority of Correggio in this particular. But he did not deign to mention Rembrandt. Nothing Germanic or Northern pleased him. He was a Latin among Latins, and his passion for Italy and the Italians was not assumed. He had asked of his executor that he be buried in the little Protestant cemetery at Rome. Then he changed his mind and ordered that the

49

cemetery of Andilly, near Montmorency, be his last resting-place. But the fates, that burn into ashes the fairest fruits of man's ambitions, dropped Stendhal's remains in the cemetery of Montmartre, Paris, where still stands the prosaic tomb with its falsification of the writer's birth. His epitaph he doubtless discovered when fabricating his life of Haydn. In the composer's case it runs: "Veni, scripsi, vixi." And when we consider the fact that his happiest years were in Milan, that there lived the object of his deepest affection, Angela Pietragrua, this inscription was as sincere as the majority of such marble ingenuities in post-mortem politeness.

With all his critical limitations, Stendhal never gave vent to such ineptitudes as Tolstoy regarding Shakespeare. The Russian, who has spent the latter half of his life bewailing the earlier and more brilliant part, would have been abhorrent to the Frenchman, who died as he had lived, impenitent. Stendhal was a man, not a purveyor of words, or a maker of images. Not poetic, yet he did not fail to value Dante and Angelo. Virile, cynical, sensual, the greatest master of psychology of his age, he believed in action rather than thought. Literature he pretended to detest. Not a spinner of cobwebs, he left no definite system; it remained for Taine to gather together the loose strands of his sane, strong ideas and formulate them. He saw the world clearly, without sentiment — he, the most sentimental of men — and he had a horror of German mole-hill metaphysics. The

50

eighteenth century with its hard logic, its deification of Reason, its picturesque atheism, enlisted Beyle's sympathies. Socialism was for him anathema.

Love and art were his watchwords. His love of art was on a sound basis. Joyous, charming music like Mozart's, Rossini's, Cimarosa's, appealed to him; and Correggio, with his sensuous colouring and voluptuous design, was his favourite painter. He was complex, but he was not morbid. The artistic progenitor of a long line of analysts, supermen, criminals, and æsthetic ninnies, he probably would have disclaimed the entire crowd, including the faithful Stendhalians, because the latter have so widely departed from his canons of simplicity and sunniness in art.

But Stendhal left the soul out of his scheme of life; never did he knock at the gate of her dwelling-place. Believing with Napoleon that because the surgeon's scalpel did not lay bare any trace of the soul, there was none, Stendhal practically denied her existence. For this reason his windows do not open upon eternity. They command fair, charming prospects. Has he not written: " J'ai recherché avec une sensibilité exquise la vue des beaux paysages. . . . Les paysages etaient comme un archet qui jouait sur mon âme"? He meant his nerves, not his soul. Spiritual overtones are not sounded in his work. A materialist (a singularly unhappy home and maladroit education are to blame for . . much of his errors in after life), he was, at least, no hypocrite. He loved beautiful art, women, land-

scapes, brave feats. He confesses, in a letter to
Colomb, dated November 25, 1817, to planning
a History of Energy in Italy (both Taine and
Barrès later transposed the theme to France with
varying results). A tissue of contradictions, he
somehow or other emerges from the mists and
artistic embroilments of the earlier half of the
last century a robust, soldierly, yet curious, subtle
and enigmatic figure. It is best to employ in
describing him his own favourite definition — he
was "different." And has he not said that difference engenders hatred?

VI

In his brilliant and much-abused book, A Rebours, the late J.-K. Huysmans describes the
antics of a feeble-brained young nobleman who,
having saturated himself with Baedeker's London, the novels of Dickens, English roast beef and
ale, came to the comical conclusion that he might
be disappointed if he crossed the Channel, so after
a few hours spent within the hospitable walls
of a Parisian English bar he gathered up his plaids,
traps, walking-stick, and calmly returned to his
home near the French capital. He had travelled
to England in an easy-chair, as mentioned by
Goldsmith — better after all than not travelling at
all. Circumstances condemn many of us to this
mode of motion, which comes well within the
definition of our great-grandfathers, who called it .
The Pleasures of the Imagination.

HENRY BEYLE-STENDHAL

But there are, luckily for them, many who are not compelled to assist at this intellectual Barmecide's feast. They go and they come, and no man says them nay. Whether they see as much as those who voyaged in the more leisurely manner of the eighteenth and early nineteenth centuries is open to doubt. Europe or Asia through a car-window is only a series of rapidly dissolving slides, pictures that live for brief seconds. Modern travel is impressionistic. Nature viewed through a nebulous blur. Our grandfathers, if they didn't go as far as their descendants, contrived to see more, to see a lot of delightful little things, note a myriad of minute traits of the country through which they paced at such a snail's gait. Nowadays we hurriedly glance at the names of railroad stations. The ideal method of locomotion is really that of the pedestrian — shanks'-mare ought to be popular. Vernon Lee spoke thus of our hero: "'Tis the mode of travelling that constituted the delight and matured the genius of Stendhal, king of cosmopolitans and grand master of the psychologic novel."

It is interesting to turn back and flutter the pages of that perennially delightful book, Promenades dans Rome. Italy may truthfully be said to have been engraved upon the author's heart. Under the heading Manner of Travelling From Paris to Rome, dated March 25, 1828, he tells his readers, few but fit, how he made that wonderful trip.

One of the best ways, writes Stendhal, is to

53

take a post-chaise, or a *calèche*, light and made in Vienna. Carry little baggage. It only means vexation at the various custom-houses, bother with the police — who treat all travellers as spies or suspected persons — and it will surely attract bandits. Besides, prices are instantly doubled when a post-chaise arrives. There is the mail-coach. It rolls along comfortably. In its capacious interior one may sleep, watch the scenery, converse, or read. You can go to Béfort or Basel if you desire to pass the north of la Suisse, or to Pontarlier or Ferney, if desirous of reaching the Simplon. You may take the mail to Lyons or Grenoble, and pass by Mont Cenis; or until Draguignan if you wish to escape the mountains and enter Italy by the beautiful highway, the work of M. de Chabral. You arrive at Nice and pass on to Genoa. This is the ideal route for scenery.

But, continues Stendhal, the most expeditious and the interesting way, the one he usually took, begins with a forty-eight hour ride in the diligence as far as Béfort; a carriage for which you pay a dozen francs will conduct you to Basel. Once there you may take a diligence for Lucerne — that singular and dangerous lake, the theatre of William Tell's exploits, remarks Stendhal impressively (they believed in the Tell legend, those innocent times) — and attain Altdorf. Here Tell and the apple will arouse your imagination. Then Italy may be entered by Saint Gothard, Bellinzona, Como, and Milan. *Via* the Simplon was

54

more to the taste of our writer. He often took the
diligence, which at Basel went to Bern; arriving
in the Rhone valley by way of Louèche and
Tourtemagne, he would find his baggage, which
had gone around by Lausanne, Saint Maurice,
and Sion. He tells us that the conductor of the
excellent diligence plying between Lausanne and
Domo d'Ossola was a superior man; a glimpse
of his calm Swiss features drives away all fear of
danger. For ten years three times a week this
conductor has passed the Simplon. He did not
encounter avalanches. Anyhow, the Simplon
route is less dangerous than Mont Cenis; there
are fewer precipices and the edge of the road is
bordered by trees; if the horses ran away the
coach would not be overturned into the abyss.
And since the opening of the Simplon route, Stendhal gravely notes, only forty travellers have
perished, nine of them unhappy Italian soldiers
returning from Russia. Are not these details of
a savoury simplicity, like the faded odour of sandal-
wood which meets your nostrils when you open
some old secretary of your grandparents?

Kept by a man from Lyons was a fine inn on
the Simplon route in those days. Stendhal never
failed to record where could be found good wines,
cooking, and clean sheets. He usually paid twelve
francs for a carriage to Domo d'Ossola, Lac
Majeur (Lago Maggiore) *vis-à-vis* to the Borro-
mean Islands. Four hours in a boat to Sesto
Calende, and five hours in a fast coach — behold,
Milan! Or you can reach Milan *via* Varese.

55

Milan to Mantua in the regular diligence. Thence to Bologna by a carriage, there the mail-coach. You go to Rome by the superb routes of Ancona and Loreto. You must pay thirty or thirty-five francs on the coach between Milan and Bologna. Stendhal assures us that he often found good company in the carriages that traverse the distance from Bologna to Florence. It· took two days to cover twenty leagues and cost twenty francs. From Florence to Rome he consumed four or five days, going by Perugia in preference to Siena. Once he travelled in company with three priests, of whom he was suspicious until the ice was broken; then with joyous anecdotes they passed the time, and he is surprised to find these clerical men, who said their prayers openly three times a day without being embarrassed by the presence of strangers, were very human, very companionable. With his accustomed naïve expression of pleasure, he writes that they saved him considerable annoyance at the custom-house.

And to-day, eighty years later, we take a train *de luxe* at Paris and in thirty hours we are in the Eternal City. It is swifter, more comfortable, and safer, our way of travelling, than Stendhal's, but that we see as much as he did we greatly doubt. The motor-car is an improvement on the mail-coach and the express train; you may, if you will, travel leisurely and privately from Paris to Rome. Or, why not hire a stout little carriage and go through Tuscany in an old-fashioned manner as did the Chevalier de Pensieri-Vani!

56

HENRY BEYLE-STENDHAL

Few may hope to store as many memories as
Stendhal, yet we should see more than the oc-
cupants of railroad drawing-rooms that whiz by us
on the road to Rome.

VII

Even in our days of hasty production the
numerous books of Stendhal provoke respectful
consideration. What leisure they had 'in the
first half of the last century! What patience
was shown by the industrious man who worked
to ward off *ennui!* He must have written twenty-
five volumes. In 1906 the *Mercure de France*
printed nineteen newly discovered letters to his
London friend, Sutton Sharpe (Beyle visited
London occasionally; he corresponded with
Thomas Moore the poet, and once he spent an
evening at a club in the company of the humourist
Theodore Hook). But the titles of many of his
books suffice; the majority of them are negligible.
Who wishes to read his lives of Rossini, Haydn,
Mozart, Metastasio? His life of Napoleon,
posthumously published in 1876, is of more interest; Beyle had seen his subject in the flesh and
blood. His Racine et Shakespeare is worth
while for the Stendhalian; none but the fanatical
kind would care to read the History of Painting
in Italy. There is the Correspondence, capital
diversion, ringing with Stendhalian wit and prej-
udice; and Promenades dans Rome is a classic;
not inferior are Mémoires d'un Touriste, or

57

Rome, Naples, et Florence. Indeed, the influence of the Promenades has been pronounced. His three finished novels are Armance, Le Rouge et le Noir—which does not derive its title from the gambling game, but opposes the sword and the soutane, red and black—and La Chartreuse de Parme. The short stories show him at his best, his form being enforced to concision, his style suiting the brief passionate recitals of love, crime, intrigue, and adventure — for the most part, old Italian anecdotes recast; as the Italian tales of Hewlett are influenced by Stendhal. L'Abbesse de Castro could hardly have been better done by Mérimée. In the same volume are Les Cenci, Vittoria Accoramboni, Vanina Vanini, and La Duchesse de Palliano, all replete with dramatic excitement and charged with Italian atmosphere. San Francesca a Ripa is a thrilling tale; so are the stories contained in Nouvelles Inédites, Féder (le Mari d'Argent), Le Juif (Filippo Ebreo) — the latter Balzac might have signed; and the unfinished novel, Le Chasseur Vert, which was at first given three other titles: Leuwen, l'Orange de Malte, Les Bois de Prémol. It promised to be a rival to Le Rouge et le Noir. Lucien Leuwen, the young cavalry officer, is Stendhal himself, and he is, like Julien Sorel, the first progenitor of a long line in French fiction; disillusioned youths who, after the electric storms caused by the Napoleonic apparition, end in the sultry dilettantism of Jean, duc d'Esseintes of Huysmans' A Rebours and in the pages of Maurice

58

HENRY BEYLE-STENDHAL

Barrès. From Beyle to Huysmans is not such a remote modulation as might be imagined. Nor are those sick souls, Goncourt, Charles Demailly and Coriolis, without the taint of *beylisme*. Lucien Leuwen is a highly organized young man who goes to a small provincial town where his happiness, his one love-affair, is wrecked by the malice of his companions. There is a sincerer strain in the book than in some of its predecessors.

Armance, Stendhal's first attempt at fiction, is unpleasant; the theme is an impossible one — pathology obtrudes its ugly head. Yet, Armance de Zohilhoff is a creature who interests; she was sketched from life, Stendhal tells us, a companion to a lady of left-handed rank. She is an unhappy girl and her marriage to a *babilan*, Octave de Malivert, is a tragedy. Lamiel, a posthumous novel, published by Casimir Stryienski in 1888, contains an *avant-propos* by Stendhal dated from Cività Vecchia, May 25, 1840. (His prefaces are masterpieces of sly humour and ironical malice.) It is a very disagreeable fiction — Lamiel is the criminal woman with all the stigmata described by Lombroso in his Female Delinquent. She is wonderfully portrayed with her cruelty, coldness, and ferocity. She, too, like her creator, exclaimed, "Is that all?" after her first bought experience in love. She becomes attached to a scoundrel from the galleys, and sets fire to a palace to avenge his death. She is burned to cinders. A hunchback doctor, Sansfin by name, might have stepped from a page of Le Sage.

59

EGOISTS

The Stendhal heroines betray their paternity.
Madame de Renal, who sacrifices all for Julien
Sorel, is the softest-hearted, most womanly of
his characters. She is of the same sweet, maternal type as Madame Arnoux in Flaubert's
L'Education Sentimentale, though more impul-
sive. Her love passages with Julien are the
most original in French fiction. Mathilde de la
Môle, pedant, frigid, perverse, snobbish, has
nevertheless fighting blood in her veins. Lamiel
is a caricature of her. What could be more
evocative of Salome than her kneeling before
Julien's severed head? Clelia Conti in the
Chartreuse is like the conventional heroine of
Italian romance. She is too sentimental, too
prudish with her vow and its sophistical evasion.
The queen of Stendhal women is Gina, *la duchesse*
Sanseverina. She makes one of the immortal
quartet in nineteenth-century fiction — the other
three being Valérie Marneffe, Emma Bovary, and
Anna Karénina. Perhaps if Madame de Chas-
teller in Le Chasseur Vert had been a finished
portrait, she might have ranked after Gina in
interest. That lovable lady, with the morals of
a *grande dame* out of the Italian Renaissance,
will never die. She embodies all the energy,
tantalizing charm, and paradox of Beyle. And
a more vital woman has not swept through literature since the Elizabethans. At one time he
dreamed of conquering the theatre. Adolphe
Brisson saw the *ébauches* for several plays; at
least fifteen scenarios or the beginnings of them

60

have been found in his literary remains.   Nothing
came of his efforts to become a second Molière.

Zola places Le Rouge et le Noir above La
Chartreuse de Parme; so does Rod.   The first
novel is more sombre, more tragic; it contains
masterly characterisations, but it is depressing
and in spots duller than the Chartreuse.   Its
author was too absorbed in his own ego to become a master-historian of manners.   Yet what
a book is the Chartreuse 'for a long day.   What
etched landscapes are in it — notably the descriptions of Lake Como!   What evocations of enchanting summer afternoons in Italy floating
down the mirror-like stream under a blue sky,
with the entrancing Duchess!   The episodes of
Parmesan court intrigue are models of observation and irony.   Beyle's pen was never more delightful, it drips honey and gall.   He is master
of dramatic situations; witness the great scene in
which the old Duke, Count Mosca, and Gina
participate.   At the close you hear the whirring
of the theatre curtain.   Count Mosca, it is said,
was a portrait of Metternich; rather it was
Stendhal's friend, Count de Saurau.   In sooth,
he is also very much like Stendhal — Stendhal
humbly awaiting orders from the woman he loves.
That Mosca was a tremendous scoundrel we need
not doubt; yet, like Metternich and Bismarck, he
could be cynical enough to play the game honestly.
Despite the rusty melodramatic machinery of the
book, its passionate silhouettes, its Pellico prisons,
its noble bandit, its poisons, its hair-breadth es-

61

capes, duels and assassinations — these we must accept as the slag of Beyle's genius — there is ore rich enough in it to compensate us for the *longueurs*.

Of his disquisition, De l'Amour, with its famous theory of "crystallisation," much could be written. Not founded on a basic physiological truth as is Schopenhauer's doctrine of love, Beyle's is wider in scope. It deals more with manners than fundamentals. It is a manual of tactics in the art of love by a superior strategist. His knowledge of woman on the social side, at least, is unparalleled. His definitions and classifications are keener, deeper than Michelet's or Balzac's. "Femmes! femmes! vous êtes bien toujours les mêmes," he cries in a letter to a fair correspondent. It is a quotidian truth that few before him had the courage or clairvoyancy to enunciate. Crowded with crisp epigrams and worldly philosophy, this book on Love may be studied without exhausting its wisdom and machiavellianism.

Stendhal as an art or musical critic cannot be taken seriously, though he says some illuminating things; embedded in platitudes may be found shrewd *aperçus* and flashes of insight; but the trail of the "gifted amateur" is over them all. At a time when Beethoven was in the ascendant, when Berlioz — who hailed from the environs of Grenoble — was in the throes of the "new music," when Bach had been rediscovered, Beyle prattles of Cimarosa. He provoked Berlioz with his praise of Rossini — "les plus irritantes stupidités sur la musique, dont il croyait avoir le secret," wrote Berlioz of the Rossini biography. Lavoix went further: "Ecrivain d'esprit . . . fanfaron d'ignorance en musique." Poor Stendhal! He had no *flair* for the various artistic movements about him, although he had unwittingly originated several. He praised Goethe and Schiller, yet never mentioned Bach, Beethoven, Chopin; music for him meant operatic music, some other "divine adventure" to fill in the background of conversation. Conversation! In that art he was virtuoso. To dine alone was a crime in his eyes. A *gourmet*, he cared more for talk than eating. He could not make up his mind about Weber's Freischütz, and Meyerbeer he did not very much like; "he is said to be the first pianist of Europe," he wrote; at the time, Liszt and Thalberg were disputing the kingdom of the keyboard. It was Stendhal, so the story goes, who once annoyed Liszt at a *musicale* in Rome by exclaiming in his most elliptical style: "*Mon cher* Liszt, pray give us your *usual* improvisation this evening!"

As a plagiarist Stendhal was a success. He "adapted" from Goethe, translated entire pages from the *Edinburgh Review*, and the material of his history of Painting in Italy he pilfered from Lanzi. More barefaced still was his wholesale appropriation of Carpani's Haydine, which he coolly made over into French as a life of Haydn. The Italian author protested in a Paduan journal, *Giornale dell' Italiana Letteratura*, calling Sten-

63

dhal by his absurd pen-name: "M. Louis-Alex-ander-César Bombet, *soi-disant* Français auteur des Haydine." The original book appeared in 1812 at Milan. Stendhal published his plagia-rism at Paris, 1814, but asserted that it had been written in 1808. He did not stop at mere piracy, for in 1816 and in an open letter to the *Constitution-nel* he fabricated a brother for the aforesaid Bombet and wrote an indignant denial of the facts. He spoke of César Bombet as an invalid incapable of defending his good name. The life of Mozart is a very free adaptation from Schlichtegroll's. When Shakespeare, Handel, and Richard Wagner plundered, they plundered mag-nificently; in comparison, Stendhal's stealings are absurd.

Irritating as are his inconsistencies, his prank-ishness, his bombastic affectations, and preten-sions to a superior immorality, Stendhal's is nevertheless an enduring figure in French liter-ature. His power is now felt in Germany, where it is augmented by Nietzsche's popularity — Nietz-sche, who, after Mérimée, was Stendhal's great-est pupil. Pascal had his "abyss," Stendhal had his fear of *ennui* — it was almost pathologic, this obsession of boredom. One side of his many-sided nature was akin to Pepys, a French Pepys, who chronicled immortal small-beer. However, it is his heart's history that will make this protean old faun eternally youthful. As a prose artist he does not count for much. But in the current of his swift, clear narrative and under the spell of

64

HENRY BEYLE-STENDHAL

his dry magic and peptonized concision we do not miss the peacock graces and coloured splendours of Flaubert or Chateaubriand. Stendhal delivers himself of a story rapidly; he is all sinew. And he is the most seductive spiller of souls since Saint-Simon.

II

THE BAUDELAIRE LEGEND

I

For the sentimental no greater foe exists than the iconoclast who dissipates literary legends. And he is abroad nowadays. Those golden times when they gossipped of De Quincey's enormous opium consumption, of the gin absorbed by gentle Charles Lamb, of Coleridge's dark ways, Byron's escapades, and Shelley's atheism — alas! into what faded limbo have they vanished. Poe, too, Poe whom we saw in fancy reeling from Richmond to Baltimore, Baltimore to Philadelphia, Philadelphia to New York. Those familiar fascinating anecdotes have gone the way of all such jerry-built spooks. We now know Poe to have been a man suffering at the time of his death from cerebral lesion, a man who drank at intervals and but little. Dr. Guerrier of Paris has exploded a darling superstition about De Quincey's opium-eating. He has demonstrated that no man could have lived so long — De Quincey was nearly seventy-five at his death — and worked so hard, if he had consumed twelve thousand drops of laudanum as often as he said he did. Furthermore, the Eng-

66

lish essayist's description of the drug's effects is inexact. He was seldom sleepy — a sure sign, asserts Dr. Guerrier, that he was not altogether enslaved by the drug habit. Sprightly in old age, his powers of labour were prolonged until past threescore and ten. His imagination needed little opium to produce the famous Confessions. Even Gautier's revolutionary red waistcoat worn at the *première* of Hernani was, according to Gautier, a pink doublet. And Rousseau has been whitewashed. So they are disappearing, those literary legends, until, disheartened, we cry out: Spare us our dear, old-fashioned, disreputable men of genius!

But the legend of Charles Baudelaire is seemingly indestructible. This French poet himself has suffered more from the friendly malignant biographer and Parisian chroniclers than did Poe. Who shall keep the curs out of the cemetery? asked Baudelaire after he had read Griswold on Poe. A few years later his own cemetery was invaded and the world was put in possession of the Baudelaire legend; that legend of the atrabilious, irritable poet, dandy, maniac, his hair dyed green, spouting blasphemies; that grim, despairing image of a Diabolic, a libertine, saint, and drunkard. Maxime du Camp was much to blame for the promulgation of these tales — witness his Souvenirs Littéraires. However, it may be confessed that part of the Baudelaire legend was created by Charles Baudelaire. In the history of literature it is difficult to

67

parallel such a deliberate piece of self-stultifica-
tion. Not Villon, who preceded him, not Verlaine, who imitated him, drew for the astonishment
or disedification of the world like unflattering
portraits. Mystifier as he was, he must have
suffered at times from acute cortical irritation.
And, notwithstanding his desperate effort to
realize Poe's idea, he only proved Poe correct,
who had said that no man can bare his heart
quite naked; there will be always something held
back, something false too ostentatiously thrust
forward. The grimace, the attitude, the pomp
of rhetoric are so many buffers between the soul
of man and the sharp reality of published confessions. Baudelaire was no more exception to
this rule than St. Augustine, Bunyan, Rousseau,
or Huysmans; though he was as frank as any of
them, as we may see in the recently printed diary,
Mon cœur mis à nu (Posthumous Works, So-
ciété du Mercure de France); and in the Journal,
Fusées, Letters, and other fragments exhumed
by devoted Baudelarians.

To smash legends, Eugène Crépet's biographical
study, first printed in 1887, has been republished
with new notes by his son, Jacques Crépet. This
is an exceedingly valuable contribution to Baudelaire lore; a dispassionate life, however, has yet
to be written, a noble task for some young poet
who will disentangle the conflicting lies originated
by Baudelaire — that tragic comedian — from
the truth and thus save him from himself. The
new Crépet volume is really but a series of notes;

68

there are some letters addressed to the poet by the distinguished men of his day, supplementing the rather disappointing volume of Letters, 1841–1866, published in 1908. There are also documents in the legal prosecution of Baudelaire, with memories of him by Charles Asselineau, Léon Cladel, Camille Lemonnier, and others.

In November, 1850, Maxime du Camp and Gustave Flaubert found themselves at the French Ambassador's, Constantinople. The two friends had taken a trip in the Orient which later bore fruit in Salammbô. General Aupick, the representative of the French Government, received the young men cordially; they were presented to his wife, Madame Aupick. She was the mother of Charles Baudelaire, and inquired of Du Camp, rather anxiously: "My son has talent, has he not?" Unhappy because her second marriage, a brilliant one, had set her son against her, the poor woman welcomed from such a source confirmation of her eccentric boy's gifts. Du Camp tells the much-discussed story of a quarrel between the youthful Charles and his stepfather, a quarrel that began at table. There were guests present. After some words Charles bounded at the General's throat and sought to strangle him. He was promptly boxed on the ears and succumbed to a nervous spasm. A delightful anecdote, one that fills with joy psychiatrists in search of a theory of genius and degeneration. Charles was given some money and put on board a ship sailing to East India. He became a cattle-dealer in the

69

British army, and returned to France years afterward with a *Vénus noire*, to whom he addressed extravagant poems! All this according to Du Camp. Here is another tale, a comical one. Baudelaire visited Du Camp in Paris, and his hair was violently green. Du Camp said nothing. Angered by this indifference, Baudelaire asked: "You find nothing abnormal about me?" "No," was the answer. "But my hair — it is green!" "That is not singular, *mon cher* Baudelaire; every one has hair more or less green in Paris." Disappointed in not creating a sensation, Baudelaire went to a café, gulped down two large bottles of Burgundy, and asked the waiter to remove the water, as water was a disagreeable sight for him; then he went away in a rage. It is a pity to doubt this green hair legend; presently a man of genius will not be able to enjoy an epileptic fit in peace — as does a banker or a beggar. We are told that St. Paul, Mahomet, Handel, Napoleon, Flaubert, Dostoiëvsky were epileptoids; yet we do not encounter men of this rare kind among the inmates of asylums. Even Baudelaire had his sane moments.

The joke of the green hair has been disposed of by Crépet. Baudelaire's hair thinning after an illness, he had his head shaved and painted with salve of a green hue, hoping thereby to escape baldness. At the time when he had embarked for Calcutta (May, 1841), he was not seventeen, but twenty, years of age. Du Camp said he was seventeen when he attacked General Aupick.

THE BAUDELAIRE LEGEND

The dinner could not have taken place at Lyons because the Aupick family had left that city six years before the date given by Du Camp. Charles was provided with five thousand francs for his expenses, instead of twenty — Du Camp's version — and he never was a beef-drover in the British army, for a good reason — he never reached India. Instead, he disembarked at the Isle of Bourbon, and after a short stay was seized by homesickness and returned to France, being absent about ten months. But, like Flaubert, on his return home Baudelaire was seized with the nostalgia of the East; out there he had yearned for Paris. Jules Claretie recalls Baudelaire saying to him with a grimace: "I love Wagner; but the music I prefer is that of a cat hung up by his tail outside of a window, and trying to stick to the panes of glass with its claws. There is an odd grating on the glass which I find at the same time strange, irritating, and singularly harmonious." Is it necessary to add that Baudelaire, notorious in Paris for his love of cats, dedicating poems to cats, would never have perpetrated such revolting cruelty?

Another misconception, a critical one, is the case of Poe and Baudelaire. The young Frenchman first became infatuated with Poe's writings in 1846 or 1847 — he gives these two dates, though several stories of Poe had been translated into French as early as 1841 or 1842; L'Orang-Outang was the first, which we know as The Murders in the Rue Morgue; Madame Meunier also adapted several Poe stories for the reviews. Baudelaire's labours as a translator lasted over ten years. That he assimilated Poe, that he idolized Poe, is a commonplace of literary gossip. But that Poe had overwhelming influence in the formation of his poetic genius is not the truth. Yet we find such an acute critic as the late Edmund Clarence Stedman writing, "Poe's chief influence upon Baudelaire's own production relates to poetry." It is precisely the reverse. Poe's influence affected Baudelaire's prose, notably in the disjointed confessions, Mon cœur mis à nu, which recall the American writer's Marginalia. The bulk of the poetry in Les Fleurs de Mal was written before Baudelaire had read Poe, though not published in book form until 1857. But in 1855 some of the poems saw the light in the *Revue des deux Mondes*, while many of them had been put forth a decade or fifteen years before as fugitive verse in various magazines. Stedman was not the first to make this mistake. In Bayard Taylor's The Echo Club we find on page 24 this criticism: "There was a congenital twist about Poe. . . . Baudelaire and Swinburne after him have been trying to surpass him by increasing the dose; but his muse is the natural Pythia, inheriting her convulsions, while they eat all sorts of insane roots to produce theirs." This must have been written about 1872, and after reading it one would fancy Poe and Baudelaire were rhapsodic wrigglers on the poetic tripod, whereas their poetry is often reserved, even glacial. Baudelaire, like

72

THE BAUDELAIRE LEGEND

Poe, sometimes "built his nests with the birds of Night," and that was enough to condemn the work of both men with critics of the didactic school.

Once, when Baudelaire heard that an American man-of-letters (?) was in Paris, he secured an introduction and called. Eagerly inquiring after Poe, he learned that he was not considered a genteel person in America. Baudelaire withdrew, muttering maledictions. Enthusiastic poet! Charming literary person! But the American, whoever he was, represented public opinion at the time. To-day criticisms of Poe are vitiated by the desire to make him an angel. It is to be doubted whether without his barren environment and hard fortunes we should have had Poe at all. He had to dig down deeper into the pit of his personality to reach the central core of his music. But every ardent young soul entering "literature" begins by a vindication of Poe's character. Poe was a man, and he is now a classic. He was a half-charlatan as was Baudelaire. In both the sublime and the sickly were never far asunder. The pair loved to mystify, to play pranks on their contemporaries. Both were implacable pessimists. Both were educated in affluence, and both had to face unprepared the hardships of life. The hastiest comparison of their poetic work will show that their only common ideal was the worship of an exotic beauty. Their artistic methods of expression were totally dissimilar. Baudelaire, like Poe, had a harp-like

73

temperament which vibrated in the presence of strange subjects. Above all he was obsessed by sex. Woman, as angel of destruction, is the keynote of his poems. Poe was almost sexless. His aerial creatures never footed the dusty highways of the world. His lovely lines, "Helen, thy beauty is to me," could never have been written by Baudelaire; while Poe would never have pardoned the "fulgurant" grandeur, the Beethoven-like harmonies, the Dantesque horrors of that "deep wide music of lost souls" in "Femmes Damnées":

> Descendez, descendez, lamentables victimes.

Or this, which might serve as a text for one of John Martin's vast sinister mezzotints:

> J'ai vu parfois au fond d'un théâtre banal
> Qu'enflammait l'orchestre sonore,
> Une fée allumer dans un ciel infernal
> Une miraculeuse aurore;
>
> J'ai vu parfois au fond d'un théâtre banal
> Un être, qui n'était que lumière, or et gaze,
> Terrasser l'énorme Satan;
> Mais mon cœur que jamais ne visite l'extase,
> Est un théâtre où l'on attend
> Toujours, toujours en vain l'Etre aux ailes de gaze.

Professor Saintsbury thus sums up the differences between Poe and Baudelaire: "Both authors — Poe and De Quincey — fell short of Baudelaire himself as regards depth and fulness

74

of passion, but both have a superficial likeness
to him in eccentricity of temperament and affection for a certain peculiar mixture of grotesque
and horror." Poe is without passion, except a
passion for the *macabre;* for what Huysmans calls
"The October of the sensations"; whereas, there
is a gulf of despair and terror and humanity in
Baudelaire which shakes your nerves yet stimu-
lates the imagination. However, profounder as
a poet, he was no match for Poe in what might
be termed intellectual prestidigitation. The mathematical Poe, the Poe of the ingenious detective
tales, tales extraordinary, the Poe of the swift
flights into the cosmical blue, the Poe the prophet
and mystic — in these the American was more
versatile than his French translator. That
Baudelaire said, "Evil, be thou my good,"
is doubtless true. He proved all things and
found them vanity. He is the poet of original
sin, a worshipper of Satan for the sake of paradox; his Litanies to Satan ring childish to us —
in his heart he was a believer. His was "an infinite reverse aspiration," and mixed up with his
pose was a disgust for vice, for life itself. He
was the last of the Romanticists; Sainte-Beuve
called him the Kamtschatka of Romanticism; its
remotest hyperborean peak. Romanticism is dead
to-day, as dead as Naturalism; but Baudelaire is
alive, and is read. His glistening phosphorescent
trail is over French poetry and he is the begetter
of a school:— Verlaine, Villiers de l'Isle Adam,
Carducci, Arthur Rimbaud, Jules Laforgue,

75

Verhaeren, and many of the youthful crew. He affected Swinburne, and in Huysmans, who was not a poet, his splenetic spirit lives. Baudelaire's motto might be the opposite of Browning's lines: "The Devil is in heaven. All's wrong with the world."

When Goethe said of Hugo and the Romanticists that they all came from Chateaubriand, he should have substituted the name of Rousseau — "Romanticism, it is Rousseau," exclaims Pierre Lasserre. But there is more of Byron and Petrus Borel — a forgotten mad poet — in Baudelaire; though, for a brief period, in 1848, he became a Rousseau reactionary, sported the workingman's blouse, shaved his head, shouldered a musket, went to the barricades, wrote inflammatory editorials calling the proletarian "Brother!" (oh, Baudelaire!) and, as the Goncourts recorded in their diary, had the head of a maniac. How seriously we may take this swing of the pendulum is to be noted in a speech of the poet's at the time of the Revolution: "Come," he said, "let us go shoot General Aupick!" It was his stepfather that he thought of, not the eternal principles of Liberty. This may be a false anecdote; many were foisted upon Baudelaire. For example, his exclamations at cafés or in public places, such as: "Have you ever eaten a baby? I find it pleasing to the palate!" or, "The night I killed my father!" Naturally people stared and Baudelaire was happy — he had startled the bourgeois. The cannibalistic idea he may have

76

borrowed from Swift's amusing pamphlet, for this French poet knew English literature.

Gautier compares the poems to a certain tale of Hawthorne's in which there is a garden of poisoned flowers. But Hawthorne worked in his laboratory of evil wearing mask and gloves; he never descended into the mud and sin of the street. Baudelaire ruined his health, smudged his soul, yet remained withal, as Anatole France says, "a divine poet." How childish, yet how touching is his resolution — he wrote in his diary of prayer's dynamic force — when he was penniless, in debt, threatened with imprisonment, sick, nauseated with sin: "To make every morning my prayer to God, the reservoir of·all force, and all justice; to my father, to Mariette, and to Poe as intercessors." (Evidently, Maurice Barrès encountered here his theory of Intercessors.) Baudelaire loved the memory of his father as much as Stendhal hated his. His mother he became reconciled with after the death of General Aupick, in 1857. He felt in 1862 that his own intellectual eclipse was approaching, for he wrote: "I have cultivated my hysteria with joy and terror. To-day imbecility's wing fanned me as it passed." The sense of the vertiginous gulf was abiding with him; read his poem, "Pascal avait son gouffre."

In preferring the Baudelaire· translations of Poe to the original — and they give the impression of being original works — Stedman agreed with Asselineau that the French is more concise than

77

the English. The prose of Poe and Baudelaire
is clear, sober, rhythmic; Baudelaire's is more
lapidary, finer in contour, richer coloured, more
supple, though without the "honey and tiger's
blood" of Barbey d'Aurevilly's. Baudelaire's
soul was patiently built up as a fabulous bird
might build its nest — bits of straw, the sobbing
of women, clay, cascades of black stars, rags,
leaves, rotten wood, corroding dreams, a spray
of roses, a sparkle of pebble, a gleam of blue sky,
arabesques of incense and verdigris, despairing
hearts and music and the abomination of desolation
for ground-tones. But this soul-nest is also a cemetery of the seven sorrows. He loved the clouds
. . . . *les nuages . . . là bas.* . . . It was *là bas*
with him even in the tortures of his wretched love-
life. Corruption and death were ever floating in his
consciousness. He was like Flaubert, who saw
everywhere the hidden skeleton. Félicien Rops
has best interpreted Baudelaire: the etcher and
poet were closely knit spirits. Rodin, too, is a
Baudelarian. If there could be such an anomaly
as a native wood-note evil, it would be the lyric
and astringent voice of this poet. His sensibility
was both catholic and morbid, though he could be
frigid in the face of the most disconcerting mis-
fortunes. He was a man for whom the visible
word existed; if Gautier was pagan, Baudelaire
was a strayed spirit from mediæval days. The
spirit ruled, and, as Paul Bourget said, "he saw
God." A Manichean in his worship of evil, he
nevertheless abased his soul: "Oh! Lord God!

78

THE BAUDELAIRE LEGEND

Give me the force and courage to contemplate my heart and my body without disgust," he prays: But as some one remarked to Rochefoucauld, "Where you end, Christianity begins."

Baudelaire built his ivory tower on the borders of a poetic Maremma, which every miasma of the spirit pervaded, every marsh-light and glow-worm inhabited. Like Wagner, Baudelaire painted in his sultry music the profundities of abysms, the vastness of space. He painted, too, the great nocturnal silences of the soul.

Pacem summam tenent! He never reached peace on the heights. Let us admit that souls of his kind are encased in sick frames; their steel is too shrewd for the scabbard; yet the enigma for us is none the less unfathomable. Existence for such natures is a sort of muffled delirium. To affiliate him with Poe, De Quincey, Hoffmann, James Thomson, Coleridge, and the rest of the sombre choir does not explain him; he is, perhaps, nearer Donne and Villon than any of the others — strains of the metaphysical and sinister and supersubtle are to be discovered in him. The disharmony of brain and body, the spiritual bi-location, are only too easy to diagnose; but the remedy? *Hypocrite lecteur — mon semblable — mon frère!* When the subtlety, force, grandeur, of his poetic production be considered, together with its disquieting, nervous, vibrating qualities, it is not surprising that Victor Hugo wrote to the poet: "You invest the heaven of art with we know not what deadly rays; you create a new shudder."

79

Hugo could have said that he turned Art into an Inferno. Baudelaire is the evil archangel of poetry. In his heaven of fire, glass, and ebony he is the blazing Lucifer. "A glorious devil, large in heart and brain, that did love beauty only . . ." sang Tennyson.

II

As long ago as 1869 and in our "barbarous gaslit country," as Baudelaire named the land of Poe, an unsigned review appeared in which this poet was described as "unique and as interesting as Hamlet. He is that rare and unknown being, a genuine poet — a poet in the midst of things that have disordered his spirit — a poet excessively developed in his taste for and by beauty . . . very responsive to the ideal, very greedy of sensation." A better description of Baudelaire does not exist. The Hamlet-motive, particularly, is one that sounded throughout the disordered symphony of the poet's life.

He was, later, revealed to American readers by Henry James. This was in 1878, when appeared the first edition of French Poets and Novelists. Previous to that there had been some desultory discussion, a few essays in the magazines, and in 1875 a sympathetic paper by Professor James Albert Harrison of the University of Virginia. But Mr. James had the ear of a cultured public. He denounced the Frenchman for his reprehensible taste, though he did not

80

mention his beautiful verse or his originality in the matter of criticism. Baudelaire, in his eyes, was not only immoral, but he had, with the approbation of Sainte-Beuve, introduced Poe as a great man to the French nation. (See Baudelaire's letter to Sainte-Beuve in the newly published Letters, 1841–1866.) Perhaps Mr. Dick Minim and his projected Academy of Criticism might make clear these devious problems.

The Etudes Critiques of Edmond Schérer were collected in 1863. In them we find this unhappy, uncritical judgment: "Baudelaire, lui, n'a rien, ni le cœur, ni l'esprit, ni l'idée, ni le mot, ni la raison, ni la fantaisie, ni la verve, ni même la facture . . . son unique titre c'est d'avoir contribué à créer l'esthétique de la débauche." It is not our intention to dilate upon the injustice of this criticism. It is Baudelaire the critic of æsthetics in whom we are interested. Yet I cannot forbear saying that if all the negations of Schérer had been transformed into affirmations, only justice would have been accorded Baudelaire, who was not alone a poet, the most original of his century, but also a critic of the first rank, one who welcomed Richard Wagner when Paris hooted him and his fellow composer, Hector Berlioz, played the rôle of the envious; one who fought for Edouard Manet, Leconte de Lisle, Gustave Flaubert, Eugène Delacroix; fought with pen for the modern etchers, illustrators, Meryon, Daumier, Félicien, Rops, Gavarni, and Constantin Guys. He literally identified himself with De

81

Quincey and Poe, translating them so wonderfully well that some unpatriotic critics like the French better than the originals. So much was Baudelaire absorbed in Poe that a writer of his times asserted the translator would meet the same fate as the American poet. A singular, vigorous spirit is Baudelaire's, whose poetry with its "icy ecstasy" is profound and harmonic, whose criticism is penetrated by a catholic quality, who anticipated modern critics in his abhorrence of schools and environments, preferring to isolate the man and study him uniquely. He would have subscribed to Swinburne's generous pronouncement: "I have never been able to see what should attract man to the profession of criticism but the noble pleasure of praising." The Frenchman has said that it would be impossible for a critic to become a poet; and it is impossible for a poet not to contain a critic.

Théophile Gautier's study prefixed to the definitive edition of Les Fleurs du Mal is not only the most sympathetic exposition of Baudelaire as man and genius, but it is also the high-water mark of Gautier's gifts as an essayist. We learn therein how the young Charles, an incorrigible dandy, came to visit Hôtel Pimodan about 1844. In this Hôtel Pimodan a dilettante, Ferdinand Boissard, held high revel. His fantastically decorated apartments were frequented by the painters, poets, sculptors, romancers, of the day — that is, carefully selected ones such as Liszt, George Sand, Mérimée, and others whose verve or genius gave

82

them the privilege of saying Open Sesame! to this cave of forty Supermen. Balzac has in his Peau de Chagrin pictured the same sort of scenes that were supposed to occur weekly at the Pimodan. Gautier eloquently describes the meeting of these kindred artistic souls, where the beautiful Jewess Maryx, who had posed for Ary Scheffer's Mignon and for Paul Delaroche's La Gloire, met the superb Mme. Sabatier, the only woman that Baudelaire loved, and the original of that extraordinary group of Clésinger's — the sculptor and son-in-law of George Sand — la Femme au Serpent, a Salammbô *à la mode* in marble. Hasheesh was eaten, so Gautier writes, by Boissard and by Baudelaire. As for the creator of Mademoiselle Maupin, he was too robust for such nonsense. He had to work for his living at journalism, and he died in harness an irreproachable father, while the unhappy Baudelaire, the inheritor of an intense, unstable temperament, soon devoured his patrimony of 75,000 francs and for the remaining years of his life was between the devil of his dusky Jenny Duval and the deep sea of debt.

It was at these Pimodan gatherings, which were no doubt much less wicked than the participants would have us believe, that Baudelaire encountered Emile Deroy, a painter of skill, who made his portrait, and encouraged the fashionable young fellow to continue his art studies. We have seen an album containing sketches by the poet. They betray talent of about the same order as Thack-

eray's, with a superadded note of the horrific —
that favourite epithet of the early Poe critics.
Baudelaire admired Thackeray, and when the
Englishman praised the illustrations of Guys,
he was delighted. Deroy taught his pupil the
commonplaces of a painter's technique; also how
to compose a palette — a rather meaningless
phrase nowadays. At least he did not write
of the arts without some technical experience.
Delacroix took up his enthusiastic disciple, and
when the Salons of Baudelaire appeared in 1845,
1846, 1855, and 1859, the praise and blame they
evoked were testimonies to the training and knowledge of their author. A new spirit had been born.

The names of Diderot and Baudelaire were
coupled. Neither academic nor spouting the
jargon of the usual critic, the Salons of Baudelaire
are the production of a humanist. Some would
put them above Diderot's. Mr. Saintsbury,
after Mr. Swinburne the warmest advocate of
Baudelaire among the English, thinks that the
French poet in his picture criticism observed too
little and imagined too much. "In other words,"
he adds, "to read a criticism of Baudelaire's without the title affixed is by no means a sure method
of recognizing the picture afterward." Now,
word-painting was the very thing that Baudelaire
avoided. It was his friend Gautier, with the
plastic style, who attempted the well-nigh impossible feat of competing in his verbal descriptions
with the certitudes of canvas and marble. And
if he with his verbal imagination did not entirely

84

succeed, how could a less adept manipulator of the vocabulary? We do not agree with Mr. Saintsbury. No one can imagine too much when the imagination is that of a poet. Baudelaire divined the work of the artist and set it down scrupulously in prose of rectitude. He did not paint pictures in prose. He did not divagate. He did not overburden his pages with technical terms. But the spirit he did disengage in a few swift phrases. The polemics of historical schools were a cross for him to bear, and he bore all his learning lightly. Like a true critic, he judged more by form than theme. There are no types; there is only life, he had cried before Jules Laforgue. He was ever for art-for-art, yet, having breadth of comprehension and a Heine-like capacity for seeing both sides of his own nature and its idiosyncrasies, he could write: "The puerile utopia of the school of art for art, in excluding morality, and often even passion, was necessarily sterile. All literature which refuses to advance fraternally between science and philosophy is a homicidal and a suicidal literature."

Baudelaire, then, was no less sound a critic of the plastic arts than of music and literature. Like his friend Flaubert, he had a horror of democracy, of the democratisation of the arts, of all the sentimental fuss and fuddle of a pseudo-humanitarianism. During the 1848 agitation the former dandy of 1840 put on a blouse and spoke of barricades. These things were in the air. Wagner rang the alarm-bells during the Dresden uprising.

85

Chopin wrote for the pianoforte a revolutionary étude. Brave lads! Poets and musicians fight their battles best in the region of the ideal. Baudelaire's little attack of the equality-measles soon vanished. He lectured his brother poets and artists on the folly and injustice of abusing or despising the bourgeois (being a man of paradoxes, he dedicated a volume of his Salons to the bourgeois), but he would not have contradicted Mr. George Moore for declaring that "in art the democrat is always reactionary. In 1830 the democrats were against Victor Hugo and Delacroix." And Les Fleurs du Mal, that book of opals, blood, and evil swamp-flowers, can never be savoured by the mob.

In his Souvenirs de Jeunesse, Champfleury speaks of the promenades in the Louvre he enjoyed in company with Baudelaire. Bronzino was one of the latter's preferences. He was also attracted to El Greco — not an unnatural admiration, considering the sombre extravagance of his own genius. Goya he has written of in exalted phrases. Velasquez was his touchstone. Being of a perverse nature, his nerves ruined by abuse of drink and drugs, the landscapes of his imagination or those by his friend Rousseau were more beautiful than Nature herself. The country, he declared, was odious. Like Whistler, whom he often met — see the Hommage à Delacroix by Fantin-Latour, with its portraits of Whistler, Baudelaire, Manet, Bracquemond the etcher, Legros, Delacroix, Cordier, Duranty the

86

critic, and De Balleroy — he could not help show-
ing his aversion to "foolish sunsets." In a word,
Baudelaire, into whose brain had entered too
much moonlight, was the father of a lunar school
of poetry, criticism and fiction. His Samuel
Cramer, in La Fanfarlo, is the literary progenitor
of Jean, Duc d'Esseintes, of Huysmans's A
Rebours. Huysmans modelled at first himself on
Baudelaire. His Le Drageoir aux Epices is a
continuation of Petits Poèmes en Prose. And to
Baudelaire's account must be laid much artificial
morbid writing. Despite his pursuit of perfection
in form, his influence has been too often baneful to
impressionable artists in embryo. A lover of
Gallic Byronism, and high-priest of the Satanic
school, there was no extravagance, absurd or terrible, that he did not commit, from etching a four-
part fugue on ice to skating hymns in honour of
Lucifer. In his criticism alone was he the sane,
logical Frenchman. And while he did not live to
see the success of the Impressionist group, he
would have surely acclaimed their theories and
practice. Was he not an impressionist himself?

As Richard Wagner was his god in music, so
Delacroix quite overflowed his æsthetic consciousness. Read Volume II. of his collected works,
Curiositiés Esthétiques, which contains his Salons;
also his essay, De l'Essence du Rire (worthy to be
placed side by side with George Meredith's essay on Comedy). Caricaturists, French and
foreign, are considered in two chapters at the close
of the volume. Baudelaire was as conscientious

87

as Gautier. He toiled around miles of mediocre canvas, saying an encouraging word to the less talented, boiling over with holy indignation, glacial irony, before the rash usurpers occupying the seats of the mighty, and pouncing on new genius with promptitude. Upon Delacroix he lavished the largesse of his admiration. He smiled at the platitudes of Horace Vernet, and only shook his head over the Schnetzes and other artisans of the day. He welcomed William Hausoullier, now so little known. He praised Devéria, Chasseriau — who waited years before he came into his own; his preferred landscapists were Corot, Rousseau and Troyon. He impolitely spoke of Ary Scheffer and the "apes of sentiment"; while his discussions of Hogarth, Cruikshank, Pinelli and Breughel proclaim his versatility of vision. In his essay Le Peintre de la Vie Moderne he was the first among critics to recognize the peculiar quality named "modernity," that nervous, naked vibration which informs the novels of Goncourt, Flaubert's L'Education Sentimentale, and the pictures of Manet, Monet, Degas and Raffaelli with their evocations of a new, nervous Paris. It is in his Volume III., entitled, L'Art Romantique, that so many things dear to the new century were then subjects of furious quarrels. This book contains much just and brilliant writing. It was easy for Nietzsche to praise Wagner in Germany in 1876, but dangerous at Paris in 1861 to declare war on Wagner's critics. This Baudelaire did.

THE BAUDELAIRE LEGEND

The relations of Baudelaire and Edouard Manet were exceedingly cordial. In a letter to Théophile Thoré, the art critic (Letters, p. 361), we find Baudelaire defending his friend from the accusation that his pictures were *pastiches* of Goya. He wrote: "Manet has never seen Goya, never El Greco; he was never in the Pourtalés Gallery." Which may have been true at the time, 1864, but Manet visited Madrid and spent much time studying Velasquez and abusing Spanish cookery. (Consider, too, Goya's Balcony with Girls and Manet's famous Balcony.) Raging at the charge of imitation, Baudelaire said in this same epistle: "They accuse even me of imitating Edgar Poe. . . . Do you know why I so patiently translated Poe? *Because he resembled me.*" The poet italicised these words. With stupefaction, therefore, he admired the mysterious coincidences of Manet's work with that of Goya and El Greco.

He took Manet seriously. He wrote to him in a paternal and severe tone. Recall his reproof when urging the painter to exhibit his work. "You complain about attacks, but are you the first to endure them? Have you more genius than Chateaubriand and Wagner? They were not killed by derision. And in order not to make you too proud I must tell you that they are models, each in his way, and in a very rich world, while *you are only the first in the decrepitude of your art.*" (Letters, p. 436.)

Would Baudelaire recall these prophetic words if he were able to revisit the glimpses of the

89

Champs Elysées at the autumn Salons? What would he think of Césanne? Odilon Redon he would understand, for he is the transposer of Baudelairianism to terms of design and colour. And perhaps the poet whose verse is saturated with tropical hues — he, when young, sailed in southern seas — might appreciate the monstrous debauch of form and colour in the Tahitian canvases of Paul Gauguin.

Baudelaire's preoccupation with pictorial themes may be noted in his verse. He is *par excellence* the poet of æsthetics. To Daumier he inscribed a poem; and to the sculptor Ernest Christophe, to Delacroix (Sur Le Tasse en Prison), to Manet, to Guys (Rêve Parisien), to an unknown master (Une Martyre); and Watteau, a Watteau *à rebours*, is seen in Un Voyage à Cythère; while in Les Phares this poet of ideal, spleen, music, and perfume shows his adoration for Rubens, Leonardo da Vinci, Michaelangelo, Rembrandt, Puget, Goya, Delacroix — "Delacroix, lac de sang hanté des mauvais anges." And what could be more exquisite than his quatrain to Lola de Valence, a poetic inscription for the picture of Edouard Manet, with its last line as vaporous, as subtle as Verlaine: Le charme inattendu d'un bijou rose et noir! Heine called himself the last of the Romantics. The first of the "Moderns" and the last of the Romantics was the many-sided Charles Baudelaire.

THE BAUDELAIRE LEGEND

III

He was born at Paris April 9, 1821 (Flaubert's
birth year), and not April 21st as Gautier has it.
His father was Joseph Francis Baudelaire, or
Beaudelaire, who occupied a government position. A cultivated art lover, his taste was apparent in the home he made for his second wife,
Caroline Archimbaut-Dufays, an orphan and
the daughter of a military officer. There was a
considerable difference in the years of this pair;
the mother was twenty-seven, the father sixty-two,
at the birth of their only child. By his first marriage the elder Baudelaire had one son, Claude,
who, like his half-brother Charles, died of paralysis, though a steady man of business. That great
neurosis, called Commerce, has its mental wrecks,
too, but no one pays attention; only when the
poet falls by the wayside is the chase begun by
neurologists and other soul-hunters seeking for
victims. After the death of Baudelaire's father,
the widow, within a year, married the handsome,
ambitious Aupick, then *chef de bataillon*, lieu-
tenant-colonel, decorated with the Legion of
Honour, and later general and ambassador to
Madrid, Constantinople, and London. Charles
was a nervous, frail youth, but unlike most children of genius, he was a scholar and won brilliant
honours at school. His step-father was proud of
him. From the Royal College of Lyons, Charles
went to the Lycée Louis-le-Grand, Paris, but was

expelled in 1839. Troubles soon began at home
for him. He was irascible, vain, very precocious,
and given to dissipation. He quarrelled with
General Aupick, and disdained his mother. But
she was to blame, she has confessed; she had quite
forgotten the boy in the flush of her second love.
He could not forget, or forgive what he called her
infidelity to the memory of his father. Hamlet-
like, he was inconsolable. The good bishop of
Montpellier, who knew the family, said that
Charles was a little crazy — second marriages
usually bring woe in their train. "When a
mother has such a son, she doesn't remarry,"
said the young poet. Charles signed himself
Baudelaire-Dufays, or sometimes, Dufais. He
wrote in his journal: "My ancestors, idiots or
maniacs . . . all victims of terrible passions";
which was one of his exaggerations. His grandfather on the paternal side was a Champenois
peasant, his mother's family presumably Norman, but not much is known of her forbears.
Charles believed himself lost from the time his
half-brother was stricken. He also believed that
his instability of temperament — and he studied
his "case" as would a surgeon — was the result
of his parents' disparity in years.

After his return from the East, where he did
not learn English, as has been said — his mother
taught him as a boy to converse in and write the
language — he came into his little inheritance,
about fifteen thousand dollars. Two years later
he was so heavily in debt that his family asked

for a guardian on the ground of incompetency. He had been swindled, being young and green. How had he squandered his money? Not exactly on opera-glasses, like Gérard de Nerval, but on clothes, pictures, furniture, books. The remnant was set aside to pay his debts. Charles would be both poet and dandy. He dressed expensively but soberly, in the English fashion; his linen dazzling, the prevailing hue of his habiliments black. In height he was medium, his eyes brown, searching, luminous, the eye of a nyctalops, "eyes like ravens'"; nostrils palpitating, cleft chin, mouth expressive, sensual, the jaw strong and square. His hair was black, curly, and glossy, his forehead high, square, white. In the Deroy portrait he wears a beard; he is there, what Catulle Mendès nicknamed him: His Excellence, Monseigneur Brummel! Later he was the elegiac Satan, the author of L'Imitation de N. S. le Diable; or the Baudelaire of George Moore: "the clean-shaven face of the mock priest, the slow cold eyes and the sharp cunning sneer of the cynical libertine who will be tempted that he may better know the worthlessness of temptation." In the heyday of his blood he was perverse and deliberate. Let us credit him with contradicting the Byronic notion that *ennui* could be best cured by dissipation; in sin Baudelaire found the saddest of all tasks. Mendès laughs at the legend of Baudelaire's violence, of his being given to explosive phrases. Despite Gautier's stories about the Hôtel Pimadon and its club of hasheesh-

93

caters, M. Mendès denies that Baudelaire was a victim of the hemp. What the majority of mankind does not know concerning the habits of literary workers is this prime fact: men who work hard, writing verse — and there is no mental toil comparable to it—cannot drink, or indulge in opium, without the inevitable collapse. The old-fashioned ideas of "inspiration," spontaneity, easy improvisation, the sudden bolt from heaven, are delusions still hugged by the world. To be told that Chopin filed at his music for years, that Beethoven in his smithy forged his thunderbolts, that Manet toiled like a labourer on the dock, that Baudelaire was a mechanic in his devotion to poetic work, that Gautier was a hard-working journalist, is a disillusion for the sentimental. Minerva springing full-fledged from Jupiter's skull to the desk of the poet is a pretty fancy; but Balzac and Flaubert did not encourage this fancy. Work literally killed Poe, as it killed Jules de Goncourt, Flaubert, and Daudet. Maupassant went insane because he would work and he would play the same day. Baudelaire worked and worried. His debts haunted him his life long. His constitution was flawed — Sainte-Beuve told him that he had worn out his nerves — from the start, he was *détraqué;* but that his entire life was one huge debauch is a nightmare of the moral police in some white cotton night-cap country.

His period of mental production was not brief or barren. He was a student. Du Camp's 'charge that he was an ignorant man is disproved

94

by the variety and quality of his published work. His range of sympathies was large. His mistake, in the eyes of his colleagues, was to write so well about the seven arts. Versatility is seldom given its real name — which is protracted labour. Baudelaire was one of the elect, an aristocrat, who dealt with the quintessence of art; his delicate air of a bishop, his exquisite manners, his modulated voice, aroused unusual interest and admiration. He was a humanist of distinction; he has left a hymn to Saint Francis in the Latin of the decadence. Baudelaire, like Chopin, made more poignant the phrase, raised to a higher intensity the expressiveness of art.

Women played a commanding rôle in his life. They always do with any poet worthy of the name, though few have been so frank in acknowledging this as Baudelaire. Yet he was in love more with Woman than the individual. The legend of the beautiful creature he brought from the East resolves itself into the dismal affair with Jeanne Duval. He met her in Paris, after he had been in the East. She sang at a café-concert in Paris. She was more brown than black. She was not handsome, not intelligent, not good; yet he idealized her, for she was the source of half his inspiration. To her were addressed those marvellous evocations of the Orient, of perfume, tresses, delicious mornings on strange far-away seas and "superb Byzant" domes that devils built. Baudelaire is the poet of perfumes; he is also the patron saint of *ennui*. No one has so chanted the praise

95

of odours. His soul swims on perfume as do other souls on music, he has sung. As he grew older he seemed to hunt for more acrid odours; he often presents an elaborately chased vase the carving of which transports us, but from which the head is quickly averted. Jeanne, whom he never loved, no matter what may be said, was a sorceress. But she was impossible; she robbed, betrayed him; he left her a dozen times only to return. He was a capital draughtsman with a strong nervous line and made many pen-and-ink drawings of her. They are not prepossessing. In her rapid decline, she was not allowed to want; Madame Aupick paying her expenses in the hospital. A sordid history. She was a veritable flower of evil for Baudelaire. Yet poetry, like music, would be colourless, scentless, if it sounded no dissonances. Fancy art reduced to the beatific and banal chord of C major!

He fell in love with the celebrated Madame Sabatier, a reigning beauty, at whose salon artistic Paris assembled. She had been christened by Gautier *Madame la Presidente*, and her sumptuous beauty was portrayed by Ricard in his La Femme au Chien. She returned Baudelaire's love. They soon parted. Again a riddle that the published letters hardly solve. One letter, however, does show that Baudelaire had tried to be faithful, and failed. He could not extort from his exhausted soul the sentiment; but he put its music on paper. His most seductive lyrics were addressed to Madame Sabatier: "A la très chère,

96

à la très-belle," a hymn saturated with love. Music, spleen, perfumes — "colour, sound, perfumes call to each other as deep to deep; perfumes like the flesh of children, soft as hautboys, green like the meadows" — criminals, outcasts, the charm of childhood, the horrors of love, pride, and rebellion, Eastern landscapes, cats, soothing and false; cats, the true companions of lonely poets; haunted clocks, shivering dusks, and gloomier dawns — Paris in a hundred phases — these and many other themes this strange-souled poet, this "Dante, pacer of the shore," of Paris has celebrated in finely wrought verse and profound phrases. In a single line he contrives atmosphere; the very shape of his sentence, the ring of the syllables, arouses the deepest emotion. A master of harmonic undertones is Baudelaire. His successors have excelled him in making their music more fluid, more singing, more vapourous — all young French poets pass through their Baudelarian green-sickness — but he alone knows the secrets of moulding those metallic, free sonnets. which have the resistance of bronze; and of the despairing music that flames from the mouths of lost souls trembling on the wharves of hell. He is the supreme master of irony and troubled voluptuousness.

Baudelaire is a masculine poet. He carved rather than sang; the plastic arts spoke to his soul. A lover and maker of images. Like Poe, his emotions transformed themselves into ideas. Bourget classified him as mystic, libertine, and

97

analyst. He was born with a wound in his soul, to use the phrase of Père Lacordaire. (Curiously enough, he actually contemplated, in 1861, becoming a candidate for Lacordaire's vacant seat in the French Academy. Sainte-Beuve dissuaded him from this folly.) Recall Baudelaire's prayer: "Thou, O Lord, my God, grant me the grace to produce some fine lines which will prove to myself that I am not the last of men, that I am not inferior to those I contemn." Individualist, egoist, anarchist, his only thought was of letters. Jules Laforgue thus described Baudelaire: "Cat, Hindoo, Yankee, Episcopal, alchemist." Yes, an alchemist who suffocated in the fumes he created. He was of Gothic imagination, and could have said with Rolla: *Je suis venu trop tard dans un monde trop vieux*. He had an unassuaged thirst for the absolute. The human soul was his stage, he its interpreting orchestra.

In 1857 The Flowers of Evil was published by the devoted Poulet-Malassis, who afterward went into bankruptcy — a warning to publishers with a taste for fine literature. The titles contemplated were Limbes, or Lesbiennes. Hippolyte Babou suggested the one we know. These poems were suppressed on account of six, and poet and publisher summoned. As the municipal government had made a particular ass of itself in the prosecution of Gustave Flaubert and his Madame Bovary, the Baudelaire matter was disposed of in haste. He was condemned to a fine of three hundred francs, a fine which was never paid, as

98

the objectionable poems were removed. . They were printed in the Belgian edition, and may be read in the new volume of Œuvres Posthumes.

Baudelaire was infuriated over the judgment, for he knew that his book was dramatic in expression. He had expected, like Flaubert, to emerge from the trial with flying colours; to be classed as one who wrote objectionable literature was a shock. "Flaubert had the Empress back of him," he complained; which was true; the Empress Eugénie, also the Princess Mathilde. But he worked as ever and put forth those polished intaglios called Poems in Prose, for the form of which he had taken a hint from Aloys Bertrand's Gaspard de la Nuit. He filled this form with a new content; not alone pictures, but moods, are to be found in these miniatures. Pity is their keynote, a tenderness for the abject and lowly, a revelation of sensibility that surprised those critics who had discerned in Baudelaire only a sculptor of evil. In one of his poems he described a landscape of metal, of marble and water; a babel of staircases and arcades, a palace of infinity, surrounded by the silence of eternity. This depressing yet magical dream was utilised by Huysmans in his A Rebours. But in the tiny landscapes of the Prose Poems there is nothing rigid or artificial. Indeed, the poet's deliberate attitude of artificiality is dropped. He is human. Not that the deep fundamental note of humanity is ever absent in his poems; the eternal diapason is there even when least overheard. Baudelaire is more human than

99

Poe. His range of sympathy is wider. In this he transcends him as a poet, though his subject-matter often issues from the very dregs of life. Brother to pitiable wanderers, there is, nevertheless, no trace of cant, no "Russian pity" *à la* Dostoiëvsky, no humanitarian or socialistic rhapsodies in his work. Baudelaire is an egoist. He hated the sentimental sapping of altruism. His prose-poem, Crowds, with its "bath of multitude," may have been suggested by Poe; but in Charles Lamb we find the idea: "Are there no solitudes out of caves and the desert? or, cannot the heart, in the midst of crowds, feel frightfully alone?"

His best critical work is the Richard Wagner and Tannhäuser, a more significant essay than Nietzsche's Richard Wagner in Bayreuth; Baudelaire's polemic appeared at a more critical period in Wagner's career. Wagner sent a brief, hearty letter of thanks to the critic and made his acquaintance. To Wagner Baudelaire introduced a young Wagnerian, Villiers de l'Isle Adam. This Wagner letter is included in the volume of Crépet; but there are no letters published from Baudelaire to Franz Liszt, though they were friends. In Weimar I saw at the Liszt house several from Baudelaire which should have been included in the Letters. The poet understood Liszt and his reforms as he understood Wagner's. The German composer admired the French poet, and his Kundry, of the sultry second act, Parsifal, has a Baudelairian hue, especially in the temptation scene.

THE BAUDELAIRE LEGEND

The end was at hand. Baudelaire had been steadily, rather, unsteadily, going downhill; a desperate figure, a dandy in shabby attire. He went out only after dark, he haunted the exterior boulevards, associated with birds of nocturnal plumage. He drank without thirst, ate without hunger, as he has said. A woeful decadence for this aristocrat of life and letters. Most sorrowful of sinners, his morose delectation scourged his nerves and extorted the darkest music from his lyre. He fled to Brussels, there to rehabilitate his dwindling fortunes. He gave a few lectures, and met Rops, Lemonnier, drank to forget, and forgot to work. He abused Brussels, Belgium, its people. A country where the trees are black, the flowers without odour, and where there is no conversation. He, the brilliant *causeur*, the chief *blaguer* of a circle in which young James McNeill Whistler was reduced to the rôle of a listener — this most *spirituel* among artists found himself a failure in the Belgium capital. It may not be amiss to remind ourselves that Baudelaire was the creator of most of the paradoxes attributed, not only to Whistler, but to an entire school — if one may employ such a phrase. The frozen imperturbability of the poet, his cutting enunciation, his power of blasphemy, his hatred of Nature, his love of the artificial, have been copied by the æsthetic blades of our day. He it was who first taunted Nature with being an imitator of art, with being always the same. Oh, the imitative sunsets! Oh, the quotidian eating and drinking! And as pessimist, too, he led the mode. Baudelaire, like Flaubert, grasped the murky torch of pessimism once held by Chateaubriand, Benjamin Constant, and Senancour. Doubtless all this stemmed from Byronism. To-day it is all as stale as Byronism.

His health failed rapidly, and he didn't have money enough to pay for doctor's prescriptions; he owed for the room in his hotel. At Namur, where he was visiting the father-in-law of Félicien Rops (March, 1866), he suffered from an attack of paralysis. He was removed to Brussels. His mother, who lived at Honfleur, in mourning for her husband, came to his aid. Taken to France, he was placed in a sanatorium. Aphasia set in. He could only ejaculate a mild oath, and when he caught sight of himself in the mirror he would bow pleasantly as if to a stranger. His friends rallied, and they were among the most distinguished people in Paris, the *élite* of souls. Ladies visited him, one or two playing Wagner on the piano — which must have added a fresh *nuance* to death — and they brought him flowers. He expressed his love for flowers and music to the last. He could not bear the sight of his mother; she revived in him some painful memories, but that passed, and he clamoured for her when she was absent. If anyone mentioned the names of Wagner or Manet, he smiled. Madame Sabatier came; so did the Manets. And with a fixed stare, as if peering through some invisible window opening upon eternity, he died, August 31, 1867, aged forty-six.

Barbey d'Aurevilly, himself a Satanist and dandy (oh, those comical old attitudes of literature!), had prophesied that the author of Fleurs du Mal would either blow out his brains or prostrate himself at the foot of the cross. (Later he said the same of Huysmans.) Baudelaire had the latter course forced upon him by fate after he had attempted spiritual suicide for how many years? (He once tried actual suicide, but the slight cut in his throat looked so ugly that he went no farther.) His soul had been a battle-field for the powers of good and evil. That at the end he brought the wreck of both soul and body to his God is not a subject of comment. He was an extraordinary poet with a bad conscience, who lived miserably and was buried with honours. Then it was that his worth was discovered (funeral orations over a genius are a species of public staircase wit). His reputation waxes with the years. He is an exotic gem in the crown of French poetry. Of him Swinburne has chanted Ave Atque Vale:

> Shall I strew on thee rose or rue or laurel,
> Brother, on this that was the veil of thee?

III

THE REAL FLAUBERT

Ah, did you once see Shelley plain,
And did he stop and speak to you . . .

I

It was some time in the late spring or early summer of 1879. I was going through the Chaussée d'Antin when a huge man, a terrific old man, passed me. His long straggling gray hair hung low. His red face was that of a soldier or a sheik, and was divided by drooping white moustaches. A trumpet was his voice, and he gesticulated freely to the friend who accompanied him. I did not look at him with any particular interest until some one behind me — if he be dead now may he be eternally blest! — exclaimed: "C'est Flaubert!" Then I stared; for though I had not read Madame Bovary I adored the verbal music of Salammbô, secretly believing, however, that it had been written by Melchior, one of the three Wise Kings who journeyed under the beckoning star of Bethlehem — how else account for its planturous Asiatic prose, for its evocations of a vanished past? But I knew the name

104

of Flaubert, that magic collocation of letters, and I .gazed at him. He returned my glance from prominent eyeballs, the colour of the pupil a bit of faded blue sky. He did not smile. He was too tender-hearted, despite his appreciation of the absurd. Besides, he knew, He, too, had been young and foolish. He, too, had worn a velvet coat and a comical cap, and had dreamed. I must have been a ridiculous spectacle. My hair was longer than my technique. I was studying Chopin or lunar rainbows then — I have forgotten which — and fancied that to be an artist one must dress like a cross between a brigand and a studio model. But I was happy. Perhaps Flaubert knew this, for he resisted the temptation to smile. And then he passed from my view. To be frank, I was not very much impressed, because earlier in the day I had seen Paul de Cassagnac and that famous duellist was romantic-looking, which the old Colossus of Croisset was not. When I returned to the Batignolles I told the *concièrge* of my day's outing.

"Ah!" he remarked, "M. Flaubert! M. Paul de Cassagnac! — a great man, Monsieur P-paul!" He stuttered a little. Now I only remember "M. Flaubert," with his eyes like a bit of faded blue sky. Was it a dream? Was it Flaubert? Did some stranger cruelly deceive me? But I'll never relinquish the memory of my glorious mirage.

Where was he going, Gustave Flaubert, on that sunny afternoon? It was at the time when Jules Ferry appointed him an assistant-librarian at

105

the Mazarine; *hors cadre*, a sinecure, a veiled pension with 3,000 francs a year; a charity, as the great writer bitterly complained. He was poor. He had given up, without a murmur, his entire fortune to his niece, then Madame Caroline Commainville, and through the influence of Turgenev and a few others this position had been created for him. He had no duties, yet he insisted on arriving at his post as early as half-past seven in the morning. He planned later that the government should be reimbursed for its outlay. His brother, Dr. Achille Flaubert, of Rouen, gave him a similar allowance, so the unhappy man had enough to live upon. Perhaps he was going to the Gare Saint-Lazare to take a train for Croisset; perhaps he was starting for Ancient Corinth — I thought — to see once more his Salammbô veiled by the sacred Zaïmph; or he might have been on the point of departing for Taprobana, the Ceylon of the antique world; that island whose very name he repeated with the same pleasure as did the old woman the blessed name of "Mesopotamia."

Taprobana! Taprobana! would cry Gustave Flaubert, to the despair of his friends. He was a man in love with beautiful sounds. He filled his books with them and with beautiful pictures. You must go to Beethoven or Liszt for a like variety in rhythms; the Flaubertian prose rhythms change in every sentence, like a landscape alternately swept by sunlight or shadowed by clouds. They vary with the moods and movements of the characters. They are music for ear and eye. And they can

106

never be translated. He is poet, painter, and composer, and he is the most artistic of novelists. If his work is deficient in sentiment; if he fails to strike the chords of pity of Dostoïevsky, Turgenev, and Tolstoy; if he lacks the teeming variety of Balzac, he is superior to them all as an artist. Because of his stern theories of art, he renounced the facile victories of sentimentalism. He does not invite his readers to smile or weep with him. He is not a manipulator of marionettes. And he can compress in a page more than Balzac in a volume. In part he derives from Chateaubriand, Gautier, and Hugo, and he was a lover of Rabelais, Shakespeare, and Montaigne. His psychology is simple; he believed that character should express itself by action. His landscapes in the Dutch, "tight," miniature style, or the large, luminous, "loose" manner of Hobbema; or again full of the silver repose of Claude and the dark romantic beauty of Rousseau — witness the forest of Fontaine-bleau in Sentimental Education — are ravishing. He has painted interiors incomparably — this novel is filled with them: balls, café-life, political meetings, receptions, ladies in their drawing-rooms, Meissonier-like virtuosity in details or the bourgeois elegance of Alfred Stevens. As a portraitist Flaubert recalls Velasquez, Rembrandt, or Hals, and not a little of the *diablerie* to be found in the Flemish masters of grotesque. Emma Bovary is the most perfectly finished portrait in fiction and Frédéric Moreau is nearly as life-like — the eternal middle-class Young Man. Madame

108

Arnoux, chiefly rendered by marvellous evasions, is in the clear-obscure of Rembrandt. Homais stands alone, a subject the delineation of which Swift would have envied. And Rosannette Bron — the truest record of her class ever depicted, and during the same decade that saw the odious sentimental and false Camille. Or Salome in Hérodias, that vision, cruel, feline, exquisite, which lesser writers have sought vainly to imitate. (Gustave Moreau alone transposed her to paint—Moreau, too, was a cenobite of art.) Or Félicité in Trois Contes. Or the perpetual journalist, Hussonet, the swaggering politician, Regimbart, Pellerin, the dilettante painter, the socialist, Sénecal, and Arnoux, the immortal charlatan. Whatever subject Flaubert attacked, a masterpiece emerged. He left few books; each represents the pinnacle of its *genre:* Bovary, Salammbô, Sentimental Education, Hérodias, Bouvard and Pécuchet — this last-named an epitome of human stupidity. Not an original philosophic intellect, nevertheless a philosophy has been drawn from Flaubert's work by the brilliant French philosopher Jules Gaultier, who defines *Bovaryisme* as that tendency in mankind to appear other than it is; a tendency which is an important factor in our mental and social evolution. Without illusions mankind would take to the trees, the abode, we are told, of our prehistoric arboreal ancestors. Nevertheless, Emma Bovary as a philosophic symbol would have greatly astonished Gustave Flaubert.

II

"Since Goethe," might be a capital title for an essay on the epics that were written after the death of the noblest German of them all. The list would be small. In France there are only the rather barren rhetorical exercise of Edgar Quinet's Ahasvérus, the surging insurrectionary poems of Hugo, and the faultlessly frigid performance of Leconte de Lisle. But a work of such heroic power and proportions as Faust there is not, except Flaubert's Temptation of Saint Antony, which is so impregnated by the Faustian spirit — though poles apart from the German poem in its development — that, when we hear the youthful Gustave was a passionate admirer and student of Goethe, even addressing a long poem in alexandrines to his memory, we are not surprised. The real Flaubert is only beginning to be revealed. His four volumes of correspondence, his single volume of letters addressed to George Sand, and the recently published letters to his niece Caroline — now Madame Franklin Grout of Antibes — have shown us a very different Flaubert from the legend chiefly created by Maxime du Camp. Dr. Félix Dumesnil, in his remarkable study, has told us of the Rouen master's neurasthenia and has utterly disproved Du Camp's malicious yarns about epilepsy. Above all, Flaubert's devotion to Goethe and the recent publication of the first version of his Saint Antony have presented a novel picture of his personality. We now know that, striving to become impersonal in art, he is personal and present in every page he ever wrote; furthermore that, despite his incessant clamours and complaints, he, in reality, loved his galley-like, self-imposed labours.

The Temptation of Saint Antony is the only modern poem of epical largeness that may be classed with Brand or Zarathustra. It recalls at times the Second Part of Faust in its sweep and grandeur, in its grandiose visions; but though it is superior in verbal beauty it falls short of Goethe in its presentation of the problems of human will. Faust is a man who wills; Antony is static, not dynamic; the one is tempted by the Devil and succumbs, but does not lose his soul; Flaubert's hermit resists the Devil at his subtlest, yet we do not feel that his soul is as much worth the saving as Faust's. Ideas are the heroes in Flaubert's prose epic. Saint Antony is a metaphysical drama, not a human one like Faust; nevertheless, to Faust alone may we compare it.

Flaubert was born at Rouen, December 12, 1821, where he died May 18, 1880. That he practically passed his years at Croisset, his mother's home, below Rouen facing the Seine, and in his study toiling like a titan over his books, should be recorded in every text-book of literature. For he is the patron-saint of all true literary men. He had a comfortable income. He thought, talked, lived literature. His friends Du Camp, Louis Bouilhet, Turgenev, Taine, Baudelaire,

III

Zola, the Goncourts, Daudet, Renan, Maupassant, Henry James, have testified to his absorption in his art. It is almost touching in these times when a man goes into the writing business as if vending tripe, to recall the example of Flaubert for whom art was more sacred than religion. Naturally, he has been proved by the madhouse doctors to have been half cracked. Perhaps he was not as sane as a stockbroker, but it takes all sorts to make a world and a writer of Flaubert's rank should not be weighed in the same scales with, say, a successful politician.

He was endowed with a nervous temperament, though up to his twenty-second year he was as handsome and as free from sickness as a god. He was very tall and his eyes were sea-green. A nervous crisis supervened and at wide intervals returned. It was almost fatal for Gustave. He became pessimistic and afraid of life. However, the talk of his habitual truculent pessimism has been exaggerated. Naturally optimistic, with a powerful constitution and a stout heart, he worked like the Trojan he was. His pessimism came with the years during his boyhood — Byronic literary spleen was in the air. He was a grumbler and rather overdid the peevish pose. As Zola asked: "What if he had been forced to earn his living by writing?" But, even in his blackest moods, he was glad to see his friends at Croisset, glad to go up to Paris for recreation. His letters, so free, fluent, explosive, give us the true Flaubert who childishly roared yet was so hearty, so friendly, so loving to his mother, niece, and intimates. His heredity was puzzling. His father was, like Baudelaire's grandfather, of Champenois stock; bourgeois, steady, a renowned surgeon. From him Gustave inherited his taste for all that pertained to medicine and science. Recall his escapades as a boy when he would peep for hours into the dissecting-room of the Rouen hospital. Such matters fascinated him. He knew more about the theory and practice of medicine than many professional men. An air of mortality exhales from his pages. He is in Madame Bovary the keen soul-surgeon. His love of a quiet, sober existence came to him from his father. He clung to one house for nearly a half century. He has said that one must live like a bourgeois and think like an artist; to be ascetic in life and violent in art — that was a Flaubert maxim. "I live only in my ideas," he wrote. But from the mother's side, a Norman and aristocrat she was, he inherited his love of art, his disdain for philistines, his adventurous disposition — transposed because of his malady to the cerebral region, to his imagination. He boasted Canadian blood, "red skin," he called it, but that was merely a mystification. The dissonance of temperament made itself felt early. He was the man of Gòethe with two spirits struggling within him. Dual in temperament, he swung from an almost barbaric Romanticism to a cruel analysis of life that made him the pontiff of the Realistic school. He hated realism, yet an inner force set him to the disagreeable task of writing Madame Bovary and Sentimental Education — the latter, with its daylight atmosphere, the supreme exemplar of realism in fiction. So was it with his interior life. He was a mystic who no longer believed. These dislocations of his personality he combated all his life, and his books show with what success. "Flaubert," wrote Turgenev, his closest friend, to George Sand, "has tenacity without energy, just as he has self-love without vanity." But what tenacity!

Touching on the question of epilepsy, a careful reading of Dumesnil convinces anyone, but the neurologist with a fixed idea, that Flaubert was not a sufferer from genuine epilepsy. Not that there is any reason why epilepsy and genius should be divorced; we know in many cases the contrary is the reverse. Take the case of Dostoievsky — his epilepsy was one of the most fruitful of motives in his stories. Nearly all his heroes and heroines are attainted. (Read The Idiot or the Karamsoff Brothers.) But Flaubert's epilepsy was arranged for him by Du Camp, who thought that by calling him an epilept in his untrustworthy Memoirs he would belittle Flaubert. And he did, for in his time the now celebrated — and discredited — theory of genius and its correlation with the falling-sickness had not been propounded. Flaubert had hystero-neurasthenia. He was rheumatic, asthmatic, predisposed to arterio-sclerosis and apoplexy. He died of an apoplectic stroke. His early nervous fits were without the *aura* of epilepsy; he did not froth at the mouth nor were there mus-

cular contractions; not even at his death. Dr.
Tourneaux, who hastened to aid him in the absence of his regular physician, Dr. Fortin, denied
the rumours of epilepsy that were so gaily spread
by that sublime old gossip, Edmond de Goncourt,
also by Zola and Du Camp. The contraction of
Flaubert's hands was caused by the rigidity of
death; most conclusive of all evidence against the
epileptic theory is the fact that during his occasional fits Gustave never lost consciousness.
Nor did he suffer from any attacks before he had
attained his majority, whereas epilepsy usually
begins at an early age. He studied with intense
zeal his malady and in a dozen letters refers to it,
tickets its symptoms, tells of plans to escape
the crises, and altogether, has furnished students
of pathology many examples of nerve-exhaustion
and its mitigation. His first attacks began at
Pont-Audemar, in 1843. In 1849 he had a fresh
attack. His trip to the Orient relieved him.
He was a Viking, a full-blooded man, who scorned
sensible hygiene; he took no exercise beyond a
walk in the morning, a walk in the evening on
his terrace, and in summer an occasional swim
in the Seine. He ate copiously, was moderate
in drinking, smoked fifteen or twenty pipes a
day, abused black coffee, and for months at a
stretch worked fifteen hours out of the twenty-
four at his desk. He warned his disciple, Guy
de Maupassant, against too much boating as
being destructive of mental productivity. After
Nietzsche read this he wrote: "Sedentary applica-

115

tion is the very sin against the Holy Ghost. Only thoughts won by walking are valuable." In 1870 another crisis was brought on by protracted labours over the revision of the definitive version of the Saint Antony. His travels in Normandy, in the East, his visits to London (1851) and to Righi-Kaltbad, together with sojourns in Paris — where he had a little apartment — make up the itinerary of his fifty-eight years. Is it any wonder that he died of apoplexy, stricken at his desk, he of a violently sanguine temperament, bull-necked, and the blood always in his face?

Maurice Spronck, who took too seriously the saying of Flaubert — a lover of extravagant paradox — thinks the writer had a cerebral lesion, which he called *audition colorée*. It is a malady peculiar to imaginative natures, which transposes tone to colour, or odour to sound. As this "malady" may be found in poets from the dawn of creation, "coloured audition" must be a necessary quality of art. Flaubert took pains to exaggerate his speech when in company with the Goncourts. He suspected their diary-keeping weakness and he humoured it by telling fibs about his work. "I have finished my book, the cadence of the last paragraph has been found. Now I shall write it." Aghast were the brothers at the idea of an author beginning his book backward. Flaubert boasted that the colour of Salammbô was purple. Sentimental Education (a bad title, as Turgenev wrote him; Withered Fruits, his first title, would have been better) was gray, and

116

Madame Bovary was for him like the colouring of certain mouldy wood-vermin. The Goncourts solemnly swallowed all this, as did M. Spronck. Which moved Anatole France to exclaim: "Oh these young clinicians!"

But what is all this when compared with the magnificent idiocy of Du Camp, who asserted that if Flaubert had not suffered from epilepsy *he would have become a genius! Hénaurme!* as the man who made such masterpieces as Madame Bovary, Sentimental Education, Temptation of Saint Antony, the Three Tales, Bouvard et Pécuchet, had a comical habit of exclaiming. Enormous, too, was Guy de Maupassant's manner of avenging his master's memory. In the final edition — eight volumes long — Maupassant, with the unerring eye of hatred, affixed an introduction to Bouvard et Pécuchet. Therein he printed Maxime du Camp's letters to Flaubert during the period when Madame Bovary was appearing in the *Revue de Paris*. Du Camp was one of its editors. He urged Flaubert to cut the novel — the concision of which is so admirable, the organic quality of which is absolute. Worse still remains. If Flaubert couldn't perform the operation himself, then the aforesaid Du Camp would hire some experienced hack to do it for the sensitive author; wounded vanity Du Camp believed to be the cause of indignant remonstrances. They eliminated the scene of the agricultural fair and the operation on the hostler's foot—one scene as marvellous as a *genre* paint-

ing by Teniers with its study of the old farm
servant, and psychologically more profound; the
other necessary to the development of the story.
Thus Madame Bovary was slaughtered serially
by a man ignorant of art, that Madame Bovary
which is one of the glories of French literature,
as Mr. James truly says. Flaubert scribbled on
Du Camp's letters another of his favourite ex-
pletives, *Gigantesque!* Flaubert never forgave
him, but they were apparently reconciled years
later. Du Camp went into the Academy;
Flaubert refused to consider a candidacy, though
Victor Hugo — wittily nicknamed by Jules Laforgue "Aristides the Just" — urged him to do
so. Even the mighty Balzac was too avid of
glory and gold for Flaubert, to whom art and its
consolations were all-sufficing.

III

Bouvard et Pécuchet was never finished. Its
increasing demands killed Flaubert. In his desk
were found many cahiers of notes taken to illus-
trate the fatuity of mankind, its stupidity, its
bêtise. He was as pitiless as Swift or Schopenhauer in his contempt for low ideals and vulgar
pretensions, for the very bourgeois from whom
he sprung. In the collection we find this gem of
wisdom uttered by Louis Napoleon in 1865:
"The richness of a country depends on its general prosperity." To it should be included the
Homais-like dictum of Maxime du Camp that

118

if Flaubert had not been an epilept he would have been a genius! Or, the following hospital criticism; Flaubert was denied creative ability! Who has denied it to him? Homais alone in his supreme asininity should be a beacon-light of warning for any one of these inept critics. Flaubert once wrote: "I am reading books on hygiene; how comical they are! What impertinence these physicians have! What asses for the most part they are!" And he, the son of a celebrated surgeon and the brother of another, a medical student himself, might have made Homais a psychiatrist instead of a druggist, if he had lived longer.

Du Camp—who, clever and witty as well as inexact and reckless in statement, was a man given to envies and literary jealousies — never got over Flaubert's startling success with Madame Bovary. He once wrote a fanciful epitaph for Louise Colet, a French woman of mediocrity, the "Muse" of Flaubert, a general trouble-breeder and a recipient of Flaubert's correspondence. The Colet had embroiled herself with De Musset and published a spiteful romance in which poor Flaubert was the villain. This the Du Camp inscription: "Here lies the woman who compromised Victor Cousin, made Alfred de Musset ridiculous, calumniated Gustave Flaubert, and tried to assassinate Alphonse Karr: *Requiescat in pace.*" A like epitaph suggests itself for Maxime du Camp: *Hic jacet* the man who slandered Baudelaire, traduced his loving friend

119

Gustave Flaubert, and was snuffed out of critical existence by Guy de Maupassant.

The massive-shouldered Hercules, Flaubert, a Hercules spinning prose for his exacting Dejanira of art, was called unintelligent by Anatole France. He had not, it is true, the subtle critical brain and thorough scholarship of M. France; yet Flaubert was learned. Brunetière even taxed him with an excess of erudition. But his multitudinous conversation, his lack of logic, his rather gross sense of humour, are not to be found in his work. Without that work, without Salammbô, for example, should we have had the pleasure, thrice-distilled, of reading Anatole France's Thaïs? (See a single instance in the definitive edition Temptation, page 115, the episode of the Gymnosophist.) All revivals of the antique world are unsatisfactory at best, whether Chateaubriand's Martyrs, or the unsubstantial lath and plaster of Bulwer's Last Days of Pompeii, or the flabbiness and fustian of Quo Vadis. The most perfect attempt is Salammbô, an opera in words, and its battlements of purple prose were riddled by Sainte-Beuve, by Froehner, and lately by Maurice Pézard — who has proved to his own satisfaction that Flaubert was sadly amiss in his Punic archæology. Well, who cares if he was incorrect in details? His partially successful reconstruction of an epoch is admitted, though the human element is somewhat obliterated. Flaubert was bound to be more Carthaginian than Carthage.

THE REAL FLAUBERT

After the scandal caused by the prosecution of Madame Bovary Flaubert was afraid to publish his 1856, second version of Saint Antony. He had been advised by the sapient Du Camp to cast the manuscript into the fire, after a reading before Bouilhet and Du Camp lasting thirty-three hours. He refused. This was in September, 1849. Du Camp declares that he asked him to essay "the Delaunay affair," meaning the Delamarre story. This Flaubert did, and the result was the priceless history of Charles and Emma Bovary. D'Aurevilly attacked the book viciously; Baudelaire defended it. Later Turgenev wrote to Flaubert: "After all you are Flaubert!" George Sand was a motherly consoler. Their letters are delightful. She did not quite understand the bluff, naïve Gustave, she who composed so flowingly, and could turn on or off her prose like the tap of a kitchen hydrant (the simile is her own). How could she fathom the tormented desire of her friend for perfection, for the blending of idea and image, for the eternal pursuit of the right word, the shapely sentence, the cadenced *coda* of a paragraph? And of the larger demands of style, of the subtle tone of a page, a chapter, a book, why should this fluent and graceful writer, called George Sand, concern herself with such superfluities! It was always *O altitudo* in art with Flaubert — the most copious, careless of correspondents. He had set for himself an impossible standard of perfection and an ideal of impersonality neither of which he realized.

But there is no outward sign of conflict in his work; all trace of the labour bestowed upon his paragraphs is absent. His style is simple, direct, large, above all, clear, the clarity of classic prose.

His declaiming aloud his sentences has been adduced to prove his absence of sanity. Beethoven, too, was pronounced crazy by his various landladies because he sang and howled in his voice of a composer his compositions in the making. Flaubert was the possessor of an accurate musical ear; not without justice did Coppée call him the "Beethoven of French prose." His sense of rhythm was acute; he carried it so far that he would sacrifice grammar to rhythmic flow. He tested his sentences aloud. Once in his apartment, Rue Murillo, overlooking Parc Monceau, he rehearsed a page of a new book for hours. Belated coachmen, noting the open windows, hearing an outrageous vocal noise, concluded that a musical *soirée* was in progress. Gradually the street filled on either side with carriages in search of passengers. But the guests never emerged from the house. In the early morning the lights were extinguished and the oaths of the disappointed ones must have been heard by Flaubert.

He would annotate three hundred volumes for a page of facts. His bump of scrupulousness was large. In twenty pages he sometimes saved three or four from destruction. He did not become, however, as captious as Balzac in the handling of proofs. A martyr of style, he was not altogether an enameller in precious stones, not a patient

122

mosaic-maker, superimposing here and there a precious verbal jewel. First, the image, and then its appropriate garb; sometimes image and phrase were born simultaneously, as was the case with Richard Wagner. These extraordinary things may happen to men of genius, who are neither opium-eaters nor lunatics. The idea that Flaubert was ever addicted to drugs — beyond the quinine with which his good father dosed him after the fashion of those days — is ridiculous. The gorgeous visions of Saint Antony are the results of stupendous preparatory studies, a stupendous power of fantasy, and a stupendous concentration. Opium superinduces visions, but not the power and faculty of attention to record them in terms of literature for forty years. George Saintsbury has pronounced Saint Antony the most perfect specimen of dream literature extant. And because of its precision in details, its architectonic, its deep-hued waking hallucinations.

Flaubert was a very nervous man, "as hysterical as an old woman," said Dr. Hardy of the hospital Saint-Louis, but neither mad nor epileptic. His mental development was not arrested in his youth, as asserted by Du Camp; he had arranged his life from the time he decided to become a writer. He was one with the exotic painter, Gustave Moreau, in his abhorrence of the mob. He was a poet who wrote a perfect prose, not prose-poetry. Enamoured of the antique, of the Orient, of mystical subjects, he spent a lifetime in the elaboration of his beloved themes. That he was ob-

123

sessed by them is merely to say that he was the possessor of mental energy and artistic gifts. He was not happy. He never brought his interior and exterior lives into complete harmony. An unparalleled observer, an imaginative genius, he was a child outside the realm of art. Soft of heart, he raised his niece as a daughter; a loving son, he would console himself after his mother's death by looking at the dresses she once wore. Flaubert a sentimentalist! He outlived his family and his friends, save a few; death was never far away from his thoughts; he would weep over his souvenirs. At Croisset I have talked with the faithful Colange, whose card reads: "E. Colange, ex-cook of Gustave Flaubert!" The affection of the novelist for cats and dogs, he told me, was marked. The study pavilion is to-day a Flaubert Memorial. The parent house is gone, and in 1901 there was a distillery on the grounds, which is now a printing establishment. Flaubert cherished the notion that Pascal had once stopped in the old Croisset homestead; that Abbé Prévost had written Manon Lescaut within its walls. He had many such old-fashioned and darling *tics*, and he is to be envied them.

Since Madame Bovary French fiction, for the most part, has been Flaubert with variations. His influence is still incalculable. François Coppée wrote: "By the extent and the magnificence of his prose, Gustave Flaubert equals Bossuet and Chateaubriand. He is destined to become a great classic. And several centuries hence — ev-

124

erything perishes — when the French language shall have become only a dead language, candidates for the bachelor's degree will be able to obtain it only by expounding (along with the famous exordium, He Who Reigns in the Heavens, etc., or The Departure of the Swallows, of René) the portrait of Catharine le Roux, the farm servant, in Madame Bovary, or the episode of the Crucified Lions in Salammbô."

IV

With the critical taste that uncovers bare the bones of the dead I have no concern, nor shall I enter the way which would lead me into the dusty region of professional ethics. Every portrait painter from Titian to John Sargent, from Velasquez to Zuloaga, has had a model. Novelists are no less honest when they build their characters upon human beings they have known and studied, whether their name be Fielding or Balzac or Flaubert.

The curiosity which seeks to unveil the anonymity of a novelist's personages may not be exactly laudable; it is yet excusable. I am reminded of its existence by a certain Parisian journalist who, acting upon information that appeared in the pages of a well-known French literary review, went to Normandy in search of the real Emma Bovary. Once called wicked, the novel has been pronounced as moral as a Sunday-school tract. Thackeray admired its style, but deplored, with his accustomed streak of sentimentalism, the cold-blooded analysis which hunted Emma to an ignominious grave. Yet the author of Vanity Fair did not hesitate to pursue through many chapters his mercurial Rebecca Sharp.

The story of Emma Bovary would hardly attract, if published in the daily news columns, much attention nowadays. A good-looking young provincial woman tires of her honest, slow-going husband. She reads silly novels, as do thousands of silly married girls to-day. Emma lived in a little town not far from Rouen. Flaubert named it Yonville. We read that Emma flirted with a country squire who in order to escape eloping with the romantic goose suddenly disappeared. She consoled herself with a young law student, but when he tired of her the consequences were lamentable. Harassed by debt, Emma took poison. Her stupid husband, a hard-working district doctor, was aghast at her death and puzzled by the ruin which followed fast at its heels. He found it all out, even the love-letters of the squire. He died suddenly.

A sordid tale, but perfectly told and remarkable not only for the fidelity of the landscapes, the chaste restraint of the style, but also because there are half a dozen marvellously executed characters, several of which have entered into the living current of French speech. Homais, the vainglorious, yet human and likable Homais, is a synonym for pedantic bragging mediocrity. He is a druggist. He would have made an ideal

126

politician. He stands for a shallow "modernity" but is more superstitious than a mediæval sexton. Flaubert's novel left an indelible mark in French fiction and philosophy. Even Balzac did not create a Homais.

Now comes the curious part of the story. It was the transcription of a real occurrence. Flaubert did not invent it. In a town near Rouen named Ry there was once a young physician, Louis Delamarre. He originally hailed from Catenay, where his father practised medicine. In the novel Ry is called Yonville. Delamarre paid his addresses to Delphine Couturier, who in 1843 was twenty-three years of age. She was comely, had a bright though superficial mind, spoke in a pretentious manner, and overdressed. From her father she inherited her vanity and the desire to appear as occupying a more exalted position than she did. The elder Couturier owned a farm, though heavily mortgaged, at Vieux-Château. He was a close-fisted Norman anxious to marry off his daughters— Emma had a sister. He objected to the advances of the youthful physician, chiefly because he saw no great match for his girl. Herein the tale diverges from life.

But love laughs at farmers as well as locksmiths, and by a ruse worthy of Paul de Kock, Delphine, by feigning maternity, got the parental permission. She soon regretted her marriage. The husband, Louis, was prosaic. He earned the daily bread and butter of the household, and even economised so that his pretty wife could buy fallals and foolish books. She hired a servant and had her day at home — Fridays. No one visited her. She was only an unimportant spouse of a poverty-stricken country doctor. At Saint-Germain des Essours there still lives an octogenarian peasant woman once the domestic of the Delamarres-Bovarys. She said, when asked to describe her mistress: "Heavens, but she was pretty. Face, figure, hair, all were beautiful."

In Ry there was a druggist named Jouanne. He is the original Homais. Delphine's, or rather Emma Bovary's, first admirer was a law clerk, Louis Bottet. He is described as a small, impatient, alert old man at the time of his death. The faithless Rodolphe — what a name for sentimental melodrama — was really a proprietor named Campion. He lost his farm and revenue after Emma's death and went to America to make his fortune. Unsuccessful, he returned to Paris, and about 1852 shot himself on the boulevard. Who may deny, after this, that truth is stranger than Flaubert's fiction?

The good, sensible old Abbé Bournisien, who advised Emma Bovary, when she came to him for spiritual consolation, to consult her doctor husband, was, in reality, an Abbé Lafortune. The irony of events is set forth in sinister relief by the epitaph which the real Emma's husband had carved on her tomb: "She was a good mother, a good wife." Gossips of Ry aver that

128

after the truth came to Dr. Delamarre he took a slow poison. But this seems turning the screw a trifle too far. Mme. Delamarre, or Emma Bovary, was buried in the graveyard of the only church at Ry. To-day the tomb is no longer in existence. She died March 6, 1848. The inhabitants still show the church, — the porch of which was too narrow to allow the passage of unlucky Emma's coffin — the house of her husband, and the apothecary shop of M. Homais. The latter survived for many years the unhappy heroine, who stole the ·poison that killed her from his stock. A delightful touch of Homais-like humour was displayed — one that exonerated Flaubert from the charge of exaggeration in portraying Homais — when the novel appeared. The characters were at once recognized, both in Rouen and Ry. This druggist, Jouanne-Homais, was flattered at the lengthy study of himself, of course missing its relentless ironic strokes. He regretted openly that the author had not consulted him; for, said he, "I could have given him many points about which he knew nothing." The epitaph which the real Homais composed for the tomb of his wife — surely you can never forget her after reading the novel — is magnificent in its bombast. Flaubert knew his man.

The distinguished writer is a sober narrator of facts. His is not a domain of delicate thrills. His women are neither doves nor devils. He does not paint those acrobats of the soul so dear to psychological fiction. Despite his pretended

129

impassibility, he is tender-hearted; the pity he felt for his characters is not effusively expressed. But the larger rhythms of humanity are ever present. If he had been hard of heart, he would have related the Bovary tale as it happened in life. Charles Bovary finds the love-letters and meets Rodolphe. Nothing happens. The real Charles never knew of the real Emma's treachery. Madame d'Epinay was not far amiss when she wrote: "The profession of woman is very hard.

V

No less a masterpiece than Don Quixote has been cited in critical comparison with Madame Bovary. Flaubert was called the Cervantes who had ridiculed from the field the Romantic School. This irritated him, for he never posed as a realist; indeed, he confessed that he had intended to mock the Realistic School — then headed by Champfleury — in his Bovary. The very name of this book would arouse a storm of abuse from him. He knew that he had more than one book in him, he believed better books; the indifference of the public to Sentimental Education and the Temptation he never understood. Much astonishment was expressed, after the appearance of Bovary, that such a mature work of art should have been the author's first. But Beethoven, Chopin, Brahms did not permit their juvenile efforts to see the light; the same was the case with Flaubert. In 1835 — he was fourteen at the time — he wrote Mort du Duc de Guise; in 1836 another historical study. Short stories in the style of Hoffmann, with thrilling titles, such as Rage et Impuissance, Le Rêve d'Enfer (1837), and a psychologic effort, Agonies (dedicated to Alfred le Poittevin — as are both versions of the Temptation; Alfred's sister later became the mother of Guy de Maupassant): all these exercises, as is a Dance of Death, are still in manuscript. But in 1839 a scenario of a mystery bearing the cryptic title of Smarh was written; and this with Novembre, and a study of Rabelais, and Nuit de Don Juan, have been published in the definitive edition; with a record of travels in Normandy. The Memoirs of a Madman appeared a few years ago in a Parisian magazine. It was a youthful effort. There is also in the collection of Madame Grout a 300-page manuscript (1843–1845) named L'Education Sentimentale — vaguely inspired by Wilhelm Meister — which has nothing in common with his novel of the same name published in 1869.

Flaubert's taste in the matter of titles was lamentable. He made a scenario for a tale called Spiral, and he often asserted that he hankered to write in marmoreal prose the Combat of Thermopylæ; he meditated, too, a novel the scene and characters laid in the Second Empire, and dilated upon the beauty of a portrait executed in microscopic detail of that immortal

131

character, M. le Préfet. We might have had
a second Homais if he had made this project
a reality. He told Turgenev that he had another idea, a sort of modern Matron of Ephesus
— in the Temptation there is an episode that
suggests the Ephesus. He did not lack invention
and he was an extremely rapid writer — but his
artistic conscience was morbidly sensitive. It
pained him to see Zola throwing his better self
to the dogs in his noisy, inartistic novels — in
which, he said, was neither poetry nor art. And
he wrote this opinion to Zola, who promptly
called him an idiot. In that correct but colourless book of Faguet's on Flaubert, the critic makes
note of all the novelist's grammatical errors and
reaches the conclusion that he was a stylist
unique, but not careful in his grammar. Now,
while this is piffling pedantry, the facts are in
Faguet's favour; Faguet, who holds the critical
scales nicely, as he always does, though listlessly.
But in the handling of such a robust, red-blooded
subject as Flaubert the college professor was
hardly a wise selection. The Faguet study is
clear and painstaking but not sympathetic. Mr.
James has praised it, possibly because Faguet
agrees with him as to the psychology of Sentimental Education. Not a study, Faguet's, for
Flaubertians, who see the faults of their Saint
Polycarp — his favourite self-appellation — and
love him for his all-too-human imperfections.

In 1845 Flaubert, on a visit to Italy, stopped
at Genoa. There, in the Palace Balbi-Sena-

rega — and not at the Doria, as Du Camp wrote, with his accustomed carelessness — the young Frenchman saw an old picture by Breughel (probably by Piéter the Younger, surnamed Hell-Breughel) that represents a temptation of Saint Antony. It is hardly a masterpiece, this Breughel, and is dingy in colour. But Flaubert, who loved the grotesque, procured an engraving of this picture and it hung in his study at Croisset until the day of his death. It was the spring-board of his own Temptation. The germ may be found in his mystery, Smarh, with its Demon and metaphysical colouring. Breughel set into motion the mental machinery of the Temptation that never stopped whirring until 1874. The first *brouillon* of the Temptation was begun May 24, 1848, and finished September 12, 1849. It numbered 540 pages of manuscript. Set aside for Bovary, Flaubert took up the draft again and made the second version in 1856. When he had done with it, the manuscript was reduced to 193 pages. Not satisfied, he returned to the work in 1872, and when ready for publication in 1874 the number of pages were 136. He even then cut, from ten chapters, three. Last year the French world read the second version of 1856 and was aston-ished to find it so different from the definitive one of 1874. The critical sobriety and courage of Flaubert were vindicated. In 1849, reading to Bouilhet and Du Camp, he had been advised to burn the stuff; instead he boiled it down for

133

the 1856 version. To Turgenev he had submitted the 1872 draft, and thus it came that this wonderful coloured-panorama of philosophy, this Gulliver-like travelling amid the master ideas of the antique and the early Christian worlds, was published.

All the youthful romantic Flaubert — the "spouter" of blazing phrases, the lover of jewelled words, of monstrous and picturesque ideas and situations — is in the first turbulent version of the Temptation. In the later version he is more critical and historical. Flaubert had grown intellectually as his emotions had cooled with the years. The first Temptation is romantic and religious; the 1874 version cooler and more sceptical. Dramatic, arranged more theatrically than the first, the author's affection for mysticism, the East, and the classic world shows more in this version. Psychologic gradations of character and events are clearer in the second version. I cannot agree with Louis Bertrand, who edited the 1856 version, that it is superior in interest to the 1874 version. It is a novelty, but Flaubert was never so much the surgeon as when he operated upon his own manuscript. He often hesitated, he always suffered, and he never flinched when his mind was finally satisfied. Faguet calls the Temptation an abstract pessimistic novel. He also complains that the philosophic ideas are not novel; a new philosophy would be a veritable phœnix. Why should they be? Flaubert does not enunciate a new philos-

134

ophy. He is the artist who shows us apocalyptic visions of all philosophies, all schools, ethical systems, cultures, religions. The gods from every land defile by and are each in turn swept away by the relentless Button-Moulder, Oblivion. There was a talking and amusing pig in the first version; he is not present in the second — possibly because Flaubert discovered that it was not Saint Antony of Egypt, but Saint Antony of Padua, who had a pig. (Rops has remembered the animal in his etching of Flaubert's Antony.) The Antony of 1856 has a more modern soul; the second reveals the determinism of Flaubert. He is phlegmatic, almost stupid, a supine Faust incapable of self-irony. Everything revolves about him — the multi-coloured splendours of Alexandria, of the Queen of Sheba; Satan, Death and Luxury, Hilarion, Simon Magus and Apollonius of Tyana tempt him; upon his ears fall the enchanting phrases of the eternal dialogue between Sphinx and Chimera — we dream of the Songs of Solomon when reading: " Je cherche des parfums nouveaux, des fleurs plus larges, des plaisirs inéprouvés"; the speech of the Chimera. Flaubert knew the Old Testament rhythms and beauty of phrase; witness this speech of Death's: "et on fait la guerre avec de la musique, des panaches, des drapeaux, des harnais d'or . . ." You seem to overhear the golden trumpets of Bayreuth.

The demon retires baffled at the end of the first version. He is diabolic and not a little

135

theatrical. The Devil of 1874 is more artful.
He shows Antony the Cosmos, but he is not the
victor in the duel. The new Antony studies the
protean forms of life and at the end is ravished
by the sight of protoplasm. "O bliss!" he cries,
and longs to be transformed into every species
of energy, "to be matter." Then the dawn comes
up like the uplifted curtains of a tabernacle —
Flaubert's image — and in the very disc of the
sun shines the face of Jesus Christ. "Antony
makes the sign of the cross and resumes his prayers." Thus ends the 1874 edition, ends a book
of irony, dreams, and sumptuous landscapes.
A sense of the nothingness of human thought,
human endeavour, assails the reader, for he has
traversed all the metaphysical and religious ideas
of the ages, has viewed all the gods, idols, demi-
gods, ghosts, heresies, and heresiarchs; Jupiter
on his throne and the early warring Christian
sects vanish into smoke, crumble into the gulf
of *Néant.* A vivid episode was omitted in the
definitive version. At the close of the gods'
procession the Saviour appears. He is old,
white-haired, and weary from the burden of the
cross and the sins of mankind. Some mock him;
He is reproached by kings for propounding the
equality of the poor; but by the majority He is
unrecognised; and, spurned, the Son of Man falls
into the dust of life. A poignant page, the spirit
of which may be recognised in some latter-day
French pictures and in the eloquent phrases of
Jehan Rictus. M. Bertrand has pointed out

136

that the 1849 version of the Temptation contains colour and imagery similar to the Légendes des Siècles, though written ten years before Hugo's poem. The Temptation of Saint Antony was neither a popular nor a critical success in 1874. France realises that in Flaubert's prose epic she has a masterpiece of intellectual power, profound irony, and unsurpassed beauty. The reader is alternately reminded of the Apocalypse, of Dante's grim visions, and of the second Faust.

Almost numberless are the studies of Flaubert's method in composing his books. A small library could be filled by books about his style. We have seen the reproductions of the various drafts that he made in the description of Emma Bovary's visit to Rouen. Armand Weil, with a patience that is itself Flaubertian, has shown us the variations in the manuscript of Salammbô (see, *Revue Universitaire*, April 15, 1902). Yet, compared with Balzac's spider-haunted, scribbled-over proofs, Flaubert's seem virginal of corrections. The one reproduced here is from two pages of original manuscript that I was lucky enough to secure at Paris in 1903. They contain instructions to the printer, as may be seen, and demonstrate Flaubert's sharp eye; in every instance his changes are an improvement. One of the arguments in favour of the last version of the Temptation is its shrinkage in bulk from the 1856 manuscript. The letter, hitherto unpublished — for it will not be found in the six volumes of the Correspondence

— is possibly addressed to his niece, Caroline Hamard. Unusual for Flaubert is the absence of any date; he was scrupulous in giving hour, day, month, and year, in his letters. The princess referred to is the Princess Mathilde Bonaparte-Demidoff, the patron of artists and literary men, an admirer of Flaubert's. He often dined with her at Saint-Gratien. Madame Pasca the actress was also a friend and visited Croisset when he fractured his leg. He had a genius for friendships with both women and men. His mother, often telling him that his devotion to style had dried up his natural affections, admitted that he had a bigger heart than head. And, after all, this motherly estimate gives us the measure of the real Flaubert.

IV

ANATOLE FRANCE

I

In the first part of that great, human Book,
dear to all good Pantagruelists, is this picture:
"From the Tower Anatole to the Messembrine
were faire spacious galleries, all coloured over
and painted with the ancient prowesses, histories and descriptions of the world." The
Tower Anatole is part of the architecture of the
Abbey of Thélème, in common with the other
towers named, Artick, Calaer, Hesperia, and
Caiere.

For lovers of the exquisite and whimsical
artist, Anatole France, a comparison to Rabelais
may not appear strained. Anatole, the man,
has written much that contains, as did the gracious
Tower Anatole, "faire spacious galleries . . .
painted with ancient . . . histories." He has
in his veins some infusion of the literary blood
of that "bon gros libertin," Rabelais, a figure in
French literature who refuses to be budged from
his commanding position, notwithstanding the
combined prestige of Pascal, Voltaire, Rousseau,
Chateaubriand, Hugo, and Balzac. And the

139

gentle Anatole has a pinch of Rabelais's *esprit gaulois*, which may be found in both Balzac and Maupassant.

To call France a sceptic is to state a commonplace. But he is so many other things that he bewilders. The spiritual stepson of Renan, a partial inheritor of his gifts of irony and pity, and a continuator of the elder master's diverse and undulating style, France displays affinities to Heine, Aristophanes, Charles Lamb, Epicurus, Sterne, and Voltaire. The "glue of unanimity" — to use an expression of the old pedantic Budæus — has united the widely disparate qualities of his personality. His outlook upon life is the outlook of Anatole France. His vast learning is worn with an air almost mocking. After the bricks and mortar of the realists, after the lyric pessimism of the morally and politically disillusioned generation following the Franco-German war, his genius comes in the nature of a consoling apparition. Like his own Dr. Trublet, in Histoire Comique, he can say: "*Je tiens boutique de mensonges. Je soulage, je console. Peut-il consoler et soulager sans mentir ?*" And he does deceive us with the resources of his art, with the waving of his lithe wand which transforms whales into weasels, mosques into cathedrals.

Perhaps too much stress has been set upon his irony. Ironic he is with a sinuosity that yields only to Renan. It is irony rather in the shape of the idea, than in its presentation; atmospheric is it rather than surface antithesis, or the witty

140

inversion of a moral order; he is a man of sentiment, Shandean sentiment as it is at times.
But the note we always hear, if distantly reverber-
ant, is the note of pity. To be all irony is to
mask one's humanity; and to accuse Anatole
France of the lack of humanity is to convict oneself of critical colour-blindness. His writings
abound in sympathetic overtones. His pity is
without Olympian condescension. He is a most
lovable man in the presence of the eternal spectacle
of human stupidity and guile. It is not alone that
he pardons, but also that he seeks to comprehend.
Not emulating the cold surgeon's eye of a Flaubert, it is with the kindly vision of a priest he
studies the maladies of our soul. In him there
is an ecclesiastical *fond*. He forgives because
he understands. And after his tenderest bene-
diction he sometimes smiles; it may be a smile of
irony; yet it is seldom cruel. He is an adroit de-
terminist, yet sets no store by the logical faculties.
Man is not a reasoning animal, he says, and
human reason is often a mirage.

But to label him with sentimentalism *à la
russe* — the Russian pity that stems from Dickens — would shock him into an outburst. Conceive him, then, as a man to whom all emotional
extravagance is foreign; as a detester of rhetoric,
of declamation, of the phrase facile; as a thinker
who assembles within the temple of his creations
every extreme in thought, manners, sentiment,
and belief, yet contrives to fuse this chaos by the
force of his sober style. His is a style more linear

141

than coloured, more for the eye than the ear; a style so pellucid that one views it suspiciously — it may conceal in its clear, profound depths strange secrets, as does some mountain lake in the shine of the sun. Even the simplest art may have its veils.

In the matter of clarity, Anatole France is the equal of Renan and John Henry Newman, and if this same clarity was at one time a conventional quality of French prose, it is rarer in these days. Never syncopated, moving at a moderate *tempo*, smooth in his transitions, replete with sensitive rejections, crystalline in his diction, a lover and a master of large luminous words, limpid and delicate and felicitous, the very marrow of the man is in his unique style. Few writers swim so easily under such a heavy burden of erudition. A loving student of books, his knowledge is precise, his range wide in many literatures. He is a true humanist. He loves learning for itself, loves words, treasures them, fondles them, burnishes them anew to their old meanings — though he has never tarried in the half-way house of epigram. But, over all, his love of humanity sheds a steady glow. Without marked dramatic sense, he nevertheless surprises mankind at its minute daily acts. And these he renders for us as candidly "as snow in the sunshine"; as the old Dutch painters stir our nerves by a simple shaft of light passing through a half-open door, upon an old woman polishing her spectacles. M. France sees and notes many gestures, inutile or

142

tragic, notes them with the enthralling simplicity
of a complicated artist. He deals with ideas so
vitally that they become human; yet his characters
are never abstractions, nor serve as pallid alle-
gories; they are all alive, from Sylvestre Bonnard
to the group that meets to chat in the Foro Romano
of Sur la Pierre Blanche. He can depict a cat
or a dog with fidelity; his dog Riquet bids fair
to live in French literature. He is an interpreter
of life, not after the manner of the novelist, but
of life viewed through the temperament of a
tolerant poet and philosopher.

This modern thinker, who has shed the despot-
ism of the positivist dogma, boasts the soul of a
chameleon. He understands, he loves, Christianity
with a knowledge and a fervour that surprise
until one measures the depth of his affection for ·
the antique world. To further confuse our per-
ceptions, he exhibits a sympathy for Hebraic lore
that can only be set down to a remote lineage.
He has rifled the Talmud for its forgotten stories;
he delights in juxtaposing the cultured Greek and
the strenuous Paul; he adores the contrast of
Mary Magdalen with the pampered Roman
matron. Add to this a familiarity with the proceeds of latter-day science, astronomy in particular,
with the scholastic speculation of the Renaissance,
mediæval piety, and the Pyrrhonism of a boulevard philosopher. So commingled are these contradictory elements, so many angles are there
exposed to numerous cultures, so many surfaces
avid for impressions, that we end in admiring the

exercise of a magic which blends into a happy synthesis such a variety of moral dissonances, such moral preciosity. It is magic — though there are moments when we regard the operation as intellectual legerdemain of a superior kind. We suspect dupery. But the humour of France is not the least of his miraculous solvents; it is his humour that often transforms a doubtful campaign into a radiant victory. We see him, the protagonist of his own psychical drama, dancing on a tight rope in the airiest manner, capering deliciously in the void, and quite like a prestidigitator bidding us doubt the existence of his rope.

His life long, Renan, despite his famous phrase, "the mania of certitude," was pursued by the idea of an absolute. He cried for proofs. To Berthelot he wrote: "I am eager for mathematics." It promised finality. As he aged, he was contented to seek an atmosphere of moral feeling; though he declared that "the real is a vast outrage on the ideal." He tremulously participated in the ritual of social life, and in the worship of the unknown god. He at last felt that Nature abhorred an absolute; that Being was ever a Becoming; that religion and philosophy are the result of a partial misunderstanding. All is relative, and the soul of man must ever feed upon chimeras! The Breton harp of Renan became sadly unstrung amid the shallow thunders of agnostic Paris.

But France, his eyes quite open and smiling, gayly Pagan Anatole, does not demand proofs.

He rejoices in a philosophic indifference, he has the gift of paradox. To Renan's plea for the rigid realities of mathematics, he might ask, with Ibsen, whether two and two do not make five on the planet Jupiter! To Montaigne's "What Know I?" he opposes Rabelais's "Do What Thou Wilt!" And then he adorns the wheel of Ixion with garlands.

He believes in the belief of God. He swears by the gods of all times and climes. His is the cosmical soul. A man who unites in his tales something of the Mimes of Herondas, La Bruyère's Characters, and the Lucian Dialogues, with faint flavours of Racine and La Fontaine, may be pardoned his polygraphic faiths. With Baudelaire he knows the tremours of the believing atheist; with Baudelaire he would restrain any show of irreverence before an idol, be it wooden or bronze. It might be the unknown god! — as Baudelaire once cried.

This pleasing chromatism in beliefs, a belief in all and none, is not a new phenomenon. The classical world of thought has several matches for Anatole France, from the followers of Aristippus to the Sophists. But there is a specific note of individuality, a *roulade* quite Anatolian in the Frenchman's writings. No one but this accomplished Parisian sceptic could have framed The Opinions of Jerome Coignard and his wholly delightful scheme for a Bureau of Vanity; "man is an animal with a musket," he declares; Sylvestre Bonnard and M. Bergeret are new with a dynamic novelty.

145

EGOISTS

As Walter Pater was accused of a silky dilettanteism, so France, as much a Cyrenaic as the English writer, was nevertheless forced to step down
from his ivory tower to the dusty streets and there
demonstrate his sincerity by battling for his convictions. After the imbecile Dreyfus affair had
rolled away, there was little talk in Paris of Anatole France, Epicurean. He was saluted with
every variety of abuse, but this amateur of fine
sensations had forever settled the charge of morose
aloofness, of voluptuous cynicism. (Though to-
day he is regarded with a certain suspicion by all
camps.) At a similar point where the endurance
of Ernest Renan had failed him, Anatole France
proved his own faith. Renan during the black
days of the Commune retired to Versailles, there
to meditate upon the shamelessness of the brute,
Caliban, with his lowest instincts unleashed.
But France believes in the people, he has said
that the future belongs to Caliban, and he would
scout his master's conception of the Tyrant-Sage,
a conception that Nietzsche partially transposed
later to the ecstatic key of the Superman. M.
France would probably advocate the head-chop-
ping of such wise monster-despots. An aristocrat
by culture and fastidiousness, he is without an
arrière-pensée of the snobbery of the intellect, of
the cerebral exaltation displayed by Hugo, Baudelaire, and the Goncourts.

When France published his early verse — his
débutwas as a poet and Parnassian poét — Catulle
Mendès divined the man. He wrote, "I can

146

never think of Anatole France . . . without fancying I see a young Alexandrian poet of the second century, a Christian, doubtless, who is more than half Jew, above all a neoplatonist, and further a pure theist deeply imbued with the teachings of Basilides and Valentinus, and the Perfumes of the Orphic poems of some recent rhetorician, in whom subtlety was pushed to mysticism and philosophy to the threshold of the Kabbalah."

Some critics have accused him of not being able to build a book. He knows the rhythms of poems, but he "does not know" the harmony of essences, said the late Bernard Lazare; he is an excellent Parnassian but a mediocre philosopher: he is a charming *raconteur*, but he cannot compose a book. Precise in details, diffuse in ensembles, clear and confused, neat and ambiguous, continued M. Lazare, he searches his object in concentric circles. Furthermore, he has the soul of a Greek in the decadence, and the voice of a Sistine Chapel singer — pure and irresolute. To all this admission may be made without fear of decomposing the picture which France has set up before us of his own personality — a picture, however, he does not himself hesitate to efface from the canvas whenever his perversity prompts. He is all that his critic asserts and much more. It is this moral eclecticism, this jumble of opposites, this violent contrast of traits, and these apparently irreconcilable elements of his character, which appal, interest, yet make him so

147

human. But his art never swerves; it records invariably the fluctuations of his spirit, a spirit at once desultory, savant, and subtle, records all in a style, concrete and clairvoyant.

His books are not so much novels as chronicles of designedly simple structure; his essays are confessions; his confessions, a blending of the naïve and the corrupt, for there are corroding properties in these novel persuasive disenchantments. Upon the robust of faith Anatole France makes no more impression than do Augustine, Saint Teresa, the Imitation of Christ, or the Provincial Letters. Such *nuances* of scepticism as his are for those who love the comedies of belief and disbelief. Not possessing the Huysmans intensity of temperament, France will never be betrayed into such affirmations; Huysmans, who dropped like a ripe plum into the basket of the ecclesiastical fruit-gatherer. France will never lose his balance in the fumes of a personal conversion. Of Plato himself he would ask: "What is Truth?" and if Pilate posed the same question, France would reply by handing him his Jardin d'Epicure — a veritable breviary of scepticism. In Socrates he would discover a congenial companion; yet he might mischievously allude to Montaigne "concerning cats," or quote Aristotle on the form of hats. A wilful child of philosophy and *belles-lettres*, he may be always expected to say the startling.

Be humble! he exhorts. Be without intellectual pride! for the days of man, who is naught

148

but a bit of animated pottery, are brief, and he vanishes like a spark. Thus Job — Anatole. Be humble! Even virtue may be unduly praised: "Since it is overcoming which constitutes merit, we must recognise that it is concupiscence which makes saints. Without it there is no repentance, and it is repentance which makes saints." To become a saint one must have been first a sinner. He quotes, as an example, the conduct of the blessed Pelagia, who accomplished her pilgrimage to Rome by rather unconventional means. Here, too, we recognise the amiable casuistry of Anatole — Voltaire. And there is something of Baudelaire and Barbey d'Aurevilly's piety of imagination with impiety of thought, in France's pronouncement. He is a Chrysostom reversed; from his golden mouth issue spiritual blasphemies.

Mr. Henry James has said that the province of art is "all life, all feeling, all observation, all vision." According to this rubric, France is a profound artist. He plays with the appearances of life, occasionally lifting the edge of the curtain to curdle the blood of his spectators by the sight of Buddha's shadow in some grim cavern beyond. He has the Gallic tact of adorning the blank spaces of theory and the ugly spots of reality. A student of Kant in his denial of the objective, we can never picture him as following Königsberg's sage in his admiration of the starry heavens and the moral law. Both are relative, would be the report of the Frenchman. But, if he is sceptical about things tangible, he is apt to dash off at a tangent and proclaim the existence of that "school of drums kept by the angels," which the hallucinated Arthur Rimbaud heard and beheld. His method of surprising life, despite his ingenuous manner, is sometimes as oblique as that of Jules Laforgue. And, in the words of Pater, his is "one of the happiest temperaments coming to an understanding with the most depressing of theories."

For faith he yearns. He humbles himself beneath the humblest. He excels in picturing the splendours of the simple soul; yet faith has not anointed his intellect with its chrism. He admires the golden filigree of the ciborium; its spiritual essence escapes him. He stands at the portals of Paradise; there he lingers. He stoops to some rare and richly coloured feather. He eloquently vaunts its fabulous beauty, but he will not listen to the whirring of the wings from which it has fallen. Pagan in his irony, his pity wholly Christian, Anatole France has in him something of Petronius and not a little of Saint Francis.

ANATOLE FRANCE

II

Born to the literary life, one of the elect whose career is at once a beacon of hope and despair for the less gifted or less fortunate, Anatole François Thibault first saw the heart of Paris in the year 1844. The son of a bookseller, Noël France Thibault, his childhood was spent in and around his father's book-shop, No. 9 du quai Voltaire, and his juvenile memories are clustered about books. There are many faithful pictures of old libraries and book-worms in his novels. He has a moiety of that Oriental blood which is said to have tinctured the blood of Montaigne, Charles Lamb, and Cardinal Newman. The delightful Livre de Mon Ami gives his readers many glimpses of his early days. Told with incomparable naïveté and verve, we feel in its pages the charm of the writer's personality. A portrait of the youthful Anatole reveals his excessive sensibility. His head was large, the brow was too broad for the feminine chin, though the long nose and firm mouth contradict the possible weakness in the lower part of the face. It was in the eyes, however, that the future of the child might have been discerned — they were lustrous, beautiful in shape, with the fulness that argued eloquence and imagination. He was, he tells us, a strange boy, whose chief ambition was to be a saint, a second St. Simon Stylites, and, later, the author of a history of France in fifty volumes.

Fascinating are the chapters devoted to Pierre
and Suzanne in this memoir. His tenderness of
touch and power of evoking the fairies of childhood are to be seen in Abeille. The further development of the boy may be followed in Pierre
Nozière. In college life, he was not a shining
figure, like many another budding genius. He
loved Virgil and Sophocles, and his professors
of the Stanislas College averred that he was too
much given to day-dreaming and preoccupied
with matters not set forth in the curriculum, to
benefit by their instruction. But he had wise
parents — he has paid them admirable tributes
of his love — who gave him his own way. After
some further study in L'Ecole des Chartes, he
launched himself into literature through the
medium of a little essay, La Légende de Sainte
Radégonde, reine de France. This was in 1859.
Followed nine years later a study of Alfred de
Vigny, and in 1873 Les Poëmes dorées attracted
the attention of the Parnassian group then under
the austere leadership of Leconte de Lisle.
Les Noces Corinthiennes established for him a
solid reputation with such men as Catulle Mendès,
Xavier de Ricard, and De Lisle. For this last-
named poet young France exhibited a certain
disrespect — the elder was irritable, jealous of
his dignity, and exacted absolute obedience from
his neophytes; unluckily a species of animosity
arose between the pair. When, in 1874, he accepted a post in the Library of the Senate, Leconte
de Lisle made his displeasure so heavily felt that

152

France soon resigned. But he had his revenge in an article which appeared in *Le Temps*, and one that put the pompous academician into a fury. Catulle Mendès sang the praises of the early France poems: "Les Noces Corinthiennes alone would have sufficed to place him in the first rank, and to preserve his name from the shipwreck of oblivion," declared M. Mendés.

In 1881, with The Crime of Sylvestre Bonnard he won the attention of the reading world, a crown from the Academy, and the honour of being translated into a half-dozen languages. From that time he became an important figure in literary Paris, while his reputation was further fortified by his criticisms of books — vagrom criticism, yet charged with charm and learning. He followed Jules Claretie on *Le Temps*, and there he wrote for five years (1886–1891) the *critiques*, which appeared later in four volumes, entitled La Vie Littéraire. Georg Brandes had said that, in the strict sense of the word, M. France is not a great critic. But Anatole France has said this before him. He despises pretentious official criticism, the criticism that distributes good and bad marks to authors in a pedagogic fashion. He may not be so "objective" as his one-time adversary, Ferdinand Brunetière, but he is certainly more convincing.

The quarrel, a famous one in its day, seems rather faded in our days of critical indifference. After his clever formula, that there is no such thing as objective criticism, that all criticism but

153

records the adventures of one's soul among the masterpieces, France was attacked by Brunetière — of whom the ever-acute Mr. James once remarked that his "intelligence has not kept pace with his learning." Those critical watchwords, "subjective" and "objective," are things of yester-year, and one hopes, forever. But in this instance there was much ink spilt, witty on the part of France, deadly earnest from the pen of Brunetière. The former annihilated his adversary by the mode metaphysical. He demonstrated that in the matter of judgment we are prisoners of our ideas, and he also formed a school that has hardly done him justice, for every impressionistic value is not necessarily valid. It is easy to send one's soul boating among masterpieces and call the result "criticism"; the danger lies in the contingency that one may not boast the power of artistic navigation possessed by Anatole France, a master steersman in the deeps and shallows of literature.

His own critical contributions are notable. Studies of Chateaubriand, Flaubert, Renan, Balzac, Zola, Pascal, Villiers de l'Isle Adam, Barbey d'Aurevilly, Rabelais, Hamlet, Baudelaire, George Sand, Paul Verlaine — a masterpiece of intuition and sympathy this last — and many others, vivify and adorn all they touch. A critic such as Sainte-Beuve, or Taine, or Brandes, France is not; but he exercises an unfailing spell in everything he signs. His "august vagabondage" — the phrase is Mr. Whibley's —

through the land of letters has proved a boon to all students.

In 1897 he was received at the Académie Française, as the successor of Ferdinand de Lesseps. His addresses at the tombs of Zola and Renan are matters of history. As a public speaker, France has not the fiery eloquence of Jean Jaurès or Laurent Tailhade, but he displays a cool magnetism all his own. And he is absolutely fearless.

It is not through lack of technique that the structure of the France novels is so simple, his tales plotless, in the ordinary meaning of the word. Elaborate formal architecture he does not affect. The novel in the hands of Balzac, Flaubert, Goncourt, and Zola would seem to have reached its apogee as a canvas upon which to paint a picture of manners. In the sociological novel, the old theatrical climaxes are absent, the old recipes for cooking character find no place. Even the love motive is not paramount. The genesis of this form may be found in Balzac, in whom all the modern fiction is rooted. Certain premonitions of the *genre* are also encountered in L'Education Sentimentale of Flaubert, with its wide gray horizons, its vague murmurs of the immemorial mobs of vast cities, its presentation of undistinguished men and women. Truly democratic fiction, by a master who hated democracy with creative results.

Anatole France, Maurice Barrès, Edouard Estaunie, Rosny (the brothers Bex), René

Bazin, Bertrand, and the astonishing Paul Adam are in the van of this new movement of fiction with ideas, endeavouring to exorcise the "demon of staleness." French fiction in the last decade of the past century saw the death of the naturalistic school. Paris had become a thrice-told tale, signifying the wearisome "triangle" and the chronicling of flat beer. Something new had to be evolved. Lo! the sociological novel, which discarded the familiar machinery of fiction, rather than miss the new spirit. It is unnecessary to add that in America the fiction of ideas has not been, thus far, of prosperous growth; indeed, it is viewed with suspicion.

Loosely stated, the fiction of Anatole France may be divided into three kinds: fantastic, philosophic, and realistic. This arbitrary grouping need not be taken literally; in any one of his tales we may encounter all three qualities. For example, there is much that is fantastic, philosophic, real, in that moving and wholly human narrative of Sylvestre Bonnard. France's familiarity with cabalistic and exotic literatures, his deep love and comprehension of the Latin and Greek classics, his knowledge of mediæval legends and learning, coupled with his command of supple speech, enable him to project upon a ground-plan of simple narrative extraordinary variations.

The full flowering of France's knowledge and imagination in things patristic and archæologic is to be seen in Thaïs, a masterpiece of colour and construction. Thaïs is that courtesan of Alex-

156

andria, renowned for her beauty, wit, and wickedness, who was converted by the holy Paphnutius, saint and hermit of the Thebaïd. How the devil finally dislodges from the heart of Paphnutius its accumulation of virtue, is told in an incomparable manner. If Flaubert was pleased by the first offering of his pupil, Guy de Maupassant, (Boule de Suif), what would he not have said after reading Thaïs? The ending of the wretched monk, following his spiritual victories as a holy man perched on a pillar—a memory of the author's youthful dream—is lamentable. He loves Thaïs, who dies; and thenceforth he is condemned to wander, a vampire in this world, a devil in the next. A monument of erudition, thick with pages of jewelled prose, Thaïs is a book to be savoured slowly and never forgotten. It is the direct parent of Pierre Loüys's Aphrodite, and later evocations of the antique world.

Of great emotional intensity is Histoire Comique (1903). It is a study of the histrionic temperament, and full of the major miseries and petty triumphs of stage life. It also contains a startling incident, the suicide of a lovelorn actor. The conclusion is violent and morbid. The nature of the average actress has never been etched with such acrid precision. There are various tableaux of behind and before the footlights; a rehearsal, an actor's funeral, and the life of the greenroom. Set forth in his most disinterested style, M. France shows us that he can handle with ease so-called "objective" fiction. His Doctor Trublet

157

is a new France incarnation, wonderful and kindly old consoler that he is. He is attached as house physician to the Odéon, and to him the comedians come for advice. He ministers to them body and soul. His discourse is Socratic. He has wit and wisdom. And he displays the motives of the heroine so that we seem to gaze through an open window. As vital as Sylvestre Bonnard, as Bergeret, Trublet is truly an avatar of Anatole France. Histoire Comique! The title is a rare jest aimed at mundane and bohemian vanity.

Passing Jocaste et le Chat maigre, and Le Puits de Sainte-Claire, we come to L'Etui de Nacre, a volume of tales published in 1892. This book may be selected as typical of a certain side of its author, a side in which his fantasy and historic sense meet on equal terms. The most celebrated is Le Procurateur de Judée, who is none other than Pontius Pilate, old, disillusioned of public ambition, and grumbling, as do many retired public officers, at the ingratitude of governments and princes. To his friend he confesses finally, after his memory has been vainly prompted, that he has no recollection of Jesus, a certain anarchistic prophet of Judea, condemned by him to death. His final phrases give us, as in the flare of lightning, the withering, double-edged irony of the author. He has quite forgotten the tremendous events that occurred in Jerusalem; forgotten, too, is Jesus. Not all the stories that follow, not the pious records of Sainte Euphrosine, of Sainte Oliverie et Liberetta, of Amyeus and

158

Celestin, of Scolastica, can rob the reader of this first cruel impression. In Balthasar the narratives are of a superior quality. Nothing could be better, for example, than the recital of the Ethiopian king who sought the love of Balkis, Queen of Sheba, was accepted, after proofs of his bravery, and then quietly forgotten. He studies the secrets of the spheres, and when Balkis, repenting of her behaviour, seeks Balthasar anew, it is too late. He has discovered the star of Bethlehem which leads him straightway to the crib in company with Gaspar and Melchior, there to worship the King of Kings. Powerful, too, in its fantastic evocation is La Fille de Lilith, which relates the adventure of a modern Parisian with a deathless daughter of Adam's first wife, Lilith, so named in the Talmud. Laeta Acilia tells us one of France's best anecdotes about a Roman matron residing at Marseilles during the reign of Tiberius. She encounters Mary Magdalen, who almost converts the woman by a promise of children, long desired. The conclusion is touching. It discloses admirably the psychology of the two women. L'Oeuf Rouge is a tale of Cæsarian madness, and the bizarre Le Réséda du Curé is so simply related that we are disarmed by the style.

A graceful collection is that called Clio, illustrated in the highly decorative manner of Mucha. Possibly the first is the best, a story of Homer. Some confess a preference for a Gaulish recital of the times when Cæsar went to Britain. Na-

159

poleon, too, is in the list. An interesting discussion of Napoleon and the Napoleonic legend is in a full-fledged novel, The Red Lily. "Napoleon," says one of its characters, "was violent and frivolous; therefore profoundly human. . . . He desired with singular force, all that most men esteem and desire. He had the illusions which he gave to the people. He believed in glory. He retained always the infantile gravity which finds pleasure in playing with swords and drums, and the sort of innocence which makes good military men. It is this vulgar grandeur which makes heroes, and Napoleon is the perfect hero. His brain never surpassed his hand — that hand, small and beautiful, which crumpled the world. . . . Napoleon lacked interior life. . . . He lived from the outside." In the art of attenuating great reputations Anatole France has had few superiors.

This novel displeased his many admirers, who pretend to see in it the influence of Paul Bourget. Yet it is a memorable book. Paul Verlaine is depicted in it with freshness, that poet Paul, and his childish soul so ironically, yet so lovingly distilled by his critic. There are glimpses of Florence, of Paris; the study of an English girl-poet will arouse pleasant memories of a lady well known to Italian, Parisian, and London art life. And there is the sculptor, Jacques Dechartres, who may be a mask, among many others of M. France. But Choulette-Verlaine is the lodestone of the novel.

.

Where the ingenuity and mental flexibility, not to say historical mimicry, of France are seen at their supreme, is in La Rôtisserie de la Reine Pédauque. Jacques Tournebroche, or Turnspit, is an assistant in the cook-shop of his father, in old Paris. He is of a studious mind, and becomes the pupil of the Abbé Jérôme Coignard, "who despises men with tenderness," a figure that might have stepped out of Rabelais, though baked and tempered in the refining fires of M. France's imagination. Such a man! Such an ecclesiastic! He adores his maker and admires His manifold creations, especially wine, women, and song. He has more than his share of human weakness, and yet you wonder why he has not been canonised for his adorable traits. He is a glutton and a wine-bibber, a susceptible heart, a pious and deeply versed man. Nor must the rascally friar be forgotten, surely a memory of Rabelais's Friar Jhon. There are scenes in this chronicle that would have made envious the elder Dumas; scenes of swashbuckling, feasting, and bloodshed. There is an astrologer who has about him the atmosphere of the black art with its imps and salamanders, and an ancient Jew who is the Hebraic law personified. So lifelike is Jérôme Coignard that a book of his opinions was bound to follow. His whilom pupil Jacques is supposed to be its editor. Le Jardin d'Epicure and Sur la Pierre Blanche (1905) are an excuse for the opinions of M. France on many topics — religion, politics, science, and social life. Not-

161

withstanding their loose construction, they are never inchoate. That the ideas put forth may astound by their perversity, their novelty, their nihilism, their note of cosmic pessimism, is not to be denied. Our earth, "a miserable small star," is a drop of mud swimming in space, its inhabitants mere specks, whose doings are not of importance in the larger curves of the universe's destiny. Every illustration, geological, astronomical, and mathematical, is brought to bear upon this thesis — the littleness of man and the uselessness of his existence. But France loves this harassed animal, man, and never fails to show his love. Interspersed with moralising are recitals of rare beauty, Gallion and Par la Porte de Corne ou par la Porte d'Ivoire. Here the classic scholar, that is the base of France's temperament, fairly shines.

In the four volumes of Histoire Contemporaine we meet a new Anatole France, one who has deserted his old attitude of Parnassian impassibility for a suave anarchism, one who enters the arena of contemporaneous life bent on slaughter, though his weapon is the keen blade, never the rude battle-axe of polemics. It is his first venture in the fiction of sociology; properly speaking, it is the psychology of the masses, not exactly as Paul Adam handles it in his striking and tempestuous Les Lions (a book Balzacian in its fury of execution), but with the graver temper of the philosopher. He paints for us a provincial university town with its intrigues, religious, political,

162

and social. The first of the series is L'Orme du
Mail; follow Le Mannequin d'Osier, L'Anneau
d'Améthyste, and Monsieur Bergeret à Paris (1901).
The loop that ensnares this quartet of novels is
the simple motive of ecclesiastical ambition.
Not since Ferdinand Fabre's L'Abbé Tigrane
has French literature had such portraits of the
priesthood; Zola's ecclesiastics are ill-natured
caricatures. The Cardinal Archbishop, Abbé
Lataigne, and the lifelike Abbé Guitrel, with the
silent, though none the less desperate, fight for
the vacant bishopric of Turcoing — these are the
three men who with Bergeret carry the story on
their shoulders. About them circle the entire
diocese and the tepid life of a university town.
Yet anything further from melodramatic machina-
tions cannot be imagined. Even the clerics of
Balzac seem exaggerated in comparison. The
protagonist is a professor, a master of conference
of the University Faculty, a worthy man and
earnest, though by no means of an exalted talent.
He has the misfortune of being married to a
worldly woman who does not attempt to understand him, much less to love him. She deceives
him. The discovery of this deceit is an episode
the most curious in fiction. It would be diverting
if it were not painful. It reveals in Bergeret the
preponderance of the man of thought over the
man of action. His pupil and false friend is
a classical scholar, therefore the affair might have
been worse! And he is given the scholar's excuse as a plea for forgiveness! But hesitating

163

as appears Bergeret, he utilises his wife's treachery as a springboard from which to fly his miserable household. Henceforth, with his devoted sister and daughter, he philosophises at ease and becomes a Dreyfusard. His dog Riquet is the recipient of his deepest thoughts. His monologues in the presence of this animal are the best in the book.

There are many characters in this serene and bitter tragi-comedy. A contempt, almost monastic, peeps out in the treatment of his women. They are often detestable. They behave as if an empire was at stake, though it is only a conspiracy whereby Abbé Guitrel is made Bishop of Turcoing. France always displays more pity for the frankly sinful woman than for the frivolous woman of fashion. There is also a subplot, the effort of a young Hebrew snob, Bonmont by name (Guttenberg, originally), to get into the exclusive hunting set of the Duc de Brécé. This hunt-button wins for the diplomatic Abbé Guitrel his coveted see. M. France is unequalled in his portrayal of the modern French-Hebrew millionaire, the Wallsteins and Bonmonts. He draws them without *parti-pris*. His prefect, the easy-going, cynical Worms-Clavelin, with his secret contempt of Jews and Gentiles alike, and his wife who collects ecclesiastical bric-à-brac, are executed by a great painter of character. He exposes with merciless impartiality a mob of men and women in high life. But his aristocrats are no better than his ecclesiastics or bankers.

164

There is a comic Orléanist conspiracy. There are happenings that set your hair on end, and a cynicism at times which forces one to regret that the author left his study to mingle with the world. Nor is the strain relieved when poor Bergeret goes to Paris; there he is enmeshed by the Dreyfus party. There he comes upon stormy days, though high ideals never desert him. He is as placid in the face of contemptuous epithets and opprobrious newspaper attacks as he was calm when stones were hurled at his windows in the provinces. A man obsessed by general ideas, he is lovable and never a bore, though M. Faguet and several other critics have cried him stupid. In the "fire of the footlights" M. Bergeret pales. For the drama M. France has no particular voice, though he has written several charming playlets. Even the superior acting of Guitry could not make of Crainquibille much more than a touching episode.

There is enough characterisation and incident in Histoire Contemporaine to ballast a half-dozen novelists with material. And there are treasures of humour and pathos. The success of the series has been awe-inspiring; indeed, awe-inspiring is the success of all the France books, and at a time when Parisian prophets of woe are lamenting the decline of literature. Nevertheless, here is a man who writes like an artist, whose work, web and woof, is literature, whose themes, with few exceptions, are not of the popular kind, whose politics are violently opposed to current superstition, whose very form is hybrid; yet he

165

sells, and has sold, in the hundreds of thousands. Literature cannot be called moribund in the face of such a result.   His is a case that sets one speculating without undue emphasis upon a certain superiority of French taste over English in the matter of fiction.

The Life of Jeanne d'Arc (1908), a work of scholarship and mixed prejudices, does not, I am forced to admit, unduly interest me. Whether the astonishing statements set forth therein are true is a question that may concern Mr. Lang, but hardly the lovers of the real Anatole.   The Isle of Penguins (1908) gave him back to us in all his original glory.

An art, ironical, easy, fugitive, divinely untrammelled, divinely artificial, which, like a pure flame, blazes forth in an unclouded heaven . . . *la gaya scienza;* light feet; wit; fire; grace; the dance of the stars; the tremor of southern light; the smooth sea — these Nietzschean phrases might serve as an epigraph for the work of that apostle of innocence and experience, Anatole France.

.

V

THE PESSIMIST'S PROGRESS

J.-K. HUYSMANS

"Ah! Seigneur, donnez-moi la force et le courage
De contempler mon cœur et mon corps sans dégoût."
—BAUDELAIRE.

I

JORIS-KARL HUYSMANS has been called mystic, naturalist, critic, aristocrat of the intellect; he was all these, a mandarin of letters and a pessimist besides — no matter what other qualities persist throughout his work, pessimism is never absent; his firmament is clotted with black stars. He had a mediæval monk's contempt for existence, contempt for the mangy flock of mediocrity; yet his genius drove him to describe its crass ugliness in phrases of incomparable and enamelled prose. It is something of a paradox that this man of picturesque piety should have lived to be the accredited interpreter, the distiller of its quintessence, of that elusive quality, "modernity." The "intensest vision of the modern world," as Havelock Ellis puts it, Huysmans unites to the endowment of a painter the power of a rare psychologist,

167

superimposed upon a lycanthropic nature. A collective title for his books might be borrowed from Zola: My Hatreds. He hated life and its eternal *bêtise*. His theme, with variations, is a strangling Ennui. With those devoted sons of Mother Church, Charles Baudelaire, Barbey D'Aurevilly, Villiers de l'Isle Adam, and Paul Verlaine, eccentric sons whose actions so often dismayed their fellow worshippers of less genius, Huysmans has been affiliated. He was not a poet or, indeed, a man of overwhelming imagination. But he had the verbal imagination. He did not possess the novelist's talent. His was not the flamboyant genius of Barbey, nor had he the fantastic invention of Villiers. He seems closer to Baudelaire, rather by reason of his ironic, critical temperament than because of his creative gifts. Baudelaire's oriflamme, embroidered with preciously devised letters of gold, reads: Spleen and Ideal; upon the emblematic banner of Huysmans this motto is Spleen. His work at times seems like a prolongation in prose of Baudelaire's. And by reason of his exacerbated temper he became the most personal writer of his generation. He belonged to no school, and avoided, after his beginnings, all literary groups.

He is recording-secretary of the petty miseries and ironies of the life about him. Over ugliness he becomes almost lyric. "The world is a forest of differences." His pen, when he depicts an attack of dyspepsia or neuralgia, or the nervous distaste of a hypochondriac for meeting people,

168

is like the triple sting of a hornet. He is the prose singer of neurasthenia, a Hamlet doubting his digestion, a Schopenhauer of the cook-shops. When he paints the *nuance* of rage and disgust that assails a middle-aged man at the sight of a burnt mutton-chop, his phrases are unforgettable. The tragedy of the gastric juices he has limned with a fulness of expression that almost lifts pathology to the dignity of art. A descendant of Flemish painters, sculptors, architects (Huysmans of Mechlin, the Antwerp-born painter of the seventeenth century, is said to be a forebear), he inherited their powers of envisaging exterior life; those painters for whom flowers, vegetable markets, butcher-shops, tiny gentle Dutch landscapes, gray skies, skies of rutilant flames, and homely details were surfaces to be passionately and faithfully rendered. This vision he has interpreted with pen instead of brush. He is a virtuoso of the phrase. He is a performer on the single string of self. He knows the sultry enharmonics of passion. He never improvises, he observes. All is willed and conscious, the cold-fire scrutiny of a trained eye, one keen to note the ignoble or any deviation from the normal. His pages are often sterile and smell of the lamp, but he has the candour of his chimera. Well has Remy de Gourmont called him an *eye*. In his prose, he sacrifices rhythmic variety and tone to colour. His rhythms are massive, his colour at times a furious fanfare of scarlet. Every word, like a note in a musical score, has its value and

169

position. He intoxicates because of his marvellous speech, but he seldom charms. It is a sort
of sinister verbal magic that steals upon one as
this ancient mariner from the lower moral deeps
of Paris fixes you with his glittering eye, and in
his strangely modulated language tells tales of
blasphemy and fish-wives' tales of a half-forgotten river below the bed of the Seine, of dull
cafés and dreary suburbs, of bored men and
stupid women, of sordid, opulent souls, souls
spongy and voluptuous, mean lives and meaner
alleys — such an epic of ennui, mediocrity,
bizzare sins, and neurotic, superstitious creatures
was never given the world until Huysmans wrote
Les Sœurs Vatard and A Rebours. Entire
vanished districts of Paris may be reconstructed
from his chapters. Zola declared, when Guy
de Maupassant and Huysmans appeared side
by side in Les Soirées de Médan, that the latter
was the realist.

The unity of form and substance in Huysmans
is a distinguishing trait. He had early mastered
literary technique, and the handling of his themes
varies but little. There are, however, two or
three typical varieties of description which may
be quoted as illustrations of his etched and
jewel-like prose. A cow hangs outside a butcher-
shop:

As in a hothouse, a marvellous vegetation flourished
in the carcass. Veins shot out on every side like the
trails of bindweed; dishevelled branch-work extended itself along the body, an efflorescence of en-

170

trails unfurled their violent-tinted corollas, and big clusters of fat stood out, a sharp white, against the red medley of quivering flesh.

Surely a subject for Snyders or Jan Steen.

Léon Bloy somewhere describes Huysmans's treatment of the French language as "dragging his images by the heels or the hair up and down the worm-eaten staircase of terrified syntax." Huysmans, in A Rebours, had called M. Bloy "an enraged pamphleteer whose style was at once exasperated and precious." And can magnificence of phrase in evoking a picture go further than the following which shows us Gustave Moreau's Salome:

In the perverse odour of perfumes, in the overheated atmosphere of this church, Salome, her left arm extended in a gesture of command, her bent right arm holding on the level of the face a great lotus, advances slowly to the sound of a guitar, thrummed by a woman who crouches on the floor. With collected, almost anguished countenance, she begins the lascivious dance that should waken the sleeping senses of the aged Herod; her breasts undulate, become rigid at the contact of the whirling necklets; diamonds sparkle on the dead whiteness of her skin, her bracelets, girdles, rings, shoot sparks; on her triumphal robes sewn with pearls, flowered with silver, sheeted with gold, the jewelled breast-plate, whose every stitch is a precious stone, bursts into flame, scatters in snakes of fire, swarms on the ivory-toned, tea-rose flesh, like splendid insects with dazzling wings, marbled with carmine, dotted with morning gold, diapered with steel blue, streaked with peacock green.

171

EGOISTS

Gautier,—who was for Huysmans only a prodigious reflector — Flaubert, Goncourt, could not have excelled this verbal painting, this bronze and baroque prose, which is both precise and of a splendour. Huysmans can describe a herring as would a great master of sumptuous still-life:

Thy garment is the palette of setting suns, the rust of old copper, the brown gilt of Cordovan leather, the sandal and saffron tints of the autumn foliage. When I contemplate thy coat of mail I think of Rembrandt's pictures. I see again his superb heads, his sunny flesh, his gleaming jewels on black velvet. I see again his rays of light in the night, his trailing gold in the shade, the dawning of suns through dark arches.

Or this invocation when Huysmans had begun to experience that shifting of moral emotion which we call his "conversion" — he was a Roman Catholic born, therefore was not converted; he but reverted to his early faith:

Take pity, O Lord, on the Christian who doubts, on the sceptic who desires to believe, on the convict of life who embarks alone, in the night, beneath a sky no longer lit by the consoling beacons of ancient faith.

His method is not the recital of events, but the description of a situation; a scene, not a narration, but large tableaux. Action there is little; he is more static than dynamic. His characters, like Goncourt's, suffer from paralysis of the will, from hyperæsthesia. The soul in its primordial

172

darkness interests him, and he describes it with the same penetrating prose as he does the carcass of an animal. He is a luminous mystic who speaks in terms of extravagant naturalism. A physiologist of the soul, at times his soul dwelt in a boulevard. His violent, vivid style so excellent in setting forth coloured sensations is equally admirable in the construction of metaphors which make concrete the abstract. There is the element of the grotesque, of the old, ribald Fleming, in Huysmans, though without a trace of hearty Flemish humour. He once said that the memory of the inventor of card-playing ought to be blessed, the game kept closed the mouths of imbeciles. Nor is the pepper of sophistry absent. He sculptures his ideas. He is both morose and fulgurating. He squanders his emotions with polychromatic resignation unlike a Saint Augustine or a Newman; yet we are not deeply moved by his soul-experiences. It is not vibrating sincerity that we miss; it would be wrong to question his return to Catholicism. He is more convincing than Tolstoy; for one thing, there was no dissonance between his daily life and his writings, after the publication of En Route. Lucid as is his manner, clairvoyant as the exposition of his soul at the feet of God, there is, nevertheless, an absence of unction, of tenderness, which repels. Sympathy and tenderness are *bourgeois* virtues for Huysmans. Too complicated to admire, even recognise, the sane or the simple, he remained the morbid carper after he entered La Trappe and Solesmes. As an oblate, his fastidiousness was wounded by the minor annoyances of a severe regimen; his stomach always ailed him. Perhaps to his weak digestion and a neuralgic tendency we owe the bitterness and pessimism of his art. He was not a normal man. He loathed the inevitable discords of life with a startling intensity. The venomous salt of his wit he sprinkles over the raw turpitude of men and women. Woman for him was not of the planetary sex, but either a stupid or a vicious creature; sometimes both. Impassible as he was, he could be shocked into a species of sub-acid eloquence if the theme were the inutility of mankind. No Hebraic prophet ever launched such poignant phrases of disgust and horror at the world and its works. His favourite reading was in the mystics, à Kempis, Saint Theresa, St. John of the Cross, and the Flemish Ruysbroeck.

In a new edition of A Rebours he has told us that he was not pious as a youth, having been educated not at a religious school. A Rebours came out in 1884, and it was in July, 1892, at the age of forty-four, that he went to La Trappe de Notre-Dame d'Igny, situated near Fismes, and the Aisne and Marne. He confessed that he could not discover, during the eight intervening years, why he swerved to the Church of Rome. Diminution of vital energy was not the chief reason for his reversion. The operations of divine grace in Huysmans's case may

174

be dated back to A Rebours. The modulation
by the way of art was not a difficult one. And
he had the good taste of giving us his experiences
in the guise of art. It is the history of a conversion, though he is, without doubt, the Durtal of
the books. The final explosion of grace after
years of unconscious mining, the definite illumina-
tion on some unknown Road to Damascus, took
place between the appearance of Là Bas and
En Route. We are spared the *technique* of faith
reawakened. It had become part of his cerebral
tissue. We are shown a Durtal, believer; also
a Durtal profoundly disgusted with the oily,
rancid food of La Trappe, and with the faces of
some of his companions, and a Durtal who puffs
surreptitious cigarettes. At Lourdes, in his last
book, he is the same Durtal-Huysmans, grumbling at the odours of unwashed bodies, at the perspiring crowds, at the ignorance and cupidity
of the shrine's guardians. A pessimist to the
end. And for that reason he has often outraged
the sensibilities of his coreligionists, who ques-
tioned his sincerity after such an exclamation as:
"How like a rind of lard I must look!" uttered
when he carried a dripping candle in a religious
procession. But through the dreary mists of
doubtings and black fogs of unfaith the lamp of the
Church, a shining point, drew to it from his chilly
ecstasies this hedonist. Like Taine and Nietzsche, he craved for some haven of refuge to escape
the whirring wings of Wotan's ravens. And in
the pale woven air he saw the cross of Christ.

Leslie Stephen wrote of Pascal: "Eminent
critics have puzzled themselves as to whether
Pascal was a sceptic or a genuine believer, having,
I suppose, convinced themselves, by some process
not obvious to me, that there is an incompatibility
between the two characters." Huysmans may
have been both sceptic and believer, but the dry
fervour of the later books betrays a man who willingly humiliates and depreciates the intellect
for the greater glory of God. Abbé Mugnier says
that his sincerity is itself the form of his talent.
His portrait of Simon the swineherd in En Route
is mortifying to humans with proud stomachs;
Huysmans penetrates the husks and filth and sees
only a God-intoxicated soul. Here is, indeed,
the "treasure of the humble." At first, religion
with Durtal was æsthetic, the beauty of Gothic
architecture, the pyx that ardently shines, the
bells that boom, the odours of frankincense that
rolled through the nave of some old vast cathedral
with flame-coloured windows. In L'Oblat the
feeling has widened and deepened. The walls
of life have fallen asunder, the soul glows in the
twilight of the subliminal self, glows with a spiritual phosphorescence. Huysmans is nearer, though
not face to face with, God. The object of his
prayer is the Virgin Mary; to the hem of her robe he
clings like a frightened child at its mother's dress.
All this may have been auto-suggestion, or the result
of the "will to believe," according to the formula
of Professor William James, yet it was satisfying
to Huysmans, whose life was singularly lonely.

176

He was born on February 5, 1848, in Paris, and died in that city on May 12, 1907. Christened Charles-Marie-George, he signed his books Joris-Karl. He was educated at the Lyceum Saint-Louis. His family originally resided at Breda, Holland. His father was lithographer and painter. His mother was of Burgundian stock and boasted a sculptor in her ancestral line. Huysmans came fairly by his love of art. He contemplated the profession of law; but, at the age of twenty, he entered the Ministry of the Interior, where he remained until 1897, a model, unassuming official, fond of first editions, posters, rare prints, and a few intimates. He went then to live at Ligugé, but returned to Paris after the expulsion of the Benedictines. He was elected first president of the Academy Goncourt, April 7, 1900. He was nominated chevalier of the Legion of Honour, and given the rosette of officer by Briand, though Huysmans begged that he should have no military honours at his funeral. It was for his excellent work as a civil servant that he was decorated, and not as a man of letters. At the time of his death, his reputation had suffered an eclipse; he was distrusted both by Catholics and free-thinkers. But he never wavered. Attacked by a cancerous malady, he suffered the atrocious martyrdom of his favourite Saint Lydwine. Léon Daudet, François Coppée, and Lucien Descaves were his unwearying attendants. At the last, he could still read the prayers for the dying. He was buried in his Benedictine habit.

But what an artist perished in the making of an amateur monk!

"His face," said an English friend, "with the sensitive, luminous eyes, reminded one of Baudelaire's portrait, the face of a resigned and benevolent Mephistopheles who has discovered the absurdity of the divine order, but has no wish to make improper use of his discovery. He gave me the impression of a cat, courteous, perfectly polite, most amiable, but all nerves, ready to shoot out his claws at the least word." (Huysmans, like Baudelaire, was fond of cats). When I saw him five years ago in Paris, I was struck by the essentially Semitic contour of his head — some legacy of remote ancestors from the far-away Meuse.

II

As a critic of painting Huysmans revealed himself the possessor of a temperament that was positively ferocious in the presence of an unsympathetic canvas. His vocabulary and peculiar gift of invective were then exercised with astounding verbal if not critical results. Singularly narrow in his judgments for a man of his general culture, his intensity of vision concentrated itself upon a few painters and etchers; during the latter part of his life only religious art interested him, as had the exotic and monstrous in earlier years. And even in the former sphere he restricted his admiration, rather say idolatry, to a few men; he sought for character, an ascetic type of char-

178

acter, the lean and meagre Saviours and saints of the Flemish primitives arousing in him a fire almost fanatical. Between a Roger Van der Weyden and a Giorgione there would be little doubt as to Huysmans's choice; the golden colour-music of the great Venetian harmonist would have reached deaf ears. His Flemish ancestry told in his æsthetic tastes. He once said that he preferred a Leipsic man to a Marseilles man, "the big, phlegmatic, taciturn Germans to the gesticulating and rhetorical people of the south."

Huysmans never betrayed the slightest interest in doctrines of equality; for him, as for Baudelaire, socialism, the education of the masses, or democratic prophylactics were hateful. The virus of the "exceptional soul" was in his veins. Nothing was more horrible to him than the idea of universal religion, universal speech, universal government, with their concomitant universal monotony. The world is ugly enough without the ugliness of universal sameness. Variety alone makes this globe bearable. He did not believe in art for the multitude, and the tableau of a billion humans bellowing to the moon the hymn of universal brotherhood made him shiver — as well it might. Tolstoy and his semi-idiotic mujik, to whom Beethoven was impossible, aroused in Huysmans righteous indignation. Art is for those who have the brains and patience to understand it. It is not a free port of entry for poet and philistine alike. To it, though many are called, few are chosen. So is it with religion.

That marvellous specimen of psychology, En
Route, gave more offence to Roman Catholics
than it did to sectarians of other faiths. Huysmans was a mystic, and to his temperament, as
taut as a finely attuned fiddle, the easy-going
methods of the average worshipper were absolutely blasphemous. So he could write in En
Route: "And he — Durtal — called to mind
orators petted like tenors, Monsabré, Didon,
those Coquelins of the Church, and, lower yet
than those products of the Catholic training
school, that bellicose booby the Abbé d'Hulst."
That same abbé lived to see the writer repentant
and, himself, not only to forgive, but to write
eulogistic words of the man who had abused him.

L'Art Moderne was published between covers
in 1883. It deals with the official salons of 1879,
1880-81 and the exposition of the Independents,
1880-81. The appendix, 1882, contains thumb-
nail sketches of Caillebotte, whose bequest to
the Luxembourg of impressionistic paintings,
including Manet's Olympe, stirred all artistic
and inartistic Paris; Gauguin, Mlle. Morisot,
Guillaumin, Renoir, Pissaro, Sisley, Claude
Monet, "the marine painter *par excellence*";
Manet, Roll, Redon, all men then fighting the
stream of popular and academic disfavour.
Since Charles Baudelaire's Salons, no volume on
the current Paris exhibitions has appeared of
such solid knowledge and literary power as Huysmans's. Admitting his marked prejudices, his
numerous dogmatic utterances, there is never-

180

179

theless an attractive artistic quality backed up
by the writer's stubborn convictions that persuade
where the more liberal and brilliant Théophile
Gautier never does. "Théo," who said that if
he pitched his sentences in the air they always fell
on their feet, like a cat, leaned heavily on his
verbal magic. But even in that particular he is
no match for Huysmans, who, boasting the blood of
Fleming painters, sculptors, and architects, uses
his pen as an artist his brush. Take another
bit from his study of Moreau's Salome:

"A throne, like the high altar of a cathedral,
rose beneath innumerable arches springing from
columns, thick-set as Roman pillars, enamelled
with varicoloured bricks, set with mosaics, en-
crusted with lapis-lazuli and sardonyx in a palace like the basilica of an architecture at once
Mussulman and Byzantine. In the centre of
the tabernacle surmounting the altars, fronted
with rows of circular steps, sat the Tetrarch
Herod, the tiara on his head, his legs pressed together, his hands on his knees. His face was
yellow, parchmentlike, annulated with wrinkles,
withered by age; his long beard floated like a
cloud on the jewelled stars that constellated the
robe of netted gold across his breast. Around
this statue, motionless, frozen in the sacred pose
of a Hindu god, perfumes burned, throwing out
clouds of vapour, pierced, as by the phosphorescent eyes of animals, by the fire of precious
stones set in the sides of the throne; then the
vapour mounted, unrolling itself beneath arches

where the blue smoke mingled with the powdered gold of great sun-rays fallen from the dome." . . . And of Salome he writes: "In the work of Gustave Moreau, conceived on no Scriptural data, Des Esseintes saw at last the realisation of the strange, superhuman Salome that he had dreamed. She was no more the mere dancing girl . . . she had become the symbolic deity of indestructible Lust, the goddess of immortal Hysteria; the monstrous, indifferent, irresponsible, insensible Beast, poisoning like Helen of old all that go near her, all that look upon her, all that she touches."

Not only is there an evocation of material splendour in the above passages taken from A Rebours, but a note of cenobitic contempt for woman's beauty, which sounds throughout the books of Huysmans. It may be heard at its deepest in his study of Félicien Rops, the Belgian etcher and painter, who interpreted Baudelaire's *femmes damnées*. Rops, too, regarded woman in the light of a destroyer, a being banned by the early fathers of the Church, the matrix of sin. Huysmans's incomparable study of Rops — whose great powers have never been fully recognized because of his erotic and diabolic subjects — may be found in his Certains (1889).

In his description of the Independent exposition (1880) to which Degas, Mary Cassatt and Berthe Morisot, Forain, and others sent canvases, Huysmans drifts into literary criticism; he saw analogies between the paintings of the realists, impressionists, and the modern men of fiction,

182

Flaubert, Goncourt, Zola. "Have not," he asks, "the Goncourts fixed in a style deliberate and personal, the most ephemeral of sensations, the most fugacious of *nuances* ?" So, too, have Manet, Monet, Pissaro, Raffaelli. Nor does he hesitate to make the avowal, still incomprehensible for those who are deceived by the prodigious blaring of critical trumpets, that Baudelaire is a true poet of genius; and that the *chef d'œuvre* of fiction is Flaubert's L'Education Sentimentale. Naturally Edgar Degas is the only psychological interpreter of latter-day life. There is also a careful analysis of Manet's masterpiece, the Bar at the Folies-Bergères. Huysmans recognised Manet's indebtedness to Goya.

Certains is a valuable volume. Therein are Puvis de Chavannes, Gustave Moreau, Degas, Bartholomé, Raffaelli, Stevens, Tissot, Wagner — the painter, not the composer; Huysmans admits but one form in music, the Plain Chant — Cézanne, Chéret, Whistler — which true to the tradition of Parisian carelessness is spelled "Wisthler," as Liszt years before was called "Litz" — Rops, Jan Luyken, Millet, Goya, Turner, Bianchi, and other men. He gives to Millet his just meed of praise, no more — he views him as a designer rather than as a great painter. We get Huysmans in his quintessence. Scattered through his novels — if one may dare to ascribe this title to such an amorphous form — there are eloquent and burning pages devoted to various painters, but not with the amplitude

183

and cool science displayed in his studies of Degas,
Moreau, Rops, The Monster in Art — a monstrous subject masterfully handled — and Whistler. He literally discovered Degas, and in future
books on rhetoric surely Huysmans's descriptions
of Degas's old workwomen sponging their creased
backs cannot be excluded without doing violence
to the expressive powers of the French language.
His eye mirrored the most minute details — in
that he was Dutch-Flemish; the same merciless scrutiny is pursued in the life of the soul —
he was Flemish and Spanish: Ruysbroeck and
St. John of the Cross, mystics both, with an
amazing sense of the realistic.

Without a spacious imagination, Huysmans was
a man of the subtlest sensibilities. There is a
wealth of critical divination in his studies of Moreau
and Whistler. Twenty or thirty years ago it was
not so easy to range these two enigmas. Huysmans did so, and, in company with Degas and
Rops, placed them so definitely that critics have
paraphrased his ideas ever since. Baudelaire
had recognised the glacial genius of Rops;
Huysmans definitely consecrated it in Certains.
For Huysmans the theme of love aroused his mordant wit — Flaubert, Goncourt, Baudelaire were
all summoned at one time or another in their
respective careers to answer the charge of poisoning public morals! And what malicious com-
mentaries were drawn and etched by the versatile Rops.

Extraordinary as are Rops's delineations of
184

Satan, the prose of Huysmans is not less graphic in interpreting the etched plate. In De Tout (1901) there is, literally, a little about everything. Not only are several unknown quarters of Paris sketched with a surprising freshness, but Huysmans goes far afield for his themes. He studies sleeping-cars and the sleepy city Bruges, the aquarium at Berlin — "most fastidious and most ugly" — the Gobelins, Quentin Matsys at Antwerp; but whether in illustrating with his pen the mobs at Lourdes or the intimate habits of a Parisian café, he never fails to achieve the exact phrase that illuminates. Nor is it all crass realism. His eye, the eye of a visionary as well as of a painter, penetrates to the marrow of the soul.

A Rebours is the history of a decadent soul in search of an earthly paradise. His palace of art is near Paris, and in it the Duc des Esseintes assembles all that is rare, perverse, beautiful, morbid, and crazy in modern art and literature. A Rebours is in reality a very precious work of criticism by a distinguished critical temperament, written in a prose jewelled and shining, sharp as a Damascene dagger. This French writer's admiration for Moreau has been mentioned. Luyken comes in for his share; the bizarre Luyken of Amsterdam (1649–1712). Odilon Redon, the lithographer and illustrator of Poe, is lauded by Des Esseintes. Redon's work is not lacking in subtlety, and it is sometimes disagreeable; possibly the latter quality is aimed at by the painter.

Redon certainly had in Poe a congenial subject; in Baudelaire also, for he has accomplished some shivering plates commemorating Fleurs du Mal.

Not such intractable reading as L'Oblat, withal difficult enough, is The Cathedral, which abounds in glorious chapters devoted to ecclesiastical painting, sculpture, and architecture. "It" — the Cathedral — "was as slender and colourless as Roger Van der Weyden's Virgins, who are so fragile, so ethereal, that they might blow away were they not held down to earth by the weight of their brocades and trains," is a passage in this storehouse of curious liturgical learning. Matsys, Memling, Dierck Bouts, Van der Weyden, painted great religious pictures because they possessed a naïve faith. Nowadays your painter has no faith; better, then, stick like Degas to ballet-girls and not soil canvas with profane burlesques. Always extreme, Huysmans jumped from the worldly audacities of Manet to the rebellious Christ of Grünewald. Van Eyck touched him where Van Dyck did not. He disliked the ."supersensual and sublimated Virgins of Cologne," and pronounced Botticelli's Virgins masquerading Venuses. The Van der Weyden triptych of the Nativity in the old museum, Berlin, filled him with raptures, pious and æsthetic. The "theatrical crucifixions, the fleshly coarseness of Rubens" are naught when compared to the early Flemings. His pages on Rembrandt are admirable reading, "Rembrandt, who had the soul of a Judaising Protestant . . . with his

186·

serious but fervid wit, his genius for concentration, for getting a spot of the essence of sunlight into the heart of darkness . . . has accomplished great results; and in his Biblical scenes has spoken a language which no one before him had attempted to lisp." As Huysmans loathed the rancid and voluptuous "sacred" music of Gounod and other comic-opera writers of masses and hymns in the Church, so he abominated the modern "sacred" painters. James Tissot and Munkacsy come in for a critical flagellation. What could be more dazzling than his account of a certain stained-glass window in his beloved Cathedral at Chartres:

"Up there high in the air, as they might be Salamanders, human beings, with faces ablaze and robes on fire, dwelt in a firmament of glory; but these conflagrations were enclosed and limited by an incombustible frame of darker glass which set off the youthful and radiant joy of the flames by the contrast of melancholy, the suggestion of the more serious and aged aspect presented by gloomy colouring. The bugle-cry of red, the limpid confidence of white, the repeated hallelujahs of yellow, the virginal glory of blue, all the quivering crucible of glass was dimmed as it neared this border dyed with rusty red, the tawny hues of sauces, the harsh purples of sandstone, bottle green, tinder brown, fuliginous blacks, and ashy grays." Not even Arthur Rimbaud, in his half-jesting sonnet on the "Vowels," indulged in such daring colour symbolism as Huys-

187

mans. For a specimen of his most fulgurating style read his Camïeu in Red, in a little volume edited by Mr. Howells entitled Pastels in Prose, and translated by Stuart Merrill.

"To be rich, very rich, and found in Paris in face of the triumphal ambulance, the Luxembourg, a public museum of contemporary painting!" he cries in one of his essays. He was the critic of Modernity, as Degas is its painter, Goncourt its exponent in fiction, Paul Bourget its psychologist. He lashes himself into a fine rage over the enormous prices paid some years ago by New York millionaires for the work of such artists as Bouguereau, Dubufe, Gérôme, Constant, Rosa Bonheur, Knaus, Meissonier. The Christ before Pilate, sold for 600,000 francs, sets him fulminating against its painter. "Cet indigent décor brossé par le Brésilien de la piété, par le rastaquouère de la peinture, par Munkacsy."

Joris-Karl Huysmans should have been a painter; his indubitable gift for form and colour were by some trick of nature or circumstance transposed to literature. So he brought to the criticism of pictures an eye abnormal in its keenness, and to this was superadded an abnormal power of expression.

After reading his Three Primitives you may be tempted to visit Colmar, where hang in the museum several paintings by Mathias Grünewald, who is the chief theme of the French writer's book. Colmar is not difficult to reach if you are

188

in Paris, or pass through Strasburg. It is a town of over 35,000 inhabitants, the capital of Upper Alsace and about forty miles from Strasburg. There are several admirable specimens of the Rhenish school there, Van Eyck and ·Martin Schongauer (born 1450 in Colmar), the great engraver. His statue by Bartholdi is in the town, and, as Huysmans rather delicately puts it, is an "emetic for the eyes." He always wrote what he thought, and notwithstanding the odour of sanctity in which he departed this life, his name and his books are still anathema to many of his fellow Catholics. But as to the quality of this last study there can be no mistake. It is masterly, revealing the various Huysmanses we admire: the mystic, the realist, the penetrating critic of art, and the magnificent tamer of language. Hallucinated by his phrases, you see cathedrals arise from the mist and swim so close to you that you discern every detail before the vision vanishes; or some cruel and bloody canvas of the semi-demoniacal Grünewald, on which a hideous Christ is crucified, surrounded by scowling faces. The swiftness in executing the verbal portrait allows you no time to wonder over the method; the evocation is complete, and afterward you realise the magic of Huysmans.

In his Là Bas he described the Grünewald Crucifixion, once in the Cassel Museum, now as Carlsruhe. A tragic realism invests this work of Grünewald, who is otherwise a very unequal painter. Huysmans puzzled over the Bavarian,

189

who was probably born at Aschaffenburg. Sundvart, Waagen, Goutzwiller, and Passavant have written of him. He was born about 1450 and died about 1530. He lived his later years in Mayence, lonely and misanthropic. Every one speaks of Dürer, the Cranachs, Schongauer, - Holbein, but even during his lifetime Grünewald was not famous. To-day he is esteemed by those for whom the German and Belgian Primitives mean more than all Italian art. There is a bitterness, a pessimism, a delight in torture for the sake of torture in Grünewald's treatment of sacred subjects that must have shocked his more easy-going contemporaries. Huysmans, as is his wont, does not spare us in his recital of the horrors of that Colmar Crucifixion. For me the one now at Carlsruhe suffices. It causes a shudder, and some echo of the agony of the Passion permeates that solemn scene. Grünewald must have been a painter of fierce and exalted temperament. His Christs are ugly — the ugliness symbolical of the sins of the world; — this doctrine was upheld by Tertullian and Cyprian, Cyril and St. Justin.

And the cadaverous flesh tones! Such is his fidelity, a fidelity almost pathologic, that two such eminent men as Charcot and Richet testified, after study, to the too painful verity of this early German's brushwork. He depicted with shocking realism the malady known as St. Anthony's Fire, and a still more pathological interpretation by Huysmans follows. But he warmly praises

190

the fainting mother, one of the noble figures in
German art. We allude now to the Colmar
Crucifixion, with its curious introduction of St.
John the Baptist in Golgotha, and the dark
landscape through which runs a gloomy river.
Fainting Mary, the mother of Christ, is upheld
by the disciple John. There is a mysterious
figure of a girl, an ugly but sorrowful face, and
the lamb bearing the cross is at the foot of the
cross. Audacious is the entire composition.
It wounds the soul, and that is what Grünewald
wished. His harsh nature saw in the crucifixion
not a pious symbol but the death of a god, an
unjust death. So he fulminates upon his canvas
his hatred of the outrage. How tender he can
be we see in this Virgin.

On the back of this polyptique are a Resur-
rection and Annunciation. The latter is bad.
The former is a dynamic picture representing
Christ in a vast aureole arising to the sky, His
guards tumbled over at the side of the tomb.
There is an explosion of luminosity. Christ's
face is radiant; He displays his palms upward,
pierced by the nails. The floating aerial effect
and the draperies are wonderfully handled.
The museum wherein hang these works was
formerly a convent of nuns, founded in 1232, and
in 1849 turned into a museum. Huysmans
rages, of course, over the change.

He finds among the Grünewalds at Colmar —
there are nine in all — a St. Anthony bearded,
that reminds him of a Father Hecker born in

191

Holland. What a simile, made by a man who probably never saw the American priest, except pictured!

He visits Frankfort-on-the-Main, and afterward, characteristically pouring his vials of wrath upon this New Jerusalem, he visits the Staedel Museum and goes into ecstasies over that lovely head of a young woman called the Florentine, by an unknown master. Though he admires the Van der Weyden, the Bouts, and the Virgin of Van Eyck, he really has eyes only for this exquisite, vicious androgynous creature and for the Virgin by the Master of Flemalle. After a vivid description of the Florentine Cybele he inquires into her artistic paternity, waving aside the suggestion that one of the Venezianos painted her. But which one? There are over eleven, according to Lanzi. Huysmans will not allow Botticelli's name to be mentioned, though he discerns certain Botticellian qualities. But he has never forgiven Botticelli for painting the Virgin looking like the Venus, and he hates the paganism of the Renaissance with an early Christian fervour. (Fancy the later Joris-Karl Huysmans and the early Walter Pater in a discussion about the Renaissance.) Huysmans himself was a Primitive. Much that he wrote would have been understood in the Middle Ages. The old Adam in this Fleming, however, comes to the surface as he conjectures the name of the enigmatic heroine. Is it that Giulia Farnese, called "Giulia la bella" — *puritas impuritatis* — who

192

became the favourite of Pope Alexander VI.? If it is — and then Huysmans writes some pages of perfect prose which suggest joyful depravity, as depraved as the people he paints with such marvellous colour and precision. It is a peep behind the scenes of a pagan Christian Rome.

The Master of Flemalle, whose Virgin he describes at the close of this volume, was the Jacques Daret born in the early years of the fifteenth century, a fellow student of Roger van der Weyden under Campin at Tournay. We confess that, while we enjoy the verbal rhapsodies of the author, we were not carried away by this stately Virgin and Child by Daret, though there are many Darets that once passed as the work of Roger van der Weyden. It has not the sweet melancholy, this picture, of Hans Memlinc's Madonnas, and the Van Eyck in the same gallery, as well as the Van der Weyden, are both worth a trip across Europe to gaze upon. However, on the note of a rapt devotion Huysmans ends his book. The first edition, illustrated, was published in 1905, by Vanier-Messein. But there is a new (1908) edition, published by Plon, at Paris, and called Trois Eglises et Trois Primitifs. This latter is not illustrated. The three churches discussed are Notre Dame de Paris and its symbolism, Saint Germain-l'Auxerrois, and Saint Merry.

Poor, unhappy, suffering Huysmans! He trod the Road to Damascus on foot and not in a pleasant motor-car like several of his successors. ·

193

The intimate side of the man, so hidden by him, is now being revealed to us by his friends. Recently, in the *Revue de Paris*, Mme. Myriam Harry, the writer of The Conquest of Jerusalem, tells us of her friendship with Huysmans, with a rather sentimental anecdote about his weeping over a dead love. When she met him he was already attainted with the malady which tortured him to the end. A lifetime sufferer from neuralgia and dyspepsia, he was half blind for a few months before his death. He touchingly alludes to his illness as both a punishment and a reparation for things he wrote in his Lourdes. In a letter dated January 5, 1907, he avows that nothing is more dangerous than to celebrate sorrow; all his books celebrate the physical miseries of life, the sorrows of the soul. Humbly this great writer admits that he must pay for the pages of that cruel book, the life of Sainte-Lydwine. The disease he so often described came to him at last and slew him.

III

To traverse the books of Huysmans is a true pessimistic progress; from Le Drageoir aux Epices (1874) to Les Foules de Lourdes (1906), the note, at times shrill, often profound, is never one of dulcification. The first book, a veritable little box of spices, was modelled on Baudelaire's Poemes en Prose, but revealed to the acute critic a new personal shade. Its plainness is Gallic. That amusing, ironic sketch, L'Extase, gives

194

us a key-note to the writer's disillusioned soul.
Marthe. (1876) caused a sensation. It was
speedily suppressed. La Fille Elise and Nana
the public could endure; but the cold-blooded
delineation of vice in this first novel was too
much for the Parisian, who likes a display of
sentiment or sympathy in the treatment of
unsavoury themes. Now, sympathy for sin or
suffering is missing in Huysmans. Slow veils of
pity never descend upon his sufferers. Like
a surgeon who will show you a "beautiful
disease," a "classic case," he exposed the life of
the wretched Marthe, and, while he called a cat
a cat, he forgot that certain truths are unfit for
polite ears accustomed to the rotten-ripe Dumas
fils, or the thrice-brutal Zola. It was in Marthe
that Huysmans proclaimed his adherence to
naturalism in these memorable words: "I write
what I see, what I feel, and what I have experienced, and I write it as well as I can: that is
all." This rubric he adhered to his life long,
despite his change of spiritual base. He also said
that there are writers who have talent, and others
who have not talent. All schools, groups, cliques,
whether romantic or naturalistic or decadent, need
not count.

It was 1880 before Huysmans was again heard
from, this time in collaboration with Zola, Guy
de Maupassant, Henry Céard, Léon Hennique,
and Paul Alexis. Les Soirées de Medan was
the inappropriate title of a book of interesting
tales. Huysmans's contribution, Sac au Dos, is

195

a story of the Franco-Prussian war that would have pleased Stendhal by its sardonic humour. The hero never reaches the front, but spends his time in hospitals, and the nearest he gets to the glory of war is a chronic stomach-ache. The variations on this ignoble motive showed the malice of Huysmans. War is not hell, he says in effect, but dysentery is; how often a petty ailing has unmade a heroic soul. Yet in the Brussels edition of this story there was published the following verse—the author seldom wrote poetry; he was hardly a poet, but as indicating certain religious preoccupations it is worth repeating:

"O croix qui veux l'austère, ô chair qui veux le doux,
O monde, ô évangile, immortels adversaires,   .
Les plus grands ennemis sont plus d'accord que vous,
Et les pôles du ciel ne sont pas plus contraires.
On monte dans le ciel par un chemin de pleurs,
Mais, que leur amertume a de douceurs divines!
On descend aux enfers par un chemin de fleurs,
Mais hélas! que ces fleurs nous préparent d'épines!   ·
La fleur qui, dans un jour, sèche et s'épanouit,
Les bulles d'air et d'eau qu'un petit souffle casse,
Une ombre qui paraît et qui s'évanouit
Nous représentent bien comme le monde passe."

Naturally, in the face of Maupassant's brilliant Boule de Suif, Huysmans's sly attack on patriotism was overlooked. Croquis Parisiens (1880) contains specimens of Huysmans's astounding virtuosity. No one before has ever described sundry aspects of Paris with such verisimilitude — that Paris he said was, because of the Americans,

196

fast becoming a "sinister Chicago." Balls, cafés, bars, omnibus-conductors, washerwomen, chestnut-sellers, hairdressers, remote landscapes and corners of the city, cabarets, la Bièvre, the underground river, with prose paraphrases of music, perfumes, flowers — Huysmans astonishes by his prodigality of epithet and justness of observation. What Manet, Pissaro, Raffaelli, Forain, were doing with oil and pastel and pencil, he accomplished with his pen. A Vau l'Eau followed in 1882. It is considered the typical Huysmans tale, and some see in Jean Folantin its unhappy hero, obsessed by the desire for a juicy beefsteak, the prototype of Durtal. Folantin is a poor employee in the Ministry who must exist on his annual salary of fifteen hundred francs. He haunts cheap restaurants, lives in cheap lodgings, is seedy and sour, with the nerves of a voluptuary. His sense of smell makes his life a nightmare. The sordid recital would be comical but that it is so villainously real. It is an Odyssey of a dyspeptic. Dickens would have set us laughing over the woes of this Folantin, or Dostoïevsky would have made us weep — as he did in Poor Folk. But Huysmans has no time for tears or laughter; he must register his truth, and at the end an odor of stale cheese exhales from the printed page. Wretched Monsieur Folantin. Of the official life so clearly presented in some of Maupassant's tales, we get little; Huysmans is too much preoccupied with Folantin's stomach troubles. In the same volume, though published

197

first in 1887, is Un Dilemme, which is a pitiful
tale of a girl abandoned. Huysmans, while he
came under the influence of· L'Education Sentimentale, seems to have taken as a *leit motiv* the
idiotic antics of Flaubert's Bouvard et Pécuchet.
This pair of mediocre maniacs were his models ·
for mankind at large. Les Sœurs Vatard (1879),
praised so warmly by Zola in The Experimental
Novel, is not a novel, but kaleidoscopic Parisian
pictures of intimate low life, executed with consummate finish, and closeness to fact. The two
sisters Vatard, Céline and Désirée, with their love
affairs, fill a large volume. There are minute
descriptions of proletarian interiors, sewing-shops
full of perspiring girls, railroad-yards, loco-
motives, and a gingerbread fair. The men are
impudent scamps, bullies, *souteneurs*, the women
either weak or vulgar. Veracity there often is
and an air of reality — though these swaggerers
and simpletons are silhouettes, not half as vital
as Zola's Lise or Goncourt's Germinie Lacerteux.
But atmosphere, *toujours* atmosphere — of that
Huysmans is the compeller. Not a disagreeable
scene, smell, or sound does he spare his readers.
And how many *genre* pictures he paints for us in
this book.

We reach *bourgeois* life with En Ménage (1881).
André and Cyprien the novelist and painter are
not so individual as, say, old *père* Vatard in the
preceding story. They but serve as stalking
horses for Huysmans to show the stupid miseries
of the married state; that whether a man is or

198

JORIS-KARL HUYSMANS

is not married he will regret it. Love is the supreme poison of life. André is deceived by his wife, Cyprien lives lawlessly. Neither one is contented. The novel is careful in workmanship; it is like Goncourt and Flaubert, both gray and masterful. But it leaves a bad taste in the mouth. Like the early Christian fathers, Huysmans had a conception of Woman, "the eternal feminine of the eternal simpleton," which is hardly ennobling. The painter Cyprien is said to be a portrait of the author.

A Rebours appeared at the psychologic moment. Decadence was in the air. Either were a decadent or violently opposed to the movement. Verlaine had consecrated the word — hardly an expressive one. The depraved young Jean, Duke of Esseintes, greedy of exotic sensations, who figures as the hero of this gorgeous prose mosaic, is said to be the portrait of a Parisian poet, and a fashionable dilettante of art painted by Whistler. But there is more of Huysmans — the exquisite literary critic that is Huysmans — in the work. If, as Henry James remarks: "When you have no taste you have no discretion — which is the conscience of taste," then Huysmans must be acclaimed a man of unexampled tact. His handling of a well-nigh impossible theme, his "technical heroism," above all, his soul-searching tactics in that wonderful Chapter VII, when Des Esseintes, suffering from the malady of the infinite, proceeds to examine his conscience and portrays for us the most fluctu-

ating shades of belief and feeling — his touch here
is sure, and casuistically immoral, as "all art is
immoral for the inartistic." The chief value of
the book for future generations of critics lies in
Chapters XII and XIV. Huysmans's literary
and artistic preferences are catalogued with
delicacy and erudition. More Byzantine than By-
zance, A Rebours is a storehouse of art treasures,
and it was once the battle-field of the literary
élite. It is a history of the artistic decadent, the
man of disdainful inquietudes who searches for
an earthly artificial paradise. The mouth orchestra which, by the aid of various liquors,
gives to the tongue sensations analogous to music;
the flowers and perfume concerts, the mechanical
landscape, the mock sea — all these are mysti-
fications. Huysmans the *farceur*, the Jules
Verne of æsthetics, is enjoying himself. His
liquor symphony he borrowed from La Chimie du
Goût by Polycarpe Poncelet; from Zola, perhaps,
his concert of flowers. As for the originality of
these diversions, we may turn to Goethe and
find in his Triumph der Empfindsamkeit the
mechanical landscape of the Prince, who can
enjoy sunlight or moonlight at will. He has also
a doll to whom he sighs, rhapsodises, and passes
in its silent company hours of rapture. Villiers
de l'Isle Adam evidently read Goethe: see his
Eve of the Future. All of which shows the folly
of certain critics who recognise in Huysmans the
prime exemplar of the decadent — that much
misunderstood word. But how about Goethe?

200

A Rebours, notwithstanding Huysmans's later pilgrimage to Canossa, he never excelled. It is his most personal achievement. It also contains the most beautiful writing of this Paganini of prose.

En Rade (1887) did not attract much attention. It is not dull; on the contrary, it is very Huysmansish. But it is not a subject that enthralls. Jacques Marles and his wife have lost their money. They go into the country to live cheaply. The author's detestation of nature was apparently the motive for writing the book. There are fantastic dreams worthy of H. G. Wells, and realistic descriptions of a calf's birth and a cat's agony; the last two named prove the one-time disciple of Zola had not lost his vision; the truth is, Zola's method is melodramatic, romantic, vague, when compared to Huysmans's implacable manner of etching petty facts.

But in Là-Bas he takes a leap across the ditch of naturalism and reaches another, if not more delectable, territory. This was in 1891. A new manifesto must be made — the Goncourts had printed a bookful. Symbolism, not naturalism, is now the shibboleth. Huysmans declares that:

It is essential to preserve the veracity of the document, the precision of detail, the fibrous and nervous language of Realism, but it is equally essential to become the well-digger of the soul, and not to attempt to explain what is mysterious by mental maladies. . . . It is essential, in a word, to follow the great road so deeply dug out by Zola, but it is also necessary to trace a parallel pathway in the air, another road by which we may reach the Beyond, to achieve thus a Spiritual naturalism.

And by a curious, a bizarre route Durtal, the ever-lasting Durtal, sought to achieve spiritually — a spirituality *à rebours*, for it was by devil-worship and the study of Gilles de Rais of ill-fame, that he reached his goal. We also study church bells, *incubi*, satanism, demons, witches, sacrileges of a *raffiné* sort; indeed, an enormous amount of occult lumber is dumped into the book, which is indigestible on that account. Diabolic lore *à la* Jules Dubois and other modern magi is profuse. That wicked lady, who is far from credible, Madame Chantelouve, flits through various chapters. Her final disappearance, one hopes "below" — like the devils in the pantomime — is received by Durtal and the reader with a sigh of relief. She is quite the vilest character in French fiction, and, as Stendhal would say, her only excuse is that she never existed. The Black Mass is painted by an artist adroit in the manipulation of the sombre and magnificent.

Là-Bas proved a prophetic weather-vane. En Route in 1895 did not astonish those who had been studying the spiritual fluctuations of Huysmans. Behold the miracle! He is a believing Christian. Wisely the antecedent causes were tacitly avoided. "I believe," said Durtal, simply. Of superior interest is his struggle up the ladder to perfection. This painful feat is slowly ac-

202

complished in La Cathédrale (1898), L'Oblat
(1903), and Lourdes (1906). And it must be
confessed that the more pious grew Huysmans
the less artist he — as might have been expected.
What is his art to a man who is concerned not
with the things of this world? He never lost his
acerbity, or his faculty for the phrase magical,
though his sense of proportion gradually vanished.
Luckily, he is not saccharine like the majority of
writers on religious topics. Ferdinand Brunetière
complained that Flaubert was unbearably erudite
in his three short stories — echoing what Sainte-
Beuve had said of Salammbô years before.
What must he have thought of that astonishing
Cathedral, with its chapters on the symbolism of
architecture, sculpture, gems, flowers (Sir Thomas
Browne and his quincunxes are fairly beaten
from the field), vestments, sacred vessels of the
altar, and a multitude of mysterious things,
hieroglyphics, and dark liturgical riddles? There
are ravishing pages, though none so solemn and
moving as the description of the *De profundis* and
Dies iræ in En Route.

It may prove profitable for the student after
reading La Cathédrale to take up Walter Pater's
unfinished story, Gaston De Latour, and read
the description therein of the Chartres Cathedral.
There are pages of exquisitely felt prose, but
Huysmans sees more and tells what he sees in less
musical though more lapidary phrases.

For anyone except the trailer after strange
souls The Oblate is an affliction. Madame

203

Bavoil, with her *notre ami*, is a chattering nuisance, withal a worthy creature. Durtal is always in the dumps. He speaks much of interior peace, but he gives the impression of a man sitting painfully amidst spiritual brambles. Perhaps he felt that for him after his Golgotha are the sweet-singing flames of Purgatory. We are not sorry when he returns to Paris. As for the book on Lourdes, it is like an open wound. A whiff from the operating-room of a hospital comes to you. We are edified by the childlike faith with which Huysmans accepts the report of cures that would stagger the most perfervid Christian Scientist. His Saint-Lydwine is hard reading, written by a man whose mysticism was a matter of rigid definition, a thing to be weighed and felt and verbally proved. Fleming-like, he is less melodist than harmonist — and such acrid harmonies, polyphonic variations, and fuguelike flights to the other side of good and evil.

George Moore was the first English critic to recognise Huysmans. He wrote that "a page of Huysmans is as a dose of opium, a glass of exquisite and powerful liquor." Frankly, it was his conversion that focussed upon Huysmans so much attention. No one may remain isolated in his century. He has never been a favourite with the larger Parisian public; rather, a curiosity, a spiritual ogre turned saint. And the saintship has been hotly disputed. Abbé Mugnier and Dom A. du Bourg, the prior of Sainte-Marie, since his death, have written eloquently about his conversion, his life as an oblate, and his edifying death. Huysmans refused anæsthetics because he wished to suffer for his life of sin, above all suffer for his early writings. Need it be added that, like Tolstoy, he repudiated absolutely his first books? Huysmans Intime is the title of the recollections of both Dom du Bourg and Henry Céard. His literary executors destroyed many manuscripts. He left his money principally to charities.

Huysmans was not a man possessing what are so vaguely denominated "general ideas." He was never interested in the chess-play of metaphysics, politics, or science. He was a specialist, one who had ransacked libraries for curious details, despoiled perfumers' catalogues for their odourous vocables, pored over technical dictionaries for odd-coloured words, and studied cookbooks for savoury terms. His gamut of sensations began at the violet ray. He was a perverse aristocrat who descended to the gutter there to analyse the various stratifications of filth; when he returned to his ivory cell, he had discovered, not humanity, but an anodyne, the love of God. Thenceforth, he was interested in one thing — the saving of the soul of Joris-Karl Huysmans, and being a marvellous verbal artist, his recital of the event startled us, fascinated us. Renan once wrote of Amiel: "He speaks of sin, of salvation, of redemption and conversion, as if these things were realities." Let us rather imitate Sainte-Beuve, who said: "You may not cease to be a sceptic after reading Pascal, but you must cease to treat believers with contempt." And this injunction is not difficult to obey in the case of Huysmans, for whom the things derided by Renan were the profoundest realities of his troubled life.

VI

THE EVOLUTION OF AN EGOIST

MAURICE BARRES

ONCE upon a time a youth, slim, dark, and delicate, lived in a tower. This tower was composed of ivory — the youth sat within its walls, tapestried by most subtle art, and studied his soul. As in a mirror, a fantastic mirror of opal and gold, he searched his soul and noted its faintest music, its strangest modulations, its transmutation of joy into melancholy; he saw its grace and its corruption. These matters he registered in his "little mirrors of sincerity." And he was happy in an ivory tower and far away from the world, with its rumours of dulness, feeble crimes, and flat triumphs. After some years the young man wearied of the mirror, with his spotted soul cruelly pictured therein; wearied of the tower of ivory and its alien solitudes; so he opened its carved doors and went into the woods, where he found a deep pool of water. It was very small, very clear, and reflected his face, reflected on its quivering surface his unstable soul. But soon other images of the world appeared above the pool: men's faces and women's, and the shapes of earth and

207

sky. Then Narcissus, who was young, whose soul was sensitive, forgot the ivory tower and the magic pool, and merged his own soul into the soul of his people.

Maurice Barrès is the name of the youth, and he is now a member of the Académie Française. His evolution from the Ivory tower of Egoism to the broad meadows of life is not an insoluble enigma; his books and his active career offer many revelations of a fascinating, though often baffling, personality. His passionate curiosity in all that concerns the moral nature of his fellow man lends to his work its own touch of universality; otherwise it would not be untrue to say that the one Barrès passion is love of his native land. "France" is engraved on his heart; France and not the name of a woman. This may be regarded as a grave shortcoming by the sex.

I

Paul Bourget has said of him: "Among the young people who have entered literature since 1880 Maurice Barrès is certainly the most celebrated. . . . One must see other than a decadent or a dilettante in this analyst . . . the most original who has appeared since Baudelaire." Bourget said much more about the young writer, then in his twenties, who in 1887 startled Paris with a curious, morbid, ironical, witty book, a production neither fiction nor fact. This book was called Sous l'Œil des Barbares. It made a

208

sensation. He was born on the 22nd of September,
1862, at Charmes-sur-Moselle (Vosges), and received a classical education at the Nancy (old
capital of Lorraine) Lyceum. Of good family
— among his ancestors he could boast some military men — he early absorbed a love for his native
province, a love that later was to become a species of soil-worship. His health not strong at
any time, and nervous of temperament, he nevertheless moved on Paris, for the inevitable siege of
which all romantic readers of Balzac dream during their school-days. "*A nous deux!*" muttered
Rastignac, shaking his fist at the city spread below him. *A nous deux!* exclaim countless young-
sters ever since. Maurice, however, was not
that sort of Romantic. He meant to conquer
Paris, but in a unique way; he detested melodrama. He removed to the capital in 1882. His
first literary efforts had appeared in the *Journal
de la Meurthe et des Vosges;* he could see as a
boy the Vosges Mountains; and Alsace, not far
away, was in the clutches of the hated enemy. In
Paris he wrote for several minor reviews, met distinguished men like Leconte de Lisle, Roden-
bach, Valade, Rollinat; and his Parisian début
was in *La Jeune France,* with a short story entitled Le Chemin de l'Institut (April, 1882).
Ernest Gaubert, who has given us these details,
says that, despite Leconte de Lisle's hearty support, Mme. Adam refused an essay of Barrès as
unworthy of the *Nouvelle Revue.* In 1884 appeared a mad little review, *Les Taches d'Encre,* ir-

regular in publication. Despite its literary quality, the young editor displayed some knowledge of the tactics of "new" journalism. When Morin was assassinated by Mme. Clovis Hugues, sandwich men paraded the boulevards carrying on their boards this inscription: "Morin reads no longer *Les Taches d'Encre!*" Perseverance such as this should have been rewarded; but little *Ink-spots* quickly disappeared. Barrès founded a new review in 1886, *Les Chroniques*, in company with some brilliant men. Jules Clarétie about this time remarked, "Make a note of the name of Maurice Barrès. I prophesy that it will become famous." Barrès had discovered that Rastignac's pugnacious methods were obsolete in the battle with Paris, though there was no folly he would be incapable of committing if he only could attract attention — even to walking the boulevards in the guise of primeval man. Far removed as his exquisite art now is from this blustering desire for publicity, this threat, uttered in jest or not, is significant. Maurice Barrès has since stripped his soul bare for the world's ire or edification.

Wonder-children do not always pursue their natural vocation. Pascal was miraculously endowed as a mathematician; he ended a master of French prose, a hallucinated, wretched man. Franz Liszt was a prodigy, but aspired to the glory of Beethoven. Raphael was a painting prodigy, and luckily died so young that he had not time to change his profession. Swinburne wrote faultless verse as a youth. He is a *prosateur* to-day. Maurice Barrès was born a metaphysician; he has the metaphysical faculty as some men a fiddle hand. He might say with Prosper Mérimée, "Metaphysic pleases me because it is never-ending." But not as Kant, Condillac, or William James — to name men of widely disparate systems — did the precocious thinker plan objectively. The proper study of Maurice Barrès was Maurice Barrès, and he vivisected his Ego as calmly as a surgeon trepanning a living skull. He boldly proclaimed the *culte du moi*, proclaimed his disdain for the barbarians who impinged upon his *I*. To study and note the fleeting shapes of his soul — in his case a protean psyche — was the one thing worth doing in a life of mediocrity. And this new variation of the eternal hatred for the *bourgeois* contained no menaces levelled at any class, no groans of disgust *à la* Huysmans. Imperturbable, with an icy indifference, Barrès pursued his fastidious way. What we hate we fight, what we despise we avoid. Barrès merely despised the other Egos around him, and entering his ivory tower he bolted the door; but on reaching the roof did not fail to sound his horn announcing to an eager world that the miracle had come to pass — Maurice Barrès was discovered by Maurice Barrès.

Egoism as a religion is hardly a new thing. It began with the first sentient male human. It has since preserved the species, discovered the "inferiority" of women, made civilisation, and

founded the fine arts. Any attempt to displace
the Ego in the social system has only resulted in
inverting the social pyramid. Love our neighbour
as ourself is trouble-breeding; but we must first
love ourself as a precaution that our neighbour
will not suffer both in body and in mind. The
interrogation posed on the horizon of our consciousness, regarding the perfectibility of mankind, is best answered by a definition of socialism
as that religion which proves all men to be equally
stupid. Do not let us confound the ideas of
progress and perfectibility. Since man first realised himself as man, first said, I am I, there has
been no progress. No art has progressed.
Science is a perpetual rediscovery. And what
modern thinker has taught anything new?

Life is a circle. We are imprisoned, in the
cage of our personality. Each human creates his
own picture of the world, re-creates it each day.
These are the commonplaces of metaphysics;
Schopenhauer has presented some of them to us
in tempting garb.

Compare the definitions of Man made by
Pascal and Cabanis. Man, said Pascal, is but
a reed, the feeblest of created things; yet a reed
which thinks. Man, declared the materialistic
Cabanis, is a digestive tube — a statement that
provoked the melodious indignation of Lacordaire. What am I? asks Barrès; *je suis un instant
d'une chose immortelle*. And this instant of an
immortal thing has buried within it something
eternal of which the individual has only the usu-

fruct. (Goncourt wrote, "What is life? The usufruct of an aggregation of molecules.") Before him Sénancour in Obermann — the reveries of a sick, hermetic soul — studied his malady, but offered no prophylactic. Amiel was so lymphatic of will that he doubted his own doubts, doubted all but his dreams. He, too, had fed at Hegel's ideologic banquet, where the verbal viands snared the souls of guests. But Barrès was too sprightly a spirit to remain a mystagogue. Diverse and contradictory as are his several souls, he did not utterly succumb to the spirit of analysis. Whether he was poison-proof or not to the venom that slew the peace of the unhappy Amiel (that bonze of mysticism), the young Lorrainer never lacked elasticity or spontaneity, never ceased to react after his protracted plunges into the dark pools of his subliminal self. And his volitional powers were not paralysed. Possessing a sensibility as delicate and vibrating as Benjamin Constant, he has had the courage to study its fevers, its disorders, its subtleties. He knew that there were many young men like him, not only in France, but throughout the world, highly organised, with less bone and sinew than nerves — exposed nerves; egoistic souls, weak of will. We are sick, this generation of young men, exclaimed Barrès; sick from the lying assurances of science, sick from the false promises of politicians. There must be a remedy. One among us must immolate himself, study the malady, seek its cure. I, Maurice Barrès, shall be the mirror

213

reflecting the fleeting changes of my environment, social and psychical. I repudiate the transcendental indifference of Renan; I will weigh my sensations as in a scale; I shall not fear to proclaim the result. Amiel, a Protestant Hamlet (as Bourget so finely says), believes that every landscape is a state of soul. My soul is full of landscapes. Therein all may enter and find their true selves.

All this, and much more, Barrès sang in his fluid, swift, and supple prose, without a vestige of the dogmatic. He did not write either to prove or to convince, only to describe his interior life. He did not believe, neither did he despair. There is a spiritual malice in his egoism that removes it far from the windy cosmos of Walt Whitman or the vitriolic vanity of D'Annunzio. In his fugue-like flights down the corridor of his metaphysics, he never neglects to drop some poetic rose, some precious pearl of sentiment. His little book, true spiritual memoirs, aroused both wrath and laughter. The wits set to work. He was called a dandy of psychology, nicknamed *Mlle. Renan*, pronounced a psychical harlequin, a masquerader of the emotions; he was told that, like Chateaubriand, he wore his heart in a sling. Anatole France, while recognising the eloquent art of this young man, spoke of the "perverse idealist" which is Maurice Barrès. His philosophy was pronounced a perverted pyrrhonism, the quintessence of self-worship. A *Vita Nuova* of egoism had been born.

But the dandy did not falter. He has said that

214

one never conquers the intellectual suffrages of
those who precede us in life; he made his appeal
to young France. And what was the balm in
Gilead offered by this new doctor of metaphysics?
None but a Frenchman at the end of the last century could have conceived the Barrèsian plan of
soul-saving. In Baudelaire, Barbey d'Aurevilly,
and Villiers de l'Isle Adam, the union of Roman
Catholic mysticism and blasphemy has proved to
many a stumbling-stone. These poets were believers, yet Manicheans; they worshipped at
two shrines; evil was their greater good. Barrès
plucked several leaves from their breviaries.
He proposed to school his soul by a rigid adherence
to the Spiritual Exercises of Saint Ignatius Loyola.
With the mechanism of this Catholic moralist he
would train his Ego, cure it of its spiritual dry-
ness — that malady so feared by St. Theresa —
and arouse it from its apathy. He would deliver
us from a Renan-ridden school.

This scholastic fervour urged Barrès to rein-
state man in the centre of the universe, a position
from which he had been routed by science. It
was a pious, mediæval idea. He did not, however, assert the bankruptcy of science, but the
bankruptcy of pessimism. His book is metaphysical autobiography, a Gallic transposition of
Goethe's Wahrheit und Dichtung. We may now
see that his concentrated egoism had definite
aims and was not the conceit of a callow Romantic.

Barrès imbibed from the Parnassian poetic
group his artistic remoteness. His ivory tower

215

is a borrowed phrase made by Sainte-Beuve about
De Vigny. But his mercurial soul could not be
imprisoned long by frigid theories of impeccable
art — of art for art's sake. *My soul!* that alone
is worth studying, cried Maurice. John Henry
Newman said the same in a different and more
modest dialectic. The voice of the French
youth is shriller, it is sometimes in falsetto; yet
there is no denying its fundamental sincerity of
pitch. And he has the trick of light verbal fence
beloved of his race. He is the comedian among
moralists. His is neither the frozen eclecticism
of Victor Cousin, nor the rigid determinism of
Taine. Yet he is a partial descendant of the
Renan he flouts, and of Taine — above all, of
Stendhal and Voltaire. In his early days if one
had christened him *Mlle. Stendhal*, there would
have been less to retract. Plus a delicious style,
he is a masked, slightly feminine variation of the
great mystifier who wrote La Chartreuse de
Parme, leaving out the Chartreuse. At times the
preoccupation of Barrès with the moral law approaches the borderland of the abnormal. Like
Jules Laforgue, his intelligence and his sensibility
are closely wedded. He is a sentimental ironist
with a taste for self-mockery, a Heine-like humour.
He had a sense of humour, even when he wore
the *panache* of General Boulanger, and opposed
the Dreyfus proceedings. It may rescue from the
critical executioner who follows in the footsteps
of all thinkers, many of his pages.

A dilettante, an amateur — yes! But so was

216

MAURICE BARRES

Goethe in his Olympus, so Stendhal in his Cosmopolis. He elected at first to view the spectacle of life, to study it from afar, and by the *tempo* of his own sensibility. Not the tonic egoism of Thoreau this; it has served its turn nevertheless in France. Afferent, centripetal, and other forbidding terms, have been bestowed upon his system; while for the majority this word egoism has a meaning that implies our most selfish instincts. If, however, interposes Bourget, you consider the word as a formula, then the angle of view is altered; if Barrès had said in one jet, "Nothing is more precious for a man than to guard intact his convictions, his passions, his ideal, his individuality," those who misjudged this courageous apostle of egoism, this fervent prober of the human soul, might have modified their opinions — and would probably have passed him by. It was the enigmatic message, the strained symbolism, of which Barrès delivered himself, that puzzled both critics and public. Robert Schumann once propounded a question concerning the Chopin Scherzo: "How is gravity to clothe itself if jest goes about in dark veils?" Now Barrès, who is far from being a spiritual *blagueur*, suggests this puzzle of Schumann. His employment, without a *nuance* of mockery, of the devotional machinery so marvellously devised by that captain of souls, Ignatius Loyola, was rather disquieting, notwithstanding its very practical application to the daily needs of the spirit. Ernest Hello, transported by such a spectacle,

217

may not have been far astray when he wrote of the nineteenth century as "having desire without light, curiosity without wisdom, seeking God by strange ways, ways traced by the hands of men; offering rash incense upon the high places to an unknown God, who is the God of darkness." Ernest Renan was evidently aimed at, but the bolt easily wings that metaphysical bird of gay plumage, Maurice Barrès.

II

He has published over a dozen volumes and numerous brochures, political and "psycho-therapic," many addresses, and one comedy, Une Journée Parlementaire. He calls his books metaphysical fiction, the adventures of a con-templative young man's mind. Paul Bourget is the psychologist pure and complex; Barrès has — rather, had — such a contempt for action on the "earthly plane," that at the head of each chapter of his "idealogies" he prefixed a *résumé*, a concordance of the events that were supposed to take place, leaving us free to savour the prose, enjoy the fine-spun formal texture, and marvel at the contrapuntal involutions of the hero's intellect. Naturally a reader, hungry for facts, must perish of famine in this rarefied æsthetic desert, the background of which is occasionally diversified by a sensuality that may be dainty, yet is disturbing because of its disinterested por-trayment. The Eternal Feminine is not unsung

218

in the Barrès novels. Woman for his imagination is a creature exquisitely fashioned, hardly an odalisque, nor yet the symbol of depravity we encounter in Huysmans. She is a "phantom of delight"; but that she has a soul we beg to doubt. Barrès almost endowed her with one in the case of his Bérénice; and Bérénice died very young. A young man, with various names, traverses these pages. Like the Durtal, or Des Esseintes, or Folantin, of Huysmans, who is always Huysmans, the hero of Barrès is always Barrès. In the first of the trilogy — of which A Free Man and The Garden of Bérénice are the other two — we find Philippe escaping through seclusion and revery the barbarians, his adversaries. The Adversary — portentous title for the stranger who grazes our sensitive epidermis — is the being who impedes or misleads a spirit in search of itself. If he deflects us from our destiny, he is the enemy. It may be well to recall at this juncture Stendhal, who avowed that our first enemies are our parents, an idea many an insurgent boy has asserted when his father was not present.

Seek peace and happiness with the conviction that they are never to be found; felicity must be in the experiment, not in the result. Be ardent and sceptical. Here Philippe touches hands with the lulling Cyrenaicism of Walter Pater. And Barrès might have sat for one of Pater's imaginary portraits. But it is too pretty to last, such a dream as this, in a world wherein work and sorrow rule. He is not an ascetic, Philippe.

He eats rare beefsteaks, smokes black Havanas, clothes himself in easy-fitting garments, and analyses with cordial sincerity his multicoloured soul. (And oh! the colours of it; oh! its fluctuating forms!) The young person invades his privacy — a solitary in Paris is an incredible concept. Together they make journeys "conducted by the sun." She is dreamlike until we read, "Cependant elle le suivait de loin, délicate et de hanches merveilleuses" — which delicious and dislocated phrase is admired by lovers of Goncourt syntax, but must be shocking to the old-fashioned who prefer the classic line and balance of Bossuet.

Nothing happens. Everything happens. Philippe makes the stations of the cross of earthly disillusionment. He weighs love, he weighs literature — "all these books are but pigeon-holes in which I classify my ideas concerning myself, their titles serve only as the labels of the different portions of my appetite." Irony is his ivory tower, his refuge from the banalities of his contemporaries. Henceforth he will enjoy his Ego. It sounds at moments like Bunthorne transposed to a more intense tonality.

But even beefsteaks, cigars, wine, and philosophy pall. He craves a mind that will echo his, craves a mental duo, in which the clash of character and opposition of temperaments will evoke pleasing cerebral music. In this dissatisfaction with his solitude we may detect the first rift in the lute of his egoism. He finds an old friend,

Simon by name, and after some preliminary sentimental philandering at the seashore, in the company of two young ladies, the pair agree to lead
a monastic life. To Lorraine they retire and draft
a code of diurnal obligations. "We are never so
happy as when in exaltation," and "The pleasure
of exaltation is greatly enhanced by the analysis
of it." Their souls are fortified and engineered
by the stern practices of Loyola. The woman
idea occasionally penetrates to their cells. It
distracts them — "woman, who has always possessed the annoying art of making imbeciles
loquacious." Notwithstanding these wraiths of
feminine fancy, Philippe finds himself almost
cheerful. His despondent moods have vanished.
He quarrels, of course, with Simon, who is dry, an
esprit fort.

The Intercessors now appear, the intellectual
saints who act as intermediaries between impressionable, bruised natures and the Infinite.
They are the near neighbours of God, for they are
the men who have experienced an unusual number of sensations. Philippe admits that his temperament oscillates between languor and ecstasy.
Benjamin Constant and Sainte-Beuve are the
two "Saints" of Sensibility who aid the youths
in their self-analysis; rather a startling devolu-
tion from the Imitation of Christ and Ignatius
Loyola. Tiring, finally, of this sterile analysis,
and discovering that the neurasthenic Simon is
not a companion-soul, Philippe, very illogically
yet very naturally, resolves that he must bathe

himself in new sensations, and proceeds to Venice. We accompany him willingly, for this poet who handles prose as Chopin the pianoforte, tells us of his soul in Venice, and we are soothed when he speaks of the art of John Bellini, of Titian, Veronese, above all of Tiepolo, "who was too much a sceptic to be bitter. . . . His conceptions have that lassitude which follows pleasure, a lassitude preferred by epicureans to pleasure itself." Graceful, melancholy Tiepolo. This Venetian episode is rare reading.

The last of the trilogy is The Garden of Bérénice. It is the best of the three in human interest, and its melancholy-sweet landscapes exhale a charm that is nearly new in French literature; something analogous may be found in Slavic music, or in the *Intimiste* school of painting. Several of these landscapes are redolent of Watteau: tender, doleful, sensuous, their twilights filled with vague figures, languidly joying in the mood of the moment. The impressionism which permeates this book is a veritable lustration for those weary of commonplace modern fiction. Not since has Barrès excelled this idyl of the little Bérénice and her slowly awakening consciousness to beauty, aroused by an old, half-forgotten museum in meridional France. At Arles, encompassed by the memory of a dead man, she loves her donkey, her symbolic ducks, and Philippe, who divines her adolescent sorrow, her yearning spirit, her unfulfilled dreams. Her garden upon the immemorial and paludian plains of

222

Arles is threaded by silver waters, illuminated by copper sunsets, their tones reverberating from her robes. Something of Maeterlinck's stammering, girlish, questioning Mélisande is in Bérénice. Maeterlinckian, too, is the statement that "For an accomplished spirit there is but one dialogue — that between our two Egos, the momentary Ego we are, and the ideal Ego toward which we strive." Bérénice would marry Philippe. We hold our breath, hoping that his tyrant Ego may relax, and that, off guard, he may snatch with fearful joy the chance to gain this childlike creature. Alas! there is a certain M. Martin, who is Philippe's political adversary — Philippe is a candidate for the legislature; he is become practical; in the heat of his philosophic egoism he finds that if a generous negation is good waiting ground, wealth and the participation in political affairs is a better one. M. Martin covets the hand of Bérénice. He repels her because he is an engineer, a man of positive, practical spirit, who would drain the marshes in Bérénice's garden of their beautiful miasmas, and build healthy houses for happy people. To Philippe he is the "adversary" who despises the contemplative life. "He had a habit of saying, 'Do you take me for a dreamer?' as one should say, 'Do you take me for an idiot?'" Philippe, nevertheless, more solicitous of his Ego than of his affections, advises Bérénice to marry M. Martin. This she does, and dies like a flower in a cellar. She is a lovely memory for our young idealist, who in voluptuous accents rhapsodises about her as did Sterne over his dead donkey. Sensibility, all this, to the very *ultima Thule* of egoism. Then, Philippe obtains the concession of a suburban hippodrome. Poor Bérénice! *Pauvre Petite — Secousse!* The name of this book was to have been *Qualis artifex pereo!* And there is a fitting Neronic tang to its cruel and sentimental episodes that would have justified the title. But for Barrès, it has a Goethian quality; "all is true, nothing exact."

In 1892 was published The Enemy of Law, a book of violent anarchical impulse and lyric disorder. It is still Philippe, though under another name, André, who approves of a bomb launched by the hand of an anarchist, and because of the printed expression of his sympathy he is sent to prison for a few months. A Free Man, he endures his punishment philosophically, winning the friendship of a young Frenchwoman, an *exaltee*, and also of a little Russian princess, a silhouette of Marie Bashkirtseff, and an unmistakable blood-relative of Stendhal's Lamiel. After his liberation André makes sentimental pilgrimages with one or the other, finally with both of his friends, to Germany and elsewhere. A shaggy dog, Velu, figures largely in these pages, and we are treated to some disquisitions on canine psychology. Nor are the sketches of Saint-Simon, Fourier, Karl Marx, Ferdinand Lassalle, and Ludwig of Bavaria, the Wagnerian idealist, particularly novel. They but reveal the nascent

224

223

social sympathies of Barrès, who was at the law-despising period of his development. His little princess has a touch of Bérénice, coupled with a Calmuck disregard of the *convenances;* she loves the "warm smell of stables" and does not fear worldly criticism of her conduct; the trio vanish in a too Gallic, too rose-coloured perspective. A volume of protest, The Enemy of Law served its turn, though here the phrase — clear, alert, suave — of his earlier books is transformed to a style charged with flame and acid. The moral appears to be dangerous, as well as diverting — develop your instincts to the uttermost, give satisfaction to your sensibility; then must you attain the perfection of your Ego, and therefore will not attenuate the purity of your race. The Russian princess, we are assured, carried with her the ideas of antique morality.

In the second trilogy — Du Sang, de la Volupté, et de la Mort; Amori et Dolori Sacrum; and Les Amitiés Françaises — we begin an itinerary which embraces parts of Italy, Spain, Germany, France, particularly Lorraine. Barrès must be ranked among those travellers of acute vision and æsthetic culture who in their wanderings disengage the soul of a city, of a country. France, from Count de Caylus and the Abbé Barthélemy (Voyage du Jeune Anacharsis) to Stendhal, Taine, and Bourget, has given birth to many distinguished examples. The first of the new group, Blood, Pleasure, and Death — a sensational title for a work so rich and consoling

225

in substance — is a collection of essays and tales.
The same young man describes his æsthetic and
moral impressions before the masterpieces of
Angelo and Vinci, or the tombs, cathedrals, and
palaces of Italy and Spain. Cordova is visited,
the gardens of Lombardy, Ravenna, Parma —
Stendhal's beloved city — Siena, Pisa; there are
love episodes in diaphanous keys. Barrès, ever
magnanimous in his critical judgments, pays
tribute to the memory of his dead friends, Jules
Tellier and Marie Bashkirtseff. He understood
her soul, though afterward cooled when he discovered the reality of the Bashkirtseff legend.
(He speaks of the house in which she died as 6 Rue
de Prony; Marie died at 30 Rue Ampère.) In
the succeeding volume, consecrated to love and
sorrow, the soul of Venice, the soul of a dead
city, is woven with souvenirs of Goethe, Byron,
Chateaubriand, Musset, George Sand, Taine,
Léopold Robert the painter-suicide, Théophile
Gautier, and Richard Wagner. The magic of
these prose-dreams is not that of an artist merely
revelling in description; Pierre Loti, for instance,
writes with no philosophy but that of the disen-
chanted; he is a more luscious Sénancour;
D'Annunzio has made of Venice a golden monument to his gigantic pride as poet. Not so
Barrès. The image of death and decay, the recollections of the imperial and mighty past aroused
by his pen are as so many chords in his egoistic
philosophy: Venice guarded its Ego from the
barbarians; from the dead we learn the secret of

226

life.   The note of revolt which sounded so drastic-
ally in The Enemy of Law is absent here; in that
story Barrès, mindful of Auguste Comte and
Ibsen, asserted that the dead poisoned the living.
The motive of reverence for the soil, for the past,
the motive of traditionalism, is beginning to be
overheard.   In   French   Friendships,   he   takes
his little son Philippe to Joan of Arc's country
and enforces the lesson of patriotism.   In his
Le Voyage de Sparte, the same spirit is present.
He is the man from Lorraine at Corinth, Eleusis,
or Athens, humble and solicitous for the soul of
his race, eager to extract a moral benefit from
the past.   He studies the Antigone of Sophocles,
the Helen of Goethe.   He also praises his master,
the classical scholar, Louis Ménard.   Barrès has,
in a period when France seems bent on burning
its historical ships, destroying precious relics of
its past, blown the trumpet of alarm; not the
destructive blast of Nietzsche, but one that calls
"Spare our dead!"   Little wonder Bourget pronounced him the most efficacious servitor, at the
present hour, of France the eternal.   Force and
spiritual fecundity Barrès demands of himself;
force and spiritual fecundity he demands from
France.   And, like the vague insistent thrum-
ming of the *tympani*, a ground bass in some
symphonic poem, the idea of nationalism is
gradually disclosed as we decipher these palimp-
sests of egoism.

The art of Barrès till this juncture had been of
a smoky enchantment, many-hued, of shifting
shapes, often tenuous, sometimes opaque, yet
ever graceful, ever fascinating. Whether he was
a great spiritual force or only an amazing protean acrobat, coquetting with the *Zeitgeist*, his
admirers and enemies had not agreed upon.
He had further clouded public opinion by becoming a Boulangist deputy from Nancy, and his
apparition in the Chamber must have been as
bizarre as would have been Shelley's in Parlia-
ment. Barrès but followed the illustrious lead
of Hugo, Lamartine, Lamennais. His friends
were moved to astonishment. The hater of the
law, the defender in the press of Chambige, the
Algerian homicide, this writer of "precious" literature, among the political opportunists! Yet
he sat as a deputy from 1889 to 1893, and proved
himself a resourceful debater; in the chemistry
of his personality patriotism had been at last pre-
cipitated.

His second trilogy of books was his most artistic gift to French literature. But with the
advent, in 1897, of Les Déracinés (The Uprooted)
a sharp change in style may be noted. It is the
sociological novel in all its thorny efflorescence.
Diction is no longer in the foreground. Vanished the velvety rhetoric, the musical phrase,
the nervous prose of many facets. Sharp in
contour and siccant, every paragraph is packed

with ideas. The Uprooted is formidable reading, but we at least touch the rough edges of reality. Men and women show familiar gestures;
the prizes run for are human; we are in a dense
atmosphere of intrigue, political and personal;
Flaubert's Frédéric Moreau, the young man of
confused ideas and feeble volition, once more
appears as a cork in the whirlpool of modern
Paris. The iconoclast that is in the heart of
this poet is rampant. He smashes institutions,
though his criticism is often constructive. He
strives to expand the national soul, strives to combat cynicism, and he urges decentralisation as
the sole remedy for the canker that he believes
is blighting France. Bourget holds that "Society is the functioning of a federation of organisms of which the individual is the cell"; that
functioning, says Barrès, is ill served by the
violent uprooting of the human organism from
its earth. A man best develops in his native
province. His deracination begins with the
education that sends him to Paris, there to lose
his originality. The individual can flourish only
in the land where the mysterious forces of heredity
operate, make richer his Ego, and create solidarity — that necromantic word which, in the
hands of social preachers, has become a glittering and illuding talisman. A tree does not
grow upward unless its roots plunge deeply into
the soil. A wise administrator attaches the animal to the pasture that suits it. (But Barrès
himself still lives in Paris.)

229

This nationalism of Barrès is not to be confounded with the perfidious slogan of the politicians; it is a national symbol for many youth
of his land. Nor is Barrès affiliated with some
extreme modes of socialism — socialism, that day-
dream of a retired green-grocer who sports a cultivated taste for dominoes and penny philanthropy.
To those who demand progress, he asks, Progressing toward what? Rather let us face the setting
sun. Do not repudiate the past. Hold to our
dead. They realise for us the continuity of
which we are the ephemeral expression. The
cult of the "I" is truly the cult of the dead.
Egoism must not be construed as the average
selfishness of humanity; the higher egoism is the
art — Barrès artist, always — of canalising one's
Ego for the happiness of others. Out of the
Barrès nationalism has grown a mortuary philosophy; we see him rather too fond of culling the
flowers in the cemetery as he takes his evening
stroll. When a young man he was obsessed by
the vision of death. His logic is sometimes auda-
ciously romantic; he paints ideas in a dangerously
seductive style; and he is sometimes carried away
by the electric energy which agitates his not too
robust physique. This cult of the dead, while not
morbid, smacks nevertheless of the Chinese.
Our past need not be in a graveyard, and one
agrees with Jean Dolent that man is surely matter,
but that his soul is his own work.

Latterly the patriotism of Barrès is beginning
to assume an unpleasant tinge. In his azure,

230

chauvinisme is the ugliest cloud. He loves the
fatal word "revenge." In the Service of Germany
presents a pitiable picture of a young Alsatian
forced to military service in the German army.
It is not pleasing, and the rage of Barrès will
be voted laudable until we recall the stories by
Frenchmen of the horrors of French military life.
He upholds France for the French. It is a noble
idea, but it leads to narrowness and fanatical out-
breaks. His influence was great from 1888 to
1893 among the young men. It abated, to be
renewed in 1896 and 1897. It reached its apogee
a few years ago. The Rousseau-like cry, "Back
to the soil!" made of Barrès an idol in several
camps. His election to the Academy, filling the
vacancy caused by the death of the poet De
Hérédia, was the consecrating seal of a genius
who has the gift of projecting his sympathies in
many different directions, only to retrieve as by
miraculous tentacles the richest moral and
æsthetic nourishment. We should not forget to
add, that by the numerous early Barrèsians, the
Academician is now looked upon as a backslider
from the cause of philosophic anarchy.

The determinism of Taine stems in Germany
and his theory of environment has been effectively
utilised by Barrès. In The Uprooted, the argument is driven home by the story of seven young
Lorrainers who descend upon Paris to capture it.
Their Professor Bouteiller (said to be a portrait
of Barrès's old master Burdeau at Nancy) has
educated them as if "they might some day be

called upon to do without a mother-country."
Paris is a vast maw which swallows them. They
are disorganised by transplantation. (What young
American would be, we wonder?) Some drift
into anarchy, one to the scaffold because of a
murder; all are *arrivistes;* and the centre figure,
Sturel, is a failure because he cannot reconcile
himself to new, harsh conditions. They blame
their professor. He diverted the sap of their
nationalism into strange channels. A few "arrive," though not in every instance by laudable
methods. One is a scholar. The account of
his interview with Taine and Taine's conversation with him is another evidence of the intellectual
mimicry latent in Barrès. He had astonished us
earlier by his recrudescence of Renan's very
fashion of speech and ideas; literally a feat of
literary prestidigitation. There are love, political intrigue, and a dramatic assassination —
the general conception of which recalls to us the
fact that Barrès once sat at the knees of Bourget,
and had read that master's novel, Le Disciple.
A striking episode is that of the meeting of the
seven friends at the tomb of Napoleon, there to
meditate upon his grandeur and to pledge themselves to follow his illustrious example. "Professor of Energy" he is denominated. A Professor
of Spiritual Energy is certainly Maurice Barrès.
In another scene Taine demonstrates the theory
of nationalism by the parable of a certain plane
tree in the Square of the Invalides. For the
average lover of French fiction The Uprooted

232

must prove trying. It is, with its two companions in this trilogy of The Novel of National Energy, a social document, rather than a romance. It embodies so clearly a whole cross-section of earnest French youths' moral life, that — with L'Appel au Soldat, and Leurs Figures, its sequels — it may be consulted in the future for a veridic account of the decade it describes. One seems to lean from a window and watch the agitation of the populace which swarmed about General Boulanger; or to peep through keyholes and see the end of that unfortunate victim of treachery and an ill-disciplined temperament. Barrès later reviles the friends of Boulanger who deserted him, by his delineation of the Panama scandal. Yet it is all as dry as a parliamentary blue-book. After finishing these three novels, the impression created is that the flaw in the careers of four or five of the seven young men from Lorraine was not due to their uprooting, but to their lack of moral backbone.

Paris is no more difficult a social medium to navigate in than New York; the French capital has been the battlefield of all French genius; but neither in New York nor in Paris can a young man face the conflict so loaded down with the burden of general ideas and with so scant a moral outfit as possessed by these same young men. The Lorraine band—is it a possible case?. No doubt.· Nevertheless, if its members had remained at Nancy they might have been shipwrecked for the same reason. Why does not M. Barrès

233

show his cards? The Kingdom on the table! cries Hilda Wangel to her Masterbuilder. Love of the natal soil does not make a complete man; some of the greatest patriots have been the greatest scoundrels. M. Bourget sums up the situation more lucidly than M. Barrès, who is in such a hurry to mould citizens that he omits an essential quality from his programme — God (or character, moral force, if you prefer other terms). Now, when a rationalistic philosopher considers God as an intellectual abstraction, he is not illogical. Scepticism is his stock in trade. But can Maurice Barrès elude the issue? Can he handle the tools of such pious workmen as Loyola, De Sales, and Thomas à Kempis, for the building of his soul, and calmly overlook the inspiration of those masons of men? It is one of the defects of dilettanteism that it furnishes a *point d'appui* for the liberated spirit to see-saw between freewill and determinism, between the Lord of Hosts and the Lucifer of Negation. Paul Bourget feels this spiritual dissonance. Has he not said that the day may come when Barrès may repeat the phrase of Michelet: *Je ne me peux passer de Dieu!* Has Maurice Barrès already plodded the same penitential route without indulging in an elliptical flight to a new artificial paradise?

If his moral evolution, so insistently claimed by his disciples, has been of a zigzag nature, if *lacunæ* abound in his system and paradoxical *vues d'ensemble* often distract, yet logical evolution there has been — from the maddest, ro-

234

mantic individualism to a well-defined solidarity
— and without attenuation of the dignity and
utility of the Individual in the scheme of collectivism. The Individual is the Salt of the State.
The Individual leavens the mass politic. Num-
bers will never supplant the value, psychic or
economic, of the Individual. Emerson and Matthew Arnold said all this before Barrès. Incomparable artist as is Maurice Barrès, we still must
demand of him: "In Vishnu-land what Avatar!"

235

VII

PHASES OF NIETZSCHE

I

THE WILL TO SUFFER

COLERIDGE quotes Sir Joshua Reynolds as declaring that "the greatest man is he who forms the taste of a nation; the next greatest is he who corrupts it." It is an elastic epigram and not unlike the rule which is poor because it won't work both ways. All master reformers, heretics, and rebels were at first great corrupters. It is a prime necessity in their propaganda. Aristophanes and Arius, Mohammed and Napoleon, Montaigne and Rabelais, Paul and Augustine, Luther and Calvin, Voltaire and Rousseau, Darwin and Newman, Liszt and Wagner, Kant and Schopenhauer — here are a few names of men who undermined the current beliefs and practices of their times, whether for good or evil. Rousseau has been accused of being the greatest corrupter in history; yet to him we may owe the Constitution of the United States. Pascal, in prose of unequalled limpidity, denounced the Jesuits as corrupting youth. Nevertheless, Dr. Georg

236

Brandes, an "intellectual" and a philosophic anarch, once wrote to Nietzsche: "I, too, love Pascal. But even as a young man I was on the side of the Jesuits against Pascal. Wise men, it was they who were right; he did not understand them; but they understood him and . . . they published his Provincial Letters with notes themselves. The best edition is that of the Jesuits." Were not Titian, Rubens, and Rembrandt the three unspeakable devils of painting for Blake? Loosely speaking, then, it doesn't much matter whether one considers a great man as a regenerator or a corrupter. Napoleon was called the latter by Taine after he had been saluted as demigod by his idolatrous contemporaries. Nor does the case of Nietzsche differ much from his philosophic forerunners. He scolded Schopenhauer, though borrowing his dialectic tools, as he later mocked at the one sincere friendship of his lonely life, Richard Wagner's. We know the most objective philosophies are tinged by the individual temperaments of their makers, and perhaps the chief characteristic of all philosophers is their unphilosophic contempt for their fellow-thinkers. Nietzsche displayed this trait; so did Richard Wagner — who was in a lesser fashion an amateur philosopher, his system adorned by plumes borrowed from Feuerbach, Schelling, and Schopenhauer. Arthur Schopenhauer was endowed with a more powerful intellect than either Wagner or Nietzsche. He "corrupted" them both. He was materialist enough to echo

237

the epigram attributed to Fontenelle: To be happy a man must have a good stomach and a wicked heart.

Friedrich Nietzsche was more poet than original thinker. Merely to say Nay! to all existing institutions is not to give birth to a mighty idea, though the gesture is brave. He substituted for Schopenhauer's "Will to Live" — (an ingenious variation of Kant's "Thing in Itself") the "Will to Power"; which phrase is mere verbal juggling. The late Eduard von Hartmann built his house of philosophy in the fog of the Unconscious; Nietzsche, despising Darwin as a dull grubber, returned unknowingly to the very land of metaphysics he thought he had fled forever. He was always the theologian — *toujours séminariste,* as they said of Renan. Theology was in his blood. It stiffened his bones. Abusing Christianity, particularly Protestant Christianity, he was himself an exponent of a theological odium of the virulent sort, as may be seen in his thundering polemics. He held a brief for the other side of good and evil; but a man can't so easily empty his veins of the theologic blood of his forebears. It was his Nessus shirt and ended by consuming him. He had the romantic cult of great men, yet sneered at Carlyle for his Titanism. He believed in human perfectibility. He borrowed his Superman partly from the classic pantheon, partly from the hierarchy of Christian saints — or perhaps from the very Cross he vituperated. The only Christian, he was fond of say-

238

ing, died on the Cross. The only Nietzschian, one might reply, passed away when crumbled the brilliant brain of Nietzsche. Saturated with the culture of Goethe, his Superman was sent ballooning aloft by the poetic afflatus of Nietzsche.

He was an apparition possible only in modern and rationalistic Protestant Germany. Like a voice from the Middle Ages he has stirred the profound phlegm and spiritual indifference of his fellow countrymen. But he has in him more of Savonarola than Luther — Luther, who was for him the apotheosis of all that is hateful in the German character: the self-satisfied philistinism, sensuality, beer and tobacco, unresponsiveness to all the finer issues of existence, pious tactlessness and harsh dogmatism.

His truth is enclosed in a transcendental vacuum. Whether he had Galton's science of Eugenics in his mind when he modelled his Zarathustra we need not concern ourselves. His revaluation of moral values has not shaken morality to its centre. He challenged superficial conventional morality, but the ultimate pillars of faith still stand. He reminds us of William Blake when he writes: "The path to one's heaven ever leads through the voluptuousness of one's own hell." And his psychical resemblance to Pascal is striking. Both men were physically debilitated; their nervous systems, overwhelmed by the burdens they imposed upon them, made their days and nights a continuous agony. The Nietzschian philosophy may be negligible, but the psychologi-

239

cal aspects of this singularly versatile, fascinating, and contradictory nature are not. His "Will to Power" in his own case resolves itself into the will to suffer. Compared to his, Schopenhauer's pessimism is the good-natured grumbling of a healthy, witty man, with a tremendous vital temperament. Nietzsche was delicate from youth. His experiences in the Franco-Prussian war harmed him. Headache, eye trouble, a weak stomach, coupled with his abuse of intellectual work, and, toward the last, indulgence in narcotics for insomnia, all coloured his philosophy. The personal bias was unescapable, and this bias favoured sickness, not health. Hence his frantic apotheosis of health, the dance and laughter, and his admiration for Bizet's Carmen. Hence his constant employment of joyful imagery, of bold defiance to the sober workaday world. His famous injunction: "Be hard!" was meant for his own unhappy soul, ever nearing, like Pascal's, the abyss of black melancholy.

While we believe that too much stress has been laid upon the pathologic side of Pascal's and Nietzsche's characters, there is no evading the fact that both seemed tinged with what Kurt Eisner calls *psychopathia spiritualis*. The references to suffering in Nietzsche's books are significant. There is a vibrating accent of personal sorrow on every page. He lived in an inferno, mental and physical. We are given to praising Robert Louis Stevenson for his cheerfulness in the dire straits of his illness. He was a mere

240

amateur of misery, a professional invalid, in comparison with Nietzsche. And how cruel was the German poet to himself. He tied his soul to a stake and recorded the poignant sensations of his spiritual *auto-da-fé*. At the close of his sane days we find him taking a dolorous pride in his capacity for suffering. "It is great affliction only — that long, slow affliction in which we are burned as it were with green wood, which takes time — that compels us philosophers to descend into our ultimate depth and divest ourselves of all trust, all good nature, glossing, gentleness. . . . I doubt whether such affliction improves us; but I know that it deepens us. . . . Oh, how repugnant to one henceforth is gratification, coarse, dull, drab-coloured gratification, as usually understood by those who enjoy life! . . . Profound suffering makes noble; it separates. . . . There are free, insolent minds that would fain conceal and deny that at the bottom they are disjointed, incurable souls — it is the case with Hamlet." Nietzsche has the morbidly introspective Hamlet temper, and Pascal has been called the Christian Hamlet.

We read in Overbeck's recollections that Nietzsche manifested deep interest in the personality of Pascal. Both hated hypocrisy. But the German thinker saw in the Frenchman of genius only a Christian who hugged his chains, one who for his faith suffered "a continuous suicide of reason." (Has not Nietzsche himself also said hard things about Reason?) "One is punished

241

best by one's virtues" . . . or, "He who fights
with monsters, let him be careful lest he thereby
become a monster. And if thou gaze long into
an abyss, the abyss will also gaze into thee." This
last is unquestionably a reminiscence of Pascal.
He could not endure with equanimity Pascal's
sacrifizio dell' intelletto, not realizing that the
Frenchman felt beneath his feet the solid globe
of faith. He discerned the Puritan in Pascal,
though failing to recognise the Puritan in himself.
Despite his praise of the Dionysian element in
art and life, a puritan was buried in the nerves of
Nietzsche. He never could tolerate the common
bourgeois joys. Wine, Woman, Song, and their
poets, were his detestations. Yet he hated Puritanism in Protestant Christianity. "The dangerous
thrill of repentance spasms, the vivisection of conscience," he contemns; "even in every desire for
knowledge there is a drop of cruelty." He wrote
to Brandes: "Physically, too, I lived for years in
the neighbourhood of death. This was my great
piece of good fortune; I forgot myself. I outlived myself — a shedding of the skin." Pascal
also knew the sting of the flesh and brain. From
the time he had an escape from sudden death, he
was conscious of an abyss at his side. "Men of
genius," he wrote, "have their heads higher but
their feet lower than the rest of us." With Nietzsche there was a darker *nuance* of pain; he speaks
somewhere of "the philtre of the great Circe of
mingled pleasure and cruelty." His soul was a
mysterious palimpsest. The heart has its reasons,

242

cried Pascal; of Nietzsche's heart the last word has not been written.

His criticism of Pascal was not clement. He said: "In Goethe the superabundance becomes creative, in Flaubert the hatred; Flaubert, a new edition of Pascal, but as an artist with instinctive judgment at bottom. . . . He tortured himself when he composed, quite as Pascal tortured himself when he thought." Yes, but Nietzsche was as fierce a hater as Pascal or Flaubert. He set up for Christianity a straw adversary and proceeded to demolish it. He forgot that, as Francis Thompson has it: "It is the severed head that makes the Seraph." Nietzsche would not look higher than the mud around the pedestal. He, poor sufferer, was not genuinely impersonal. His tragedy was his sick soul and body. "If a man cannot sing as he carries his cross, he had better drop it," advises Havelock Ellis. Nietzsche bore a terrible cross — like the men staggering with their chimeras in Baudelaire's poem — but he did not bear it with equanimity. We must not be deceived by his desperate gayety. As a married man he would never have enjoyed, as did John Stuart Mill, spiritual henpeckery. He was afraid of life, this dazzling Zarathustra, who went on Icarus-wings close to the sun. He could speak of women thus: "We think woman deep — why? Because we never find any foundation in her. Woman is not even shallow." Or, "Woman would like to believe that love can do all — it is a superstition peculiar to herself.

243

Alas! he who knows the heart finds out how poor, helpless, pretentious, and liable to error even the best, the deepest love is — how it rather destroys than saves."

Der Dichter spricht! Also the bachelor. Once a Hilda of the younger generation, Lou Salomé by name, came knocking at the door of the poet's heart. It was in vain. The wings of a great happiness touched his brow as it passed. No wonder he wrote: "The desert grows; woe to him who hides deserts"; "Woman unlearns the fear of man"; "Thou goest to women! Remember thy whip." (Always this resounding motive of cruelty.) "Thy soul will be dead even sooner than thy body"; "Once spirit became God; then it became man; and now it is becoming mob"; "And many a one who went into the desert and suffered thirst with the camels, merely did not care to sit around the cistern with dirty camel-drivers." Here is the aristocratic radical.

It is weakness, admitted Goethe, not to possess the capacity for noble indignation; but Nietzsche was obsessed by his indignations. His voice, that golden poet's voice, becomes too often shrill, cracked, and falsetto. Voltaire has remarked that the first man who compared a woman to a rose was a poet, the second a fool. In his attitude toward Woman, Nietzsche was neither fool nor poet; but he never called her a rose. Nor was he a cynic; he saw too clearly for that, and he had suffered. Suffering, however, should have been a bond with women. Despite his cruel

244

243

utterances he enjoyed several ideal friendships with cultivated women. "There is no happy life for woman — the advantage that the world offers her is her choice in self-sacrifice," wrote Mr. Howells. Gossip has whispered that he was hopelessly in love with Cosima Wagner. A charming theme for a' psychological novel. So was Von Bülow, once — until he married her; so, Anton Rubinstein. Both abused Wagner's music; Von Bülow after he became an advocate of Brahms; Rubinstein always. Nietzsche, just before 1876, experienced the pangs of a Wagnerian reactionary. A pretty commentary this upon masculine mental superiority if one woman (even such a remarkable creature as Cosima) could upset the stanchest convictions of these three men. And convictions, asserted Nietzsche, are prisons. He contrived to escape from many intellectual prisons. Cosima had proved the one inflexible jailer.

Merciless to himself, he did not spare others. Of Altruism, with its fundamental contradictions, he wrote:

A being capable of purely altruistic actions alone is more fabulous than the Phœnix. Never has a man done anything solely for others, and without any personal motive; how could the Ego act without Ego? . . . Suppose a man wished to do and to will everything for others, nothing for himself, the latter would be impossible, for the very good reason that he must do very much for himself, in order to do anything at all for others. Moreover, it presupposes that the

245

other is egoist enough constantly to accept these sacrifices made for him; so that the men of love and self-sacrifice have an interest in the continued existence of loveless egoists who are incapable of self-sacrifice. In order to subsist, the highest morality must positively enforce the existence of immorality.—(Menschliches, I, 137–8).

"Nietzsche's criticism on this point," remarks Professor Seth Pattison, "must be accepted as conclusive. Every theory which attempts to divorce the ethical end from the personality of the moral agent must necessarily fall into this vicious circle; in a sense, the moral centre and the moral motive must always ultimately be self, the satisfaction of the self, the perfection of the self. The altruistic virtues, and self-sacrifice in general, can only enter into the moral ideal so far as they minister to the realisation of what is recognised to be the highest type of manhood, the self which finds its own in all men's good. Apart from this, self-sacrifice, self-mortification for its own sake, would be a mere negation, and, as such, of no moral value whatever."

Hasn't this the familiar ring of Max Stirner and his doctrine of the Ego?

Nietzsche with Pascal would have assented that "illness is the natural state of the true Christian." There was in both thinkers a tendency toward self-laceration of the conscience. "Il faut s'abêtir," wrote Pascal; and Nietzsche's pride vanished in the hot fire of suffering. The Pascal injunction to stupefy ourselves was not

246

to imitate the beasts of the field, but was a counsel of humility. Montaigne in his essay on Raymond de Sebonde wrote before Pascal concerning the danger of overwrought sensibility; (Il nous faut abestir pour nous assagir, is the original old French). It would have been wise for Nietzsche to follow Pascal's advice. "We live alone, we die alone," sorrowfully wrote the greatest religious force of the past century, Cardinal Newman (a transposition of Pascal's "Nous mourrons seuls"). Nietzsche was the loneliest of poets. He lived on the heights and paid the penalty, like other exalted searchers after the vanished vase of the ideal.

II

NIETZSCHE'S APOSTASY

Although Macaulay called Horace Walpole a "wretched fribble," that gossip knew a trick or two in fancy fencing. "Oh," he wrote, "I am sick of visions and systems that shove one another aside and come again like figures·in a moving picture." This was the outburst of a man called insincere and fickle, but frank in this instance. Issuing from the mouth of Friedrich Nietzsche this cry of the entertaining, shallow Walpole would have been curiously apposite. The unhappy German poet and philosopher suffered during his intellectual life from the "moving pictures" of other men's visions and systems,

247

and when he finally escaped them all and evoked
his own dream-world his brain became over-
clouded and he passed away "trailing clouds
of glory." It is an imperative necessity for certain natures to change their opinions, to slough,
as sloughs a snake its skin, their master ideas.
Renan went still further when he asserted that
all essayists contradict themselves · sometime
during their life.

With Nietzsche the apparent contradictions
of his Wagner-worship and Wagner-hatred may
be explained if we closely examine the concepts of
his first work of importance, The Birth of Tragedy. It was a misfortune that his bitterest book,
The Wagner Case, should have been first translated into English, for Wagner is our music-maker
now, and the rude assaults of Nietzsche fall upon
deaf ears; while those who had read the earlier
essay, Richard Wagner in Bayreuth, were both
puzzled and outraged. Certainly the man who
could thus flout what he once adored must have
been mad. This was the popular verdict, a facile
and unjust verdict. What Nietzsche first postulated as to the nature of music he returned to at
the close of his life; the mighty personality of
Richard Wagner had deflected the stream of his
thought for a few years. But as early as 1872
doubts began to trouble his sensitive conscience
— this was before his pamphlet Richard Wagner
in Bayreuth — and his notebooks of that period
were sown with question-marks. In the interesting correspondence with Dr. Georg Brandes, who

248

literally revealed to Europe the genius of Nietzsche, we find this significant passage:

> I was the first to distil a sort of unity out of the two [Schopenhauer and Wagner]. . . . All the Wagnerians are disciples of Schopenhauer. Things were different when I was young. Then it was the last of the Hegelians who clung to Wagner, and "Wagner and Hegel" was still the cry in the '50s.

Nietzsche might have added the name of the philosopher Feuerbach. Wagner's English apologist, Ashton Ellis, repudiates the common belief that Wagner refashioned the latter part of the Ring so as to introduce in it his newly acquired Schopenhauerian ideas. Wagner was always a pessimist, declares Mr. Ellis; Schopenhauer but confirmed him in his theories. Wagner, like Nietzsche, was too often a weathercock. A second-rate poet and philosopher, he stands chiefly for his magnificent music. Nietzsche or any other *polemiker* cannot change the map of music by fulminating against Wagner. Time may prove his true foe — the devouring years that always show such hostility to music of the theatre, music that is not pure music.

The spirit of the letter to Brandes quoted above may be found in Nietzsche Contra Wagner (The Case of Wagner, page 72). Nietzsche wrote:

> I similarly interpreted Wagner's music in my own way as the expression of a Dionysian powerfulness of

249

248

soul. . . . It is obvious what I misunderstood, it is obvious in like manner what I bestowed upon Wagner and Schopenhauer — myself.

He read his own enthusiasms, his Hellenic ideals, into the least Greek among composers. Wagner himself was at first pleased, also not a little nonplussed by the idolatry of Nietzsche. Remember that this young philologist was a musician as well as a brilliant scholar.

Following Schopenhauer in his main contention that music is a presentative, not a representative art; the noumenon, not the phenomenon — as are, for instance, painting and sculpture — Nietzsche held that the unity of music is undeniable. There is no dualism, such as instrumental music and vocal music. Sung music is only music presented by a sonorous vocal organ; the words are negligible. A poem may be a starting-point for the composer, yet in poetry there is not the potentiality of tone (this does not naturally refer to the literary tone-quality of music). From a non-musical thing music cannot be evolved. There is only absolute music. Its beginning is absolute. All other is a masquerading. The dramatic singer is a monstrosity — the actual words of Nietzsche. Opera is a debased genre. We almost expect the author to deny, as denied Hanslick, music any content whatsoever. But this he does not. He is too much the Romantic. For him the poem of Tristan was but the "vapour" of the music.

250

PHASES OF NIETZSCHE

Music is the archetype of the arts. It is the essence of Greek tragedy and therefore pessimistic. Tragedy is pessimism. The two faces of the Greek art he calls the Apollonian and the Dionysian impulses. One is the Classic, the other the Romantic; calm beauty as opposed to bacchantic ecstasy. Wagner, Nietzsche identified with the Dionysian element, and he was not far wrong; but Greek? The passionate welter of this new music stirred Nietzsche's excitable young nerves. He was, like many of his contemporaries, swept away in the boiling flood of the Wagnerian sea. It appeared to him, the profound Greek scholar, as a recrudescence of Dionysian joy. Instead, it was the topmost crest of the dying waves of Romanticism. Nietzsche later realised this fact. To Brandes he wrote:

Your German romanticism has made me reflect how the whole movement only attained its goal in music (Schumann, Mendelssohn, Weber, Wagner, Brahms); in literature it stopped short with a huge promise — the French were more fortunate. I am afraid I am too much of a musician not to be a Romanticist. Without music life would be a mistake. . . . With regard to the effect of Tristan I could tell you strange things. A good dose of mental torture strikes me as an excellent tonic before a meal of Wagner.

Nietzsche loved Wagner the man more than Wagner the musician. The news of Wagner's death in 1883 was a terrible blow for him. He

251

wrote Frau Wagner a letter of condolence, which
was answered from Bayreuth by her daughter
Daniela von Bülow. (See the newly published
Overbeck Letters.)

Nothing could be more unfair than to ascribe
to Nietzsche petty motives in his breaking off
with Wagner. There were minor differences,
but it was Parsifal and its drift toward Rome,
that shocked the former disciple. What he wrote
of Wagner and Wagnerism may be interpreted
according to one's own views, but the Parsifal
criticism is sound. That parody of the Roman
Catholic ceremonial and ideas, and the glorifica-
tion of its psychopathic hero, with the consequent
degradation of the idea of womanhood, Nietzsche
saw and denounced. "I despise everyone who
does not regard Parsifal as an outrage on morals,"
he cried. To-day his denunciations are recognised
by wise folk as wisdom. He first heard Carmen in
Genoa, November 27, 1881. To his exacerbated
nerves its rich southern melodies were soothing.
He overpraised the opera — which is a sparkling
compound of Gounod and Spanish gypsy airs; an
olla podrida as regards style. He knew that this
was bonbon music compared with Wagner. And
the confession was wrung from his lips: "We
must first be Wagnerians." Thus, as he escaped from Schopenhauer's pessimism, he plucked
from his heart his affection for Wagner. He
had become Zarathustra. He painted Wagner
as an "ideal monster," but the severing of the
friendship cost Nietzsche his happiness. An

252

extraordinary mountain-mania attacked him on the heights of the upper Engadine. All that he had once admired he now hated. He had a positive genius for hatred, even more so than Huysmans; both writers were bilious melan-cholics, and both were alike in the display of heavy-handed irony. With Nietzsche's "ears for quarter tones" — as he told Brandes — it would have been far better for him to remain with Peter Gast in Italy, while the latter was writing that long-contemplated study on Chopin. Nietzsche loved the music of the Pole who had introduced into the heavy monochrome of Ger-man harmonies an exotic and chromatic gamut of colours.

If Wagner erred in his belief that it was the drama not the music which ruled in his own com-positions (for his talk about the welding of the different arts is an æsthetic nightmare), why should not Nietzsche have made a mistake in ascribing to Wagner his own exalted ideals? Wagner's *music* is the Wagner music drama. That is a commonplace of criticism — though not at Bayreuth. Nietzsche taught the supremacy of tone in his early book. He detested so-called musical realism. These two men became friends through a series of mutual misunderstandings. When Nietzsche discovered that music and phil-osophy had naught in common — and he had hoped that Wagner's would prove the solvent — he cooled off in his faith. It was less an apostasy than we believe. Despite his eloquent affirma-

253

tion of Wagnerism, Nietzsche was never in his innermost soul a Wagnerian. Nor yet was he insincere. This may seem paradoxical. He had felt the "pull" of Wagner's genius, and, as in the case of his Schopenhauer worship, he temporarily lost his critical bearings. This accounts for his bitterness when he found the feet of his idol to be clay. He was lashing his own bare soul in each scarifying phrase he applied to Wagner. He saw the free young Siegfried become the old Siegfried in the manacles of determinism and pessimism; then followed Parsifal and Wagner's apostasy — Nietzsche believed Wagner was going back to Çhristianity. There is more consistency in the case of Friedrich Nietzsche than has been acknowledged by the Wagnerians. He, the philosopher of decadence and romanticism, could have said to Wagner as Baudelaire to Manet: "You are only the first in the decrepitude of your art."

If Nietzsche considered the poem a vaporous background for the passionate musical mosaic of Tristan and Isolde, what would he have thought if he could have heard the tonal interpretation of his Also Sprach Zarathustra, as conceived by the mathematical and emotional brain of Richard Strauss? I recall the eagerness with which I asked an impossible question of Frau Foerster-Nietzsche when at the Nietzsche-Archive, Weimar, in 1904: Is this tone-poem by Richard Strauss truly Nietzschean? Her tact did not succeed in quite veiling a hint of dubiety, though the noble sister of the dead philosopher was too tender-hearted to suggest a formal criticism of the composer's imposing sound-palace. It is not, however, difficult to imagine Nietzsche, alive, glaring in dismay and with "embellished indignation" as he hears the dance theme in Zarathustra. Nor would he be less surprised if he had suddenly forced upon his consciousness a performance of Claude Debussy's mooning, mystic, *triste* Pélléas et Mélisande, with its invertebrate charm, its innocuous sensuousness, its absence of thematic material, its perverse harmonies, its lack of rhythmic variety, and its faded sweetness, like that evoked by musty, quaint tapestry in languid motion. (Debussy might have delved deeper into churchly modes and for novelty's sake even employed *pneumes* to lend his score a still more venerable aspect. Certainly his tonalities are on the other side of diatonic and chromatic. Why not call them *pneumatic* scales?) Surely Nietzsche could not have refrained from exclaiming: Ah! the pathos of distance! Ah! what musical sins thou must take upon thee, Richard Wagner! Strauss and Debussy are the legitimate fruits of thy evil tree of music!

Miserably happy poet, like one of those Oriental wonder-workers dancing in ecstasy on white-hot sword-blades, the tears all the while streaming down his cheeks as he proclaims his new gospel of joy: "*Il faut mediterraniser la musique.*" Alas! the pathos of Nietzsche's reality. Reality for this self-tortured Hamlet-soul was a spiritual crucifixion and a spiritual tragedy.

255

III

ANTICHRIST?

The penalty of misrepresentation and misinterpretation seems to be attached to every new idea that comes to birth through the utterances of genius. At first with Wagner it was the "noise-making Wagner" — whereas he is a master of plangent harmonies. Ibsen, we were told, couldn't write a play. His dramatic technique is nearly faultless; in reality, with its unities there is a suspicion of the academic in it and a perilous approach to the Chinese ivory mechanism of Scribe. And paint, Paris asserted, the late Edouard Manet could not. It was precisely his almost miraculous manipulation of paint that sets this artist apart from his fellows. The same tactless rating of Friedrich Nietzsche has prevailed in the general critical and popular imagination. Nietzsche has become the bugaboo of timid folk. He has been denounced as the Antichrist; yet he has been the subject of a discriminating study in such a conservative magazine as the *Catholic World*. Thanks to the conception of some writers, Nietzsche and the Nietzschians are gigantic brutes, a combination of Genghis Khan and Bismarck, terrifying apparitions wearing mustachios like yataghans, eyes rolling in frenzy, with a philosophy that ranged from pitch-and-toss to manslaughter, and with a consuming atheism as a side attraction.

256

Need we protest that this is Nietzsche misread, Nietzsche butchered to make a stupid novelist's holiday.

Ideas to be vitally effective must, like scenery, be run on during the exact act of the contemporary drama. The aristocratic individualism of Nietzsche came at a happy moment when the stage was bare yet encumbered with the débris of socialistic theories left over from the storm that first swept all Europe in 1848. It was necessary that the pendulum should swing in another direction. The small voice of Max Stirner — who, as the French would say, imitated Nietzsche in advance — was swallowed in the universal gabble of sentimental humanitarianism preached from pulpits and barricades. Nietzsche's appearance marked one of those precise psychological moments when the rehabilitation of an old idea in a new garment of glittering rhetoric would resemble a new dispensation. For over a decade now the fame and writings of the Saxon-born philosopher have traversed the intellectual life of the Continent. He was translated into a dozen languages, he was expounded, schools sprang up and his disciples fought furious battles in his name. His doctrines, because of their dynamic revolutionary quality, were impudently annexed by men whose principles would have been abhorrent to the unfortunate thinker. Nietzsche, who his life long had attacked socialism in its myriad shapes, was captured by the socialists. However, the regression of the wave of admira-

257

tion has begun not only in Germany but in France, once his greatest stronghold. The real Nietzsche, undimmed by violent partisanship and equally violent antagonism, has emerged. No longer is he a bogey man, not a creature of blood and iron, not a constructive or an academic philosopher, but simply a brilliant and suggestive thinker who, because of the nature of his genius, could never have erected an elaborate philosophic system, and a writer not quite as dangerous to established religion and morals as some critics would have us believe. He most prided himself on his common sense, on his "realism," as contradistinguished from the cobweb-spinning idealisms of his philosophic predecessors.

Early in 1908 a book was published at Jena entitled Franz Overbeck and Friedrich Nietzsche, by Carl Albrecht Bernouilli. In it at great length and with clearness was described the friendship of Overbeck — a well-known church historian and culture-novelist, born at St. Petersburg of German and English parents — and Nietzsche during their Basel period. Interesting is the story of his relations with Richard Wagner and Jacob Burckhardt, the historian of the Renaissance. As a youth Nietzsche had won the praises of both Rietschl and Burckhardt for his essay on Theognis. This was before 1869, in which year at the age of twenty-six he took his doctor's degree and accepted the chair of classical philology at Basel. His friend Overbeck noted his dangerously rapid intellectual development and does not fail to re-

258

cord, what has never been acknowledged by the dyed-in-the-wool Nietzschians, that the "Master" had read and inwardly digested Max Stirner's anarchistic work, The Ego and His Own. Not only is this long-denied fact set forth, but Overbeck, in a careful analysis, reaches the positive conclusion that, notwithstanding his profound erudition, his richly endowed nature, Friedrich Nietzsche is not one of the world's great men; that in his mad endeavour to carve himself into the semblance of his own Superman he wrecked brain and body.

The sad irony of this book lies in the fact that the sister of Nietzsche, Frau Foerster-Nietzsche, who nursed the poet-philosopher from the time of his breakdown in 1888 till his death in 1900; who for twenty years has by pen and personally made such a successful propaganda for his ideas, was in at least three letters — for the first time published by Bernouilli — insulted grievously by her brother. This posthumous hatred as expressed in the acrid prose of Nietzsche is terribly disenchanting. He calls her a meddlesome woman without a particle of understanding of his ideals. He declares that she martyred him, made him ridiculous, and in the last letter he wrote her, dated December, 1886, he wonders at the enigma of fate that made two persons of such different temperaments blood-relatives. Bernouilli, the editor of these Overbeck letters, adds insult to injury by calling the unselfish, noble-minded sister and biographer of her brother a tyrannical and not very intellectual person, who often wounded her brother with her advice and criticism.

Peter Gast doubts the authenticity of these letters, for, as he truthfully points out, the love of Nietzsche for his sister, as evidenced by an ample correspondence, was great. We recall the touching exclamation of the sick philosopher when once at his sister's house in Weimar he saw her weeping: "Don't cry, little sister, we are all so happy now." That "now" had a sinister significance, for the brilliant thinker was quite helpless and incapable of reading through the page of a book, though he was never the lunatic pictured by some of his opponents. A deep melancholy had settled upon his soul and he died without enjoying the light of a returned reason. It has not occurred to German critics that these letters even if genuine are the product of a diseased imagination. Nietzsche became a very suspicious man after his break with Wagner. He suffered from the mania of persecution. He hated mankind and fled to the heights of Sils-Maria to escape what Poe aptly described as the "tyranny of the human face."

The first thing that occurs to one after reading Beyond Good and Evil is that Nietzsche is more French than German. It is well known that his favourites were the *pensée* writers, Pascal, La Bruyère, La Rochefoucauld, Fontenelle, Chamfort, Vauvenargues. A peripatetic because of chronic ill health — he had the nerves of a Shelley and the stomach of a Carlyle — his ideas were

260

jotted down during his long walks in the Engadine. Naturally they assumed the form of aphor-
isms, epigrams, *jeux d'esprit*. With his increasing
illness came the inability to write more than a few
pages of connected thoughts. His best period was
between the years 1877 and 1882. He had attacked Schopenhauer; he wished to be free to go
up to the "heights" unimpeded by the baggage
of other men's ideas. It was with disquietude
that his friends witnessed the growing self-exalta-
tion that may be noted in the rhapsodical Zarathustra.

He felt the ground sinking under him — his
pride of intellect Luciferian in intensity — and
his latter works were a desperate challenge to
his darkening brain and the world that refused
to recognize his value.

Nietzsche had the true ascetic's temperament.
He lived the life of a strenuous saint, and his
Beyond Good and Evil might land us in a barren
desert, where austerity would rule our daily conduct. To become a Superman one must re-
nounce the world. It was the easy-going, down-
at-the-heel morality of the world, its carrying
water on both shoulders, that stirred the wrath of
this earnest man of blameless life and provoked
from him so much brilliant and fascinating prose.
He wrote a swift, golden German. He was a
stylist. The great culture hero of his day, nour-
ished on Latin and Greek, he waged war against
the moral ideas of his generation and ruined his
intellect in the unequal conflict. He turned on

261

himself and rended his soul into shreds rather than join in the affirmations of recognised faith. Yet what eloquent, touching pages he has devoted to the founder of the Christian religion. His last signature in the letter to Brandes reveals the preoccupation of his memory with the religion he despised. Nietzsche made the great renunciation of inherited faith and committed spiritual suicide. Libraries are filled with the works of his commentators, eager to make of him what he was not. He has been shamelessly exploited. He has been called the forerunner of Pragmatism. He was a poet, an artist, who saw life as a gorgeously spun dream, not as a dreary phalanstery. He belonged rather to Goethe and Faust than to Schopenhauer or the positivists. Hellenism was his first and last love.

The correspondence between Nietzsche and his famulus, the musician Peter Gast — whose real name is Heinrich Köselitz — from 1876 to 1889, appeared last autumn and comprises 278 letters. Another Nietzsche appears — gentle, suffering, as usual still hopeful. He loves Italy; at the end, Turin is his favourite city. There is little except in the final communication to show a mind cracking asunder. No doubt this correspondence was given to the world as an offset to the Overbeck-Bernouilli letters.

Leslie Stephen declared that no one ever wrote a dull autobiography, and risking a bull, added, "The very dulness would be interesting." Yet one is not afraid to maintain that Friedrich

262

PHASES OF NIETZSCHE

Nietzsche's autobiography is rather a disappoint-
ment; possibly because too much was expected.
It should not be forgotten that Nietzsche, when
at Wagner's villa Triebschen, near Lucerne, read
and corrected Wagner's autobiography, which is
yet to see the light of publication. He seems to
have violated certain confidences, for he was the
first—that is, in latter years—to revive the story of
Wagner's blood relationship to his stepfather,
Ludwig Geyer. In Leipsic this was a thrice-told
tale. Moreover, he warned us to be suspicious of
great men's autobiographies and then wrote one
himself, wrote it in three weeks, beginning October
15, 1888, the forty-fourth anniversary of his birth,
and ending with difficulty November 4. It rings
sincere, and was composed at white heat, but un-
happily for this present curious generation of
Nietzsche readers it tells very little that is new.

Notwithstanding Nietzsche's wish that the book
should not exceed in price over a mark and a half,
a limited edition de luxe has been put forth with
the acquiescence of the Nietzsche archive, Weimar,
and at a high price. This edition is limited to
1,250 copies. It is clearly printed, but the decorative element is rather bizarre. Henry Van de-
Velde of the Weimar Art School is the designer of
the title and ornaments. Raoul Richter, professor
at the Leipsic University, has written a few appre-
ciative words at the close.

Nietzsche was at Turin, November, 1888.
There he wrote the following to Professor Georg
Brandes, the celebrated Copenhagen critic: "I

263

have now revealed myself with a cynicism that will become historical. The book is called Ecce Homo and is against everything Christian. . . . I am after all the first psychologist of Christianity, and like the old artillerist I am, I can bring forward cannon of which no opponent of Christianity has even suspected the existence. . . . I lay down my oath that in two years we shall have the whole earth in convulsions. I am a fatality. Guess who it is that comes off worst in Ecce Homo? The Germans! I have said awful things to them." This was the "golden autumn" of his life, as he confessed to his sister Elizabeth. In a little over four weeks from the date of the letter to Brandes Nietzsche went mad, after a stroke of apoplexy in Turin. The collapse must have taken place between January 1 and 3, 1889. Brandes received a card signed "The Crucified One"; Overbeck, his old friend at Basel, was also agitated by a few lines in which Nietzsche proclaimed himself the King of Kings; while to Cosima Wagner at Bayreuth was sent a communication which read, "Ariadne, I love you! Dionysos." Like Tolstoy, Nietzsche suffered from theomania and prophecy madness.

These details are not in the autobiography but may be found in Dr. Mügge's excellent study just published, Nietzsche, His Life and Work. Overbeck started for Turin and there found his poor old companion giving away his money, dancing, singing, declaiming verse, and playing snatches of crazy music on the pianoforte. He was taken back

to Basel and was gentle on the trip except that in
the Saint-Gothard tunnel he sang a poem of his,
"An der Brücke," which appears in the autobiography. His mother brought him from Switzerland
to Naumburg; thence to Dr. Binswanger's establishment at Jena. Later he lived in his sister's
home at Upper Weimar, and from the balcony,
where he spent his days, he could see a beautiful
landscape. He was melancholy rather than mad,
never violent—this his sister has personally assured
me—and occasionally surprised those about him
by flashes of memory; but full consciousness was
not to be again enjoyed by him. Overwork, chloral,
and despair at the "conspiracy of silence" caused
his brain to crumble. He had attained his "Great
Noon," Zarathustra's Noon, during the closing
days of 1888. In August, 1900, came the eutha-
nasia for which he had longed.

There is internal evidence that the autobiography was written under exalted nervous conditions. The aura of insanity hovers about its pages.
Yet Nietzsche has seldom said so many brilliant,
ironical, and savage things. He melts over memories of Wagner, the one friendship of a life
crowded with friends and cursed by solitude. He
sets out to smash Christianity, but he expressed
the hope that the book would fall into the
hands of the intellectual élite. He divides his
theme into the following heads: Why I Am So
Clever: Why I Am So Sage: Why I Write Such
Good Books: Why I Am a Fatality. (You recall
here the letter to Brandes.) He ranges from the

abuse of bad German cookery to Kantian metaphysics. He calls Ibsen the typical old maid
and denounces him as the creator of the "Emancipated Woman." Yes, he does insult Germany
and the Germans, but no worse than in earlier
books; and certainly not so effectively as did
Goethe, Heine, and Schopenhauer. In calling
the Germans the "Chinese of Europe" he but
repeated the words of Goncourt in Charles Demailly. He speaks of Liszt as one "who sur-
passes all musicians by the noble accents of his
orchestration" (vague phrase); and depreciates
Schumann's "Manfred." He, Nietzsche, had
composed a counter overture which Von Bülow
declared extraordinary. True, Von Bülow did
call it something of the sort, with the advice to
throw it into the dust-bin as being an insult to
good music. He analyses his recent readings of
Baudelaire—whose diary touched him deeply—of
Stendhal, Bourget, Maupassant, Anatole France,
and others. Best of all, he minutely analyses
the mental processes of his books from The
Birth of Tragedy to The Wagner Case. He
declares Zarathustra a dithyramb of solitude and
purity, and proudly boasts that the Superman
builds his nest in the trees of the future.

What a master of invective! He often descends
to the street in his tongue-lashing, as, for instance,
when he groups "shopkeepers, Christians, cows,
women, Englishmen, and other democrats." Woman is always the enemy. The only way to tame
her is to make her a mother. As for female suf-

frage, he sets it down to psychological disorders. He is a *nuance,* and is the first German to understand women! Alas! And not the last man who will repeat this speech surely hailing from the Stone Age. He seems rather proud of his double personality, and hints at a third. Oddly enough, Nietzsche asked that his Ecce Homo (the title proves his constant preoccupation with Christianity) be translated into French by Strindberg, the Swedish poet and the first dramatist to incorporate into his plays the Nietzschian philosophy, or what he conceived to be such. (Daniel Lesueur has written of the various adaptations for gorillas of a teaching that really demands from man the utmost that is in him.) Nietzsche was a hater of Christianity; above all of Christian morals, but he was a brave and honest fighter. He raged at George Eliot, Herbert Spencer, and Carlyle for their half-heartedness. To give up the belief in Christ and His mission meant for Nietzsche to drop the moral system, to transvalue old moral values. This, he truthfully asserted, George Eliot and Spencer had not the courage to do. He did not skulk behind such masks as the Higher Criticism, Modernism, or quacksalver Christian socialism. Compromise was abhorrent to him. His Superman, with its echoes of Wagner's Siegfried, Ibsen's Brand, Stendhal's wicked heroes, the Renaissance Borgias, the second Faust of Goethe, and not a little of Hamlet, is a monster of perfection that may some day become a demigod for a new religion—and no worse than contemporary mud-gods manu-

267

factured daily. Nietzsche's particular virtue, even for the orthodox, is that though he assails their faith he also puts to rout with the fiery blasts of his rhetoric all the belly-gods, the false-culture gods, the gods who "heal," and other "ghosts"— as Max Stirner calls them. But to every generation its truths (or lies).

A recently published anecdote of Ibsen quotes a statement of his *apropos* of Brand. "The whole drama is only meant as irony. For the man who wants all or nothing is certainly crazy." Well, Friedrich Nietzsche was such a man. No half-way parleyings. Fight the Bogey. Don't go around. He went more serenely than did Brand to his ice cathedral on the heights. His prayer uttered years before came true: "Give me, ye gods, give me madness! Madness to make me believe at last in myself."

Nietzsche is the most dynamically emotional writer of his times. He sums up an epoch. He is the expiring voice of the old nineteenth-century romanticism in philosophy. His message to unborn generations we may easily leave to those unborn, and enjoy the wit, the profound criticisms of life, the bewildering gamut of his ideas; above all, pity the tragic blotting out of such a vivid intellectual life.

VIII

MYSTICS

I

ERNEST HELLO

It occurred in the beautiful gardens of the Paris exposition during that summer of 1867 when Glory and France were synonymous expressions. To the music, cynical and voluptuous, of Offenbach and Strauss the world enjoyed itself, applauding equally Renan's latest book and Thérésa's vulgarity; amused by Ponson de Terrail's fatuous indecencies and speaking of Proudhon in the same breath. Bismarck and his Prussians seemed far away. Babel or Pompeii? The tower of the Second Empire reached to the clouds; below, the people danced on the edge of the crater. A time for prophets and their lamentations. Jeremiah walked in the gardens. He was a terrible man, with sombre fatidical gaze, eyes in which were the smothered fires of hatred. His thin hair waved in the wind. He said to his friends: "I come from the Tuileries Palace; it is not yet consumed; the Barbarians delay their coming. What is Attila doing?" He passed. "A madman!" exclaimed a com-

269

panion to Henri Lasserre. "Not in the least," replied that writer. "He is Ernest Hello." After reading this episode as related by Hello's friend and editor, the disquieting figure is evoked of that son of Hanan, who prowled through the streets of the holy city in the year A.D. 62 crying aloud: "Woe, woe upon Jerusalem!" The prophecy of Hello was realized in a few years. Attila came and Attila went, and after his departure the polemical writer, who could be both a spouting volcano and a subtle doctor of theology, wrote his masterpiece, L'Homme, a remarkable book, a seed-bearing book.

Why is there so little known of Ernest Hello? He was born 1828, died 1885, and was a voluminous author, who wrote much for the *Univers* and other periodicals and passed away as he had lived, fighting in harness for the truths of his religion. Possibly the less sensitive texture of Louis Veuillot's mind and character threw the talents of Hello into shadow; perhaps his avowed hatred of mediocrity, his Old Testament power of vituperation, and his apocalyptic style militated against his acceptance by the majority of Roman Catholic readers. Notwithstanding his gifts as a writer and thinker, Hello was never popular, and it is only a few years ago that his works began to be republished. Let us hasten to add that they are rich in suggestion for lovers of apologetic or hortatory literature.

It was Huysmans and Remy de Gourmont who sent me to the amazing Hello. In A Rebours

270

Huysmans discusses him with Léon Bloy, Barbey d'Aurevilly, and Ozanam. "Hello is a cunning engineer of the soul, a skilful watchmaker of the brain, delighting to examine the mechanism of a passion and to explain the play of a wheelwork." United to his power of analysis there is the fanaticism of a Biblical prophet and the tortured ingenuity of a master of style. A little John of Patmos, one who, complex and precious, is a sort of epileptic mystic—vindictive, proud, a despiser of the commonplace. All these things was Hello to Huysmans, who did not seem to relish him very much. De Gourmont described him as one who believed with genius. A believing genius he was, Ernest Hello, and his genius, his dynamic faith—apart from any consideration of his qualities as a prose artist or his extraordinary powers of analysis. Without his faith, which was, one is tempted to add, his thematic material, he might have been a huge force vainly flapping his wings in the void, or, as Lasserre puts it, he was impatient with God because of His infinite patience. He longed to see Him strike dumb ·the enemies of His revealed word. He lived in a continuous thunder-storm of the spirit. He was a mystic, yet a warrior on the fighting line of the church militant.

Joachim of Flora has written: "The true ascetic counts nothing his own save his harp." Hello, less subjective than Newman, less lyric though a "son of thunder," counted but the harp of his faith. All else he cast away. And this faith

271

was published to the heathen with the hot rhetoric of a propagandist. The nations must be aroused from their slumber. He whirls his readers off their feet by the torrential flow of his argument. He never winds calmly into his subject, but smites vehemently the opening bars of his hardy discourse. He writes pure, untroubled prose at times, the line, if agitated, unbroken, the balance of sound and sense perfect. But too often he employs a staccato, declamatory, tropical, inflated style which recalls Victor Hugo at his worst; the short sentence; the single paragraph; the vicious abuse of antithesis; if it were not for the subject-matter whole pages might masquerade as the explosive mannerisms of Hugo. "Christianity is *naturally* impossible. However, it exists. Therefore it is supernatural!" This is Hello logic. Or, speaking of St. Joseph of Cupertino: "If he had not existed, no one could have invented him," which is a very witty inversion of Voltaire's celebrated *mot*. God-intoxicated as were St. Francis of Assisi or Père Ratisbonne, Hello was not; when absent from the tripod of vaticination he was a meek, loving man; then the walls of his *Turris eburnea* echoed the inevitable: *Ora pro nobis!* Even when the soul seems empty, it may, like a hollow shell, murmur of eternity. Hello's faith was in the fourth spiritual dimension. It demanded the affirmation of his virile intellect and the concurrence of his overarching emotional temperament.

In the black-and-white sketch by Vallotton he

272

resembles both Remenyi, the Hungarian violin virtuoso, and Louise Michel, the anarchist. The brow is vast, the expression exalted, the mouth belligerent, disputatious, and the chin slightly receding. One would say a man of violent passions, in equilibrium unsteady, a skirter of abysses, a good hater — did he not once propose a History of Hatred? Yet how submissive he was to papal decrees; many of his books contain instead of a preface his act of submission to Catholic dogma. More so than Huysmans was he a mediæval man. For him modern science did not exist. The Angelic Doctor will outlive Darwin, he cried, and the powers and principalities of darkness are as active in these days as in the age when the saints of the desert warred with the demons of doubt and concupiscence. "To wring from man's tongue the denial of his existence is proof of Satan's greatest power," was a sentiment of Père Ravignan to which Hello would have heartily subscribed. He detested Renan — *Renan, voilà l'ennemi!* Jeremy Taylor's vision of hell as an abode crowded with a million dead dogs would not be too severe a punishment for that silken sophist, whose writings are the veriest flotsam and jetsam of a disordered spiritual life. Hello has written eloquent pages about Hugo, whose poetry he admired, whose ideas he combated. Napoleon was a genius, but a foe of God.

Shakespeare for him vacillated between obscenity and melancholy; Hamlet was a character hardly sounded by Hello; doubt was a psycho-

273

logical impossibility to one of his faith. He was convinced that the John of the Apocalyptic books was not John the Presbyter, nor any one of the five Johns of the Johannic writings, but John the Apostle. He has often the colour of Bossuet's moral indignation. A master of theological odium, his favourite denunciation was "Horma, Anathema, Anathème, Amen!" His favourite symbol of confusion is Babel — Paris. He loved, among many saints, Denys the Areopagite; he extolled the study of St. Thomas Aquinas. To the unhappy Abbé de Lamenais's Paroles d'un Croyant (1834), he opposed his own Paroles de Dieu. He could have, phrase for phrase, book for book, retorted with tenfold interest to Nietzsche's vilification of Christianity. Society will again become a theocracy, else pay the penalty in anarchy. One moment beating his breast, he cries aloud: "*Maranatha! Maranatha!* Our Lord is at hand!" The next we find him with the icy contemptuousness of a mystic quoting from the Admirable Ruysbroeck (a thirteenth-century mystic whom he had translated, whose writings influenced Huysmans, and at one period of his development, Maurice Maeterlinck) these brave words: "Needs must I rejoice beyond the age, though the world has horror of my joy, and its grossness cannot understand what I say." Notwithstanding this aloofness, there are some who after reading Ernest Hello's Man may agree with Havelock Ellis: "Hello is the real psychologist of the century, not Stendhal."

MYSTICS

It is indeed a work of penetrating criticism and clairvoyance, this study of man, of life. Read his analysis of the Miser and you will recall Plautus or Molière. He has something of Saint-Simon's power in presenting a finished portrait and La Bruyère's cameo concision. He is reactionary in all that concerns modern æsthetics or the natural sciences. There is but one science, the knowledge of God. Avoiding the devious webs of metaphysics, he sets before us his ideas with a crystal clarity. Despite its religious bias, L'Homme may be recommended as a book for mundane minds. Nor is Le Siècle to be missed. Those views of the world, of men and women, are written by a shrewd observer and a profound thinker. Philosophie et Athéisme is just what its title foretells — a battering-ram of dialectic. The scholastic learning of Hello is enormous. He had at his beck the Bible, the patristic writers, the schoolmen, and all the moderns from De Maistre to Father Faber. He execrated Modernism. Physionomies de Saintes, Angelo de Foligno, and half a dozen other volumes prove how versed he was in Holy Writ. "The Scriptures are an abysm," he declared. He wrote short stories, Contes extraordinaires, which display excellent workmanship, no little fantasy, yet are rather slow reading. In literature Hello was a belated romantic, a Don Quixote of the ideal who charged ferociously the windmills of indifference.

In 1881 he was a collaborator with an American religious publication called *Propagateur Catho-*

lique (I give the French title because I do not know whether it was published here or in Canada). His contributions were incorporated later in his Words of God. I confess to knowing little of Hello but his works, the Life by Lasserre being out of print. Impressive as is his genius, it is often repellent, because love of his fellow-man is not a dominant part of it. The central flame burns brightly, fiercely; the tiny taper of charity is often missing. With his beloved Ruysbroeck (Rusbrock, he names him) he seems to be muttering too often a disdainful adieu to his gross and ignorant brethren as if abandoning them to their lies and ruin. However, his translation of this same Ruysbroeck is a genuine accession to contemplative literature. And perhaps, if one too hastily criticises the almost elemental faith of Hello and its rude assaults of the portals of pride, luxury, and worldliness, perhaps the old wisdom may cruelly rebound upon his detractors: "Dixit insipiens in corde suo: Non est Deus."

II

"MAD, NAKED BLAKE"

I

Perhaps the best criticism ever uttered offhand about the art of William Blake was Rodin's, who, when shown some facsimiles of Blake's drawings by brilliant Arthur Symons with the explanation that Blake "used literally to see those figures, they are not mere inventions," replied: "Yes. He saw them once; he should have seen them three or four times." And this acute summing up of Blake's gravest defect is further strengthened by a remark made by one of his most sympathetic commentators, Laurence Binyon. Blake once said: "The lavish praise I have received from all quarters for invention and drawing has generally been accompanied by this: 'He can conceive, but he cannot execute.' This absurd assertion has done and may still do me the greatest mischief." Now comments Mr. Binyon: "In spite of the artist's protest this continues to be the current criticism on Blake's work; and yet the truth lies rather on the other side. It is not so much in his execution as in the failure to mature his conceptions that his defect is to be found." Again: "His temperament unfitted him for success in carrying his work further; his want was not lack of skill, but lack of patience." If this sounds paradoxical we find

277

Symons admitting that Rodin had hit the nail on the head. "There, it seems to me, is the fundamental truth about the art of Blake; it is a record of vision which has not been thoroughly mastered even as vision."

Notwithstanding the neglect to which Blake was subjected during his lifetime and the misunderstanding ever since his death of his extraordinary and imaginative designs, poetry, and vaticinations, it is disquieting to see how books about Blake are beginning to pile up. He may even prove as popular as Ibsen. A certain form of genius serves as a starting-point for critical performances. Blake is the most admirable example, though Whitman and Browning are in the same class. Called cryptic by their own, they are too well understood by a later generation. Wagner once swam in the consciousness of the elect; and he was understood. Baudelaire understood him, so Liszt. Wagner to-day is the property of the man in the street, who whistles him, and Ibsen is already painfully yielding up his precious secrets to relentless "expounding" torturers. As for Maeterlinck, he is become a mere byword in literary clubs, where they discuss his Bee in company with the latest Shaw epigram. "Even caviare, it seems, may become a little flyblown," exclaims Mr. Dowden. Everything is being explained. Oh, happy age! Who once wrote: "A hundred fanatics are found to a theological or metaphysical statement, but not one for a geometric problem"?

Yet we may be too rash. Blake's prophetic books are still cloudy nightmares, for all but the elect, and not Swinburne, Gilchrist, Tatham, Richard Garnett, Ellis, Binyon, Yeats, Symons, Graham Robertson, Alfred Story, Maclagan and Russell, Elizabeth Luther Cary and the others — for there are others and there will be others — can wring from these fragments more than an occasional meaning or music. But in ten years he may be the pontiff of a new dispensation. Symons has been wise in the handling of his material. After a general and comprehensive study of Blake he brings forward some new records from contemporary sources — extracts from the diary, letters and reminiscences of Henry Crabb Robinson; from A Father's Memoir of His Child, by Benjamin Heath Malkin; from Lady Charlotte Bury's Diary (1820); Blake's horoscope, obituary notice, extract from Varley's Zodiacal Physiognomy (1828); a biographical sketch of Blake by J. T. Smith (1828), and Allan Cunningham's life of Blake (1830). In a word, for those who cannot spare the time to investigate the various and sundry Blakian exegetics, Symons's book is the best because most condensed. It is the Blake question summed up by a supple hand and a sympathetic spirit. It is inscribed to Auguste Rodin in the following happy and significant phrase: "To Auguste Rodin, whose work is the marriage of heaven and hell."

279

II

William Blake must have been the happiest man that ever lived; not the doubtful happiness of a fool's paradise, but a sharply defined ecstasy that was his companion from his earliest years to his very death-bed; that bed on which he passed away "singing of the things he saw in heaven," to the tune of his own improvised strange music. He seems to have been the solitary man in art history who really fulfilled Walter Pater's test of success in life: "To burn always with this hard gemlike flame, to maintain this ecstasy." Blake easily maintained it. His face shone with it. Withal he was outwardly sane in matters of mundane conduct, sensitive and quick to resent any personal affront, and by no means one of those awful prophets going about proclaiming their self-imposed mission. An amiable man, quick to fly into and out of a passion, a gentleman exquisite in manners, he impressed those who met him as an unqualified genius. Charles Lamb has told us of him; so have others. I possess an engraving of his head after Linnell's miniature, and while his Irish paternity has never been thoroughly established — Yeats calls him an Irishman — there can be little doubt of his Celtic origin. His is the head of a poet, a patriot, a priest. The brow is lofty and wide, the hair flamelike in its upcurling. The eyes are marvellous — true windows of a soul vividly aware of

280

its pricelessness; the mystic eye and the eye of the prophet about to thunder upon the perverse heads of his times. The full lips and massive chin make up the ensemble of a singularly noble, inspired, and well-balanced head. Symmetry is its keynote. A God-kindled face. One looks in vain for any indication of the madman — Blake was called mad during his lifetime, and ever since he has been considered mad by the world. Yet he was never mad as were John Martin and Wiertz the Belgian, or as often seems Odilon Redon, who has been called — heaven knows why! — the "French Blake." The poet Cowper said to Blake: "Oh, that I were insane always. . . . Can you not make me truly insane? . . . You retain health and yet are as mad as any of us — over us all — mad as a refuge from unbelief — from Bacon, Newton, and Locke." The arid atheism of his century was doubtless a contributory cause to the exasperation of Blake's nerves. He believed himself a Christian despite his heterodox sayings, and his belief is literal and profound. A true Citizen of Eternity, as Yeats named him, and with all his lack of academic training, what a giant he was among the Fuselis, Bartolozzis, Stothards, Schiavonettis, and the other successful mediocrities.

His life was spent in ignoble surroundings, an almost anonymous life, though a happy one because of its illuminating purpose and flashes of golden fire. Blake was born in London (1757) and died in London (1827). He was the son of

281

a hosier, whose real name was not O'Neill, as some have maintained. The boy, at the age of fourteen, was apprenticed to Ryland the engraver, but the sight of his master's face caused him to shudder and he refused to work under him, giving as a reason that Ryland would be hanged some day. And so he was, for counterfeiting. The abnormally sensitive little chap then went to the engraver Basire, with whom he remained a year. His precocity was noteworthy. In 1773 he put forth as a pretended copy of Michaelangelo a design which he called Joseph of Arimathea Among the Rocks of Albion. At that early age he had already begun to mix up Biblical characters and events with the life about him. The Bible saturated his imagination; it was not a dead record for him, but a living, growing organism that overlapped the spiritual England of his day. The grotesqueness of his titles, the mingling of the familiar with the exotic — the sublime and the absurd are seldom asunder in Blake — sacred with secular, were the results of his acquaintance with the Scriptures at a period when other boys were rolling hoops or flying kites. Blake could never have been a boy, in the ordinary sense; yet he was to the last day of his life a child in the naïveté of his vision. "I am ever the new-born child," he might have said, as did Goethe to Herder. At the age of four he said God put his face in the window, and he ran screaming to his parents to bear witness to the happening. He had seen a tree bright with angels at Peckham

282

Rye, and his life long he held converse with the spirits of Moses, Homer, Socrates, Dante, Shakespeare, and Milton. He adored Michaelangelo, and Albrecht Dürer and Swedenborg completed the conquest — perhaps the unsettlement — of his intellect. He hated Titian, Rubens, and Rembrandt. They were sensualists, they did not in their art lay the emphasis upon drawing, and as we·shall see presently, drawing was the chief factor for Blake, colour being a humble handmaiden.

In 1782 Blake married for love Catharine Boucher, or Boutcher, of whom Mr. Swinburne has said that she "deserves remembrance as about the most perfect wife on record." She was uneducated, but learned to read and write, and later proved an inestimable helpmate for the struggling and unpractical Blake. She bound his books and coloured some of his illustrations. She bore long poverty uncomplainingly, one is tempted to say with enthusiasm. Once only she faltered. Blake had his own notions about certain Old Testament customs, and he, it is said on the authority of a gossip, had proposed to add another wife to the poor little household. Mrs. Blake wept and the matter was dropped. Other gossip avers that the Adamite in Blake manifested itself in a not infrequent desire to cast aside garments and to sit in paradisiacal innocence. Whether these stories were the invention of malicious associates or were true, one thing is certain: Blake was capable of anything for which he could find a Biblical precedent. In the matter

283

of the unconventional he was the *Urvater* of English rebels. Shelley, Byron, Swinburne were timid amateurs compared to this man, who with a terrific energy translated his thoughts into art. He was not the idle dreamer of an empty day nor a mooning mystic. His energy was electric. It sounds a clarion note in his verse and prose, it reveals itself in the fiery swirlings of his line, a line swift and personal. He has been named by some 'one a heretic in the Church of Swedenborg; but like a latter-day rebel — Nietzsche, who renounced Schopenhauer — Blake soon renounced Swedenborg. But Michelangelo remained a deity for him, and in his designs the influence of Angelo is paramount.

Blake might be called an English Primitive. He stems from the Florentines, but *à la gauche*. The bar sinister on his artistic coat of arms is the lack of fundamental training. He had a Gothic imagination, but his dreams lack architectonics. Goethe, too, had dreams, and we are the richer by Faust. And no doubt there are in his works phrases that Nietzsche has seemed to repeat. It is the fashion just now to trace every idea of Nietzsche to some one else. The truth is that the language of rebellion through the ages is the same. The mere gesture of revolt, as typified in the uplifted threatening arm of a Cain, a Prometheus, a Julian the Apostate, is no more conventional than the phraseology of the heretic. How many of them have written "inspired" bibles, from Mahomet to Zarathustra. Blake, his

284

tumultuous imagination afire — remember that the artist doubled the poet in his amazing and versatile soul — poured forth for years his "sacred" books, his prophecies, his denouncements of his fellow-man. It was all sincere righteous indignation; but the method of his speech is obscure; the Mormon books of revelation are miracles of clarity in comparison. Let us leave these singular prophecies of Blake to the mystics. One thing is sure — he has affected many poets and thinkers. There are things in The Marriage of Heaven and Hell that Shaw might have said had not Blake forestalled him. Such is the cruelty of genius.

Symons makes apt comparison between Blake and Nietzsche: "There is nothing in good and evil, the virtues and vices . . . vices in the natural world are the highest sublimities in the spiritual world." This might have appeared over Nietzsche's signature in Beyond Good and Evil. And the following in his marginalia to Reynolds — Sir Joshua always professed a high regard for the genius of Blake. "The Enquiry in England is not whether a man has Talents and Genius, but whether he is Passive and Polite and a Virtuous Ass." The vocabulary of rebellion is the same. Still more bitter is his speech about holiness: "The fool shall not enter into the kingdom of heaven, let him be ever so pious." Blake glorified passion, which for him was the highest form of human energy. His tragic scrolls, emotional arabesques, are testimony to his high and subtle

285

temperament. The intellect he worshipped. Of pride we cannot have too much! As a lyric poet it is too late in the day to reiterate that he is a peer in the "holy church of English literature." The Songs of Innocence and Songs of Experience have given him a place in the anthologies and made him known to readers who have never heard of him as a pictorial genius. "Tiger, tiger, burning bright, In the forests of the night," is recited by sweet school-misses and pondered for its philosophy by their masters. And has Keats ever fashioned a lovelier image than: "Let thy west wind sleep on the lake; spread silence with thy glimmering eyes and wash the dusk with silver"? Whatever he may not be, William Blake is a great singer.

III

William Butler Yeats in his Ideas of Good and Evil has said some notable things about Blake. He calls him a realist of the imagination and first pointed out the analogy between Blake and Nietzsche. "When one reads Blake it is as though the spray of an inexhaustible fountain of beauty was blown into our faces." And "he was a symbolist who had to invent his symbols." Well, what great artist does not? Wagner did; also Ibsen and Maeterlinck. Blake was much troubled over the imagination. It was the "spirit" for him in this "vegetable universe," the Holy Ghost. All art that sets forth with any fulness the outward vesture of things is prompted by the

286

"rotten rags of memory." That is why he loathed
Rubens, why he seemingly slurs the forms of men
and things in his eagerness to portray the essential. Needless to add, the essential for him was
the soul. He believed in goading the imagination
to vision — though not with opium — and we
are led through a dream-world of his own fashion-
ing, one in which his creatures bear little correspondence to earthly types. His illustrations to
the Book of Job, to Dante, to Young's Night
Thoughts bear witness to the intensity of his vision,
though flesh and blood halts betimes in following these vast decorative whirls of flame bearing
myriad souls in blasts that traverse the very firmament. The "divine awkwardness" of his Adam
and Eve and the "Ancient of Days" recall something that might be a marionette and yet an angelic
being. To Blake they were angels; of that there
can be no doubt; but we of less fervent imagination may ask as did Hotspur of Glendower, who
had boasted that he could "call spirits from the
vasty deep." "Why, so can I, or so can any man.
But will they come when you do call for them?"
quoth the gallant Percy. We are, the majority
of us, as unimaginative as Hotspur. Blake summoned his spirits; to him they appeared; to
quote his own magnificent utterance, "The stars
threw down their spears, and watered heaven with
their tears"; but we, alas! see neither stars nor
spears nor tears, only eccentric draughtsmanship
and bizarre designs. Yet, after Blake, Doré's
Dante illustrations are commonplace; even Botti-

287

celli's seem ornamental. Such is the genius of the Englishman that on the thither side of his shadowy conceptions there shine intermittently pictures of a No Man's Land, testifying to a burning fantasy hampered by human tools. He suggests the supernatural. "How do you know," he asks, "but every bird that cuts the airy way is an immense world of delight closed by your senses five?" Of him Ruskin has said: "In expressing conditions of glaring and flickering light Blake is greater than Rembrandt." With Dante he went to the nethermost hell. His warring attributes tease and attract us. For the more human side we commend Blake's seventeen wood engravings to Thornton's Virgil. They are not so rich as Bewick's, but we must remember that it was Blake's first essay with knife and boxwood — he was really a practised copper engraver — and the effects he produced are wonderful. What could be more powerful in such a tiny space than the moon eclipse and the black forest illustrating the lines, "Or when the moon, by wizard charm'd, foreshows Bloodstained in foul eclipse, impending woes!" And the dim sunsets, the low, friendly sky in the other plates!

Blake's gospel of art may be given in his own words: "The great and golden rule of art, as of life, is this: that the more distinct, sharp and wiry the boundary line the more perfect the work of art; and the less keen and sharp, the greater is the evidence of weak imitation, plagiarism and bungling." He abominated the nacreous flesh

288

tones of Titian, Correggio, or Rubens. Reflected
lights are sinful. The silhouette betrays the soul
of the master. Swinburne in several eloquent
pages has instituted a comparison between Walt
Whitman and William Blake. (In the first edition of "William Blake: A Critical Essay," 1868.)
Both men were radicals. "The words of either
strike deep and run wide and soar high." What
would have happened to Blake if he had gone to
Italy and studied the works of the masters — for
he was truly ignorant of an entire hemisphere of
art? Turner has made us see his dreams of a
gorgeous world; Blake, as through a scarce
opened door, gives us a breathless glimpse of a
supernal territory, whether heaven or hell, or
both, we dare not aver. Italy might have calmed
him, tamed him, banished his arrogance — as it
did Goethe's. Suppose that Walt Whitman had
written poems instead of magical and haunting
headlines. And if Browning had made clear the
devious ways of Sordello — what then? "What
porridge had John Keats?" We should have
missed the sharp savour of the real Blake, the real
Whitman, the real Browning. And what a number of interesting critical books would have remained unwritten. "Oh, never star was lost here
but it arose afar." What Coleridge wrote of his
son Hartley might serve for Blake: "Exquisitely
wild, an utter visionary, like the moon among thin
clouds, he moves in a circle of his own making.
He alone is a light of his own. Of all human
beings I never saw one so utterly naked of self."

289

Naked of self! William Blake, unselfish egoist, stands before us in three words.

III

FRANCIS POICTEVIN

THERE is a memorable passage in A Rebours, the transcription of which, by Mr. George Moore, may be helpful in understanding the work of that rare literary artist, Francis Poictevin. "The poem in prose," wrote Huysmans, "handled by an alchemist of genius, should contain the quintessence, the entire strength of the novel, the long analysis and the superfluous description of which it suppresses . . . the adjective placed in such an ingenious and definite way that it could not be legally dispossessed of its place, that the reader would dream for whole weeks together over its meaning, at once precise and multiple; affirm the present, reconstruct the past, divine the future of the souls revealed by the light of the unique epithet. The novel thus understood, thus condensed into one or two pages, would be a communion of thought between a magical writer and an ideal reader, a spiritual collaboration by consent between ten superior persons scattered through the universe, a delectation offered to the most refined and accessible only to them."

This aristocratic theory of art was long ago propounded by Poe in regard to the short poem. Huysmans transposed the idea to the key of fiction

290

while describing the essential prose of Mallarmé; but some years before the author of A Rebours wrote his ideal book on decadence a modest young Frenchman had put into practice the delightfully impracticable theories of the prose poem. This writer was Francis Poictevin (born at Paris, 1854). Many there were, beginning with Edgar Poe and Louis Bertrand, who had essayed the form, at its best extremely difficult, at its worst too tempting to facile conquests: Baudelaire, Huysmans in his Le Drageoir aux Epices; Daudet, De Banville, Villiers de L'Isle Adam, Maurice de Guérin, and how many others! During the decade of the eighties the world of literature seemed to be fabricating poems in prose. Pale youths upon whose brows descended aureoles at twilight, sought fame in this ivory miniature carving addressed to the "ten superior persons" very much scattered over the globe. But like most peptonic products, the brain as does the stomach, finally refuses to accept as nourishment artificial concoctions too heavily flavoured with midnight oil. The world, which is gross, prefers its literature by the gross, and though it has been said that all the great exterior novels have been written, the majority of readers continue to read long-winded stories dealing with manners and, of course, the eternal conquest of an uninteresting female by a mediocre male. Aiming at instantaneity of pictorial and musical effect — as a picture become lyrical — the poets who fashioned their prose into artistic rhythms

291

and colours and tones ended by exhausting the patience of a public rapidly losing its faculty of attention.

Possibly these things may account for the neg·lect of a writer and thinker of such delicacy and originality as Poictevin, but he was always caviare even to the consumers of literary *caviar*. But he had a small audience in Paris, and after his · first book appeared — one hesitates to call it a novel — Daudet saluted it with the praise that Sainte-Beuve — the Sainte-Beuve of Volupté and Port-Royal — would have been delighted with La Robe du Moine. Here is a list of Poictevin's works and the years of their publication until 1894. Please note their significant and extraor-dinary names: La Robe du Moine, 1882; Ludine, 1883; Songes, 1884; Petitan, 1885; Seuls, 1886; Paysages et Nouveaux Songes, 1888; Derniers Songes, 1888; Double, 1889; Presque, 1891; Heures, 1892; Tout Bas, 1893; Ombres, 1894.

A collective title for them might be Nuances; Poictevin searches the last nuance of sensations and ideas. He is a remote pupil of Gon-court, and superior to his master in his power of recording the impalpable. (Compare any of his books with the Madame Gervaisais of Goncourt; the latter is mysticism very much in the concrete.) At the same time he recalls Amiel, Maurice de Guérin, Walter Pater, and Coventry Patmore. A mystical pantheist in his worship of nature, he is a mystic in his adoration of God. This intensity of vision in the case of Poictevin

292

did not lead to the depravities, exquisite and morose, of Baudelaire, Huysmans, and the brilliant outrageous Barbey d'Aurevilly. With his soul of ermine Poictevin is characterised by De Gourmont as the inventor of the mysticism of style. Once he saluted Edmond de Goncourt as the Velasquez of the French language, and that master, not to be outdone in politeness, told Poictevin that his prose could boast its "victories over the invisible." If by this Goncourt meant making the invisible visible, rendering in prose of crepuscular subtlety moods recondite, then it was not an exaggerated compliment. In such spiritual performances Poictevin resembles Lafcadio Hearn in his airiest gossamer-webbed phrases. A true, not a professional symbolist, the French *prosateur* sounds Debussy twilight harmonies. His speech at times glistens with the hues of a dragon-fly zigzagging in the sunshine. In the tenuous exaltation of his thought he evokes the ineffable deity, circled by faint glory. To compass his picture he does not hesitate to break the classic mould of French syntax while using all manners of strange-fangled vocables to attain effects that remind one of the clear-obscure of Rembrandt. Indeed, a mystic style is his, beside which most writers seem heavy-handed and obvious.

Original in his form, in the bizarre architecture of his paragraphs, pages, chapters, he abolishes the old endings, cadences, chapter headings. Nor, except at the beginning of his career, does

he portray a definite hero or heroine.   Even names
are avoided.   "He" or "she" suffices to indicate
the sex.   Action there is little.   Story he has
none to tell; by contrast Henry James is epical.
Exteriority does not interest Poictevin, who is
nevertheless a landscape painter; intimate and
charming.   His young man and young woman
visit Mentone, the Pyrenees, Brittany, along the
Rhine — a favourite resort — Holland, Luchon,
Montreux, and Switzerland, generally.   His palette is marvellously complicated.   We should call
him an impressionist but that the phrase is become banal.   Poictevin deals in subtle grays.
He often writes *gris-iris*.   His portraits swim in
a mysterious atmosphere as do Eugène Carrière's.
His fluid, undulating prose records landscapes in
the manner of Theocritus.

The tiny repercussions of the spirit that is re-
acted upon by life are Whistlerian notations in
the gamut of this artist's instrument.   Evocation,
not description; evocation, not narration; always evocation, yet there is a harmonious ensemble; he returns to his theme after capriciously
circling about it as does a Hungarian gypsy when
improvising upon the heart-strings of his auditors.
Verlaine once addressed a poem to Poictevin the
first line of which runs: "Toujours mécontent de
son œuvre."   Maurice Barrès evidently had read
Seuls before he wrote Le Jardin de Bérénice
(1891).   The young woman in Poictevin's tale
has the same feverish languors; her male companion, though not the egoist of Barrès, is a very

294

modern person, slightly consumptive; one of whom it may be asked, in the words of Poictevin: "Is there anything sadder under the sun than a soul incapable of sadness?" In their room hang portraits of Baudelaire and the Curé d'Ars. Odder still is the monk, P. Martin. Martin is the name of the "adversary" in The Garden of Bérénice. And the episode of the dog's death! Huysmans, too, must have admired Poictevin's descriptions of the Grünewald Christ at Colmar, and of the portrait of the Young Florentine in the Stadel Museum at Frankfort. It would be instructive to compare the differing opinions of the two critics concerning this last-named picture.

A mirror, Poictevin's soul reflects the moods of landscapes. Without dogmatism he could say with St. Anselm that he would rather go to hell sinless than be in heaven smudged by a single transgression. To his tender temperament even the reading of Pascal brought shadows of doubt. A persistent dreamer, the world for him is but the garment investing God. Flowers, stars, the wind that weeps in little corners, the placid bosom of lonely lakes, far-away mountains and their mystic silhouettes, the Rhine and its many curvings, the clamour of cities and the joy of the green grass, are his themes. Life with its frantic gestures is quite inutile. Let it be avoided. You turn after reading Poictevin to the Minoration of Emile Hennequin: "Let all that is be no more. Let glances fade and the vivacity of gestures fall. Let us be humble, soft, and slow. Let us love

295

without passion, and let us exchange weary caresses." Or hear the tragic cry of Ephraim Mikhael: "Ah! to see behind me no longer, on the lake of Eternity, the implacable wake of Time."

"Poictevin's men and women," once wrote Aline Gorren in a memorable study of French symbolism, "are subordinate to these wider curves of wave and sky; they come and go, emerging from their setting briefly and fading into it again; they have no personality apart from it; and amid the world symbols of the heavens in marshalled movements and the thousand reeded winds, they in their human symbols are allowed to seem, as they are, proportionately small. They are possessed as are clouds, waters, trees, but no more than clouds, waters, trees, of a baffling significance, forever a riddle to itself. They have bowed attitudes; the weight of the mystery they carry on their shoulders."

The humanity that secretly evaporates when the prose poet notes the attrition of two souls is shed upon his landscapes with their sonorous silences. A picture of the life contemplative, of the adventures of timorous gentle souls in search of spiritual adventures, set before us in a style of sublimated preciosity by an orchestra of sensations that has been condensed to the string quartet, the dreams of Francis Poictevin — does he not speak of the human forehead as a dream dome? — are not the least consoling of his century. He is the white-robed acolyte among mystics of modern literature.

IV

THE ROAD TO DAMASCUS

RELIGIOUS conversion and its psychology have furnished the world's library with many volumes. Perfectly understood in the ages of faith, the subject is for modern thinkers susceptible of realistic explanation. Only we pave the way now by a psychological course instead of the ancient doctrine of Grace Abounding. Nor do we confound the irresistible desire of certain temperaments to spill their innermost thoughts, with what is called conversion. There was Rousseau, who confessed things that the world would be better without having heard. He was not converted. Tolstoy, believing that primitive Christianity is almost lost to his fellow beings, preaches what he thinks is the real faith. Yet he was converted. He had been, he said, a terrible transgressor. The grace of God gave sight to his sin-saturated eyeballs. Is there the slightest analogy between his case and that of Cardinal Newman? John Henry Newman had led a spotless life before he left the Anglican fold. Nevertheless he was a convert. And Saint Augustine, the pattern of all self-confessors, the classic case, may be compared to John Bunyan or to Saint Paul! Professor William James, who with his admirable impartiality has scrutinized the psychological topsy-turvy we name conversion, has not missed the commonplace fact

297

that every man as to details varies, but at base the psychical machinery is controlled by the same motor impulses. *A chacun son infini.*

Some natures reveal a mania for confession. Dostoïevsky's men and women continually tell what they have thought, what crimes they have committed. It was an epileptic obsession with this unhappy Russian writer. Paul Verlaine sang blithely of his ghastly life, and Baudelaire did not spare himself. So it would seem that the inability of certain natures to keep their most precious secrets is also the keynote of religious confessions. But let us not muddle this with the sincerity or insincerity of the change. Leslie Stephen has said that it did not matter much whether Pascal was sincere, and instanced the Pascal wager (*le pari de Pascal*) as evidence of the great thinker's casuistry. It is better to believe and be on the safe side than be damned if you do not believe; for if there is no hereafter your believing that there is will not matter one way or the other. This is the substance of Pascal's wager, and it must be admitted that the ardent upholder of Jansenism and the opponent of the Jesuits proved himself an excellent pupil of the latter when he framed his famous proposition.

Among the converts who have become almost notorious in France during the last two decades are Ferdinand Brunetière, François Coppée, Paul Verlaine, and Joris-Karl Huysmans. But it must not be forgotten that if the quartette trod the Road to Damascus they were all returning to their early

298

City of Faith. They had been baptized Roman
Catholics. All four had strayed. And widely
different reasons brought them back to their mother
Church. We need not dwell now on the case of
Villiers de l'Isle Adam, as his was a deathbed repentance; nor with Paul Bourget, a Catholic
born and on the side of his faith since the publication of Cosmopolis. As for Maurice Barrès,
he may be a Mohammedan for all we care. He
will always stand, spiritually, on his head.

The stir in literary and religious circles over
Huysmans's trilogy, En Route, La Cathédrale,
and L'Oblat, must have influenced the succeeding generation of French writers. Of a sudden
sad young rakes who spouted verse in the æsthetic
taverns of the Left Bank fell to writing religious
verse. Mary Queen of Heaven became their
shibboleth. They invented new sins so that they
might repent in a novel fashion. They lacked
the delicious lyric gift of Verlaine and the tremendous enfolding moral earnestness of Huysmans
to make themselves believed. One, however,
has emerged from the rest, and his book, Du
Diable à Dieu (From the Devil to God), has
crossed the twenty-five thousand mark; perhaps
it is further by this time. The author is an au-
thentic poet, Adolphe Retté. For his confessions
the lately deceased François Coppée wrote a dignified and sympathetic preface. Retté's place
in contemporary poetry is high. Since Verlaine
we hardly dare to think of another poet of such
charm, verve, originality. An anarchist with

299

Sebastien Faure and Jean Grave, a Socialist of
all brands, a lighted lyric torch among the insur-
rectionists, a symbolist, a writer of "free verse"
(which is hedged in by more rules, though un-
formulated and unwritten, than the stiffest academic production of Boileau), Adolphe Retté led
the life of an individualist poet; precisely the
sort of life at which pulpit-pounders could point
and cry: "There, there is your æsthetic poet,
your man of feeling, of finer feelings than his
neighbours! Behold to what base uses he has put
this gift! See him wallowing with the swine!"
And, practically, these words Retté has employed
in speaking of himself. He insulted religion in
the boulevard journals; he hailed with joy the
separation of Church and State. He wrote not
too decent novels, though his verse is feathered
with the purest pinions. He treated his wife
badly, neglecting her for the inevitable Other
Woman. (What a banal example this is, after
all.) He once, so he tells us to his horror, mal-
treated the poor woman because of her piety.
Typical, you will say. Then why confess it in
several hundred pages of rhythmic prose, why
rehearse for gaping, indifferent Paris the threadbare, sordid tale? Paris, too, so cynical on the
subject of conversions, and also very suspicious
of such a spiritual *bouleversement* as Retté's! "No,
it won't do, Huysmans is to blame," exclaimed
many.

Yet this conversion — literally one, for he was
educated in a Protestant college — is sincere.

300

He means every word he says; and if he is copiously rhetorical, set it all down to the literary temperament. He wrote not only with the approval of
his spiritual counsellor, but also for the same
reason as Saint Augustine or Bunyan. Newman's
confession was an Apologia, an answer to Kings-
ley's challenge. With Huysmans, he is such a
consummate artist that we could imagine him
plotting ahead his cycle of novels (if novels they
are); from Là-Bas to Lourdes the spiritual modulation is harmonious. Now, M. Retté (he was
born in 1863 in Paris of an Ardennaise family),
while he has sung in his melodious voice many alluring songs, while he has shown the impressions
wrought upon his spirit by Walt Whitman and
Richard Wagner, there is little in the rich extravagance of his love for nature or the occasional
Vergilian silver calm of his verse — he can sound
more than one chord on his poetic keyboard —
to prepare us for the great plunge into the healing
waters of faith. A pagan nature shows in his
early work, apart from the hatred and contempt
he later displayed toward religion. How did
it all come about? He has related it in this book,
and we are free to confess that, though we must
not challenge the author's sincerity, his manner
is far from reassuring. He is of the brood of
Baudelaire.

Huysmans frankly gave up the riddle in his own
case. Atavism may have had its way; he had
relatives who were in convents; a pessimism that
drove him from the world also contributed its

share in the change. Personally Huysmans prefers to set it down to the mercy and grace of God — which is the simplest definition after all. When we are through with these self-accusing men; when professional psychology is tired of inventing new terminologies, then let us do as did Huysmans — go back to the profoundest of all the psychologists, the pioneers of the moderns, Saint Theresa — what actual, virile magnificence is in her Castle of the Soul — Saint John of the Cross, and Ruysbroeck. They are mystics possessing a fierce faith; and without faith a mystic is like a moon without the sun. Adolphe Retté knows the great Spanish mystics and quotes them almost as liberally as Huysmans. But with a difference. He has read Huysmans too closely; books breed books, ideas and moods beget moods and ideas. We are quite safe in saying that if En Route had not been written, Retté's Du Diable à Dieu could not have appeared in its present shape. The similarity is both external and internal. John of the Cross had his Night Obscure, so has M. Retté; Huysmans, however, showed him the way. Retté holds an obstinate dialogue with the Devil (who is a capitalized creature). Consult the wonderful fifth chapter in En Route. Naturally there must be a certain resemblance in these spiritual adventures when the Evil One captures the outposts of the soul and makes sudden savage dashes into its depths. Retté's style is not in the least like Huysmans's. It is more fluent, swifter, and more staccato. You skim his pages; in Huysmans you recognise the distilled remorse; you move as in a penitential procession, the rhythms grave, the eyes dazzled by the vision divine, the voice lowly chanting. Not so Retté, who glibly discourses on sacred territory, who is terribly at ease in Zion.

Almost gayly he recounts his misdeeds. He pelts his former associates with hard names. He pities Anatole France for his socialistic affinities. All that formerly attracted him is anathema. Even the mysterious lady with the dark eyes is castigated. She is not a truth-teller. She does not now understand the protean soul of her poet. *Retro me Sathanas!* It is very exhilarating. The Gallic soul in its most resilient humour is on view. See it rebound! Watch it ascend on high, buoyed by delicious phrases, asking sweet pardon; then it falls to earth abusing its satanic adversary with sinister energy. At times we overhear the honeyed accents, the silky tones of Renan. It is he, not Retté, who exclaims: *Mais quelles douces larmes!* Ah! Renan — also a cork soul! The Imitation is much dwelt upon — the influence of Huysmans has been incalculable in this. And we forgive M. Retté his theatricalism for the lovely French paraphrase he has made of Salve Regina. But on the whole we prefer En Route. The starting-point of Retté's change was reading some verse in the Purgatory of the Divine Comedy. A literary conversion? Possibly, yet none the less complete. All roads lead to Rome, and the Road to Damascus may be achieved from many devious side paths. But in writing with such engaging frankness the memoirs of his soul we wish that Retté had more carefully followed the closing sentence of his brilliant little book: *Non nobis, Domine, non nobis, sed nomini tuo da gloriam!*

V

FROM AN IVORY TOWER

"Their impatience," was the answer once given by Cardinal Newman to the question, What is the chief fault of heresiarchs? In this category Walter Pater never could have been included, for his life was a long patience. As Newman sought patiently for the evidences of faith, so Pater sought for beauty, that beauty of thought and expression, of which his work is a supreme exemplar in modern English literature. Flaubert, a man of genius with whom he was in sympathy, toiled no harder for the perfect utterance of his ideas than did this retiring Oxford man of letters. And, like his happy account of Raphael's growth, Pater was himself a "genius by accumulation; the transformation of meek scholarship into genius.".

Walter Pater's intimate life was once almost legendary. We heard more of him a quarter of a century ago than yesterday. This does not mean that his vogue has declined; on the contrary, he is a force at the present such as he never was either at Oxford or London. But of the living man,

· 3o4

notwithstanding his shyness, stray notes crept into print. He wrote occasional reviews. He had disciples. He had adversaries who deplored his — admittedly remote — immoral influence upon impressionable, "slim, gilt souls"; he had critics who detected the truffle of evil in savouring his exotic style. When he died, in 1894, the air was cleared by his devoted friends, Edmund Gosse, Lionel Johnson, William Sharp, Arthur Symons, and some of his Oxford associates, Dr. Bussell and Mr. Shadwell. It was proved without a possibility of doubt that the popular conception of the man was far from the reality; that the real Pater was a plain liver and an austere thinker; that he was not the impassive Mandarin of literature pictured by some; that the hedonism, epicureanism, cyrenaicism of which he had been vaguely accused had been a confounding of intellectual substances, a slipshod method of thought he abhorred; that his entire career had been spent in the pursuit of an æsthetic and moral perfection and its embodiment in prose of a rarely individual and haunting music. Recall his half-petulant, half-ironical exclamation of disgust to Mr. Gosse: "I wish they wouldn't call me a 'hedonist'; it produces such a bad effect on the minds of people who don't know Greek." He would have been quite in accord with Paul Bourget's dictum that "there is no such thing as health, or the contrary, in the world of the soul"; Bourget, who, lecturing later at Oxford, pronounced Walter Pater "un parfait prosateur."

305

Despite the attempt to chain him to the chariots of the Pre-Raphaelite brotherhood, Pater, like Chopin, during the Romantic turmoil, stood aloof from the heat and dust of its battles. He was at first deeply influenced by Goethe and Ruskin, and was a friend of Swinburne's; he wrote of the Morris poetry; but his was not the polemical cast of mind. The love of spiritual combat, the holy zeal of John Henry Newman, of Keble, of Hurrell Froude, were not in his bones. And so his scholar's life, the measured existence of a recluse, was uneventful; but measured by the results, what a vivid, intense, life it was. There is, however, very little to tell of Walter Pater. His was the interior life. In his books is his life — hasn't some one said that all great literature is autobiographical?

There are articles by the late William Sharp and by George Moore. The former in Some Personal Recollections of Walter Pater, written in 1894, gave a vivid picture of the man, though it remained for Mr. Moore to discover his ugly face and some peculiar minor characteristics. Sharp met Pater in 1880 at the house of George T. Robinson, in Gower Street, that delightful meeting-place of gifted people. Miss A. Mary F. Robinson, now Mme. Duclaux, was the tutelary genius. She introduced Sharp to Pater. The blind poet, Philip Bourke Marston, was of the party. Pater at that time was a man of medium height, stooping slightly, heavily built, with a Dutch or Flemish cast of features, a pale com-

plexion, a heavy moustache — "a possible Bismarck, a Bismarck who had become a dreamer,"
adds the keen observer. A friendship was struck
up between the pair. Pater came out of his shell,
talked wittily, paradoxically, and later at Oxford
showed his youthful admirer the poetic side of
his singularly complex nature. There are conver-
sations recorded and letters printed which would
have added to the value of Mr. Benson's memoir.

Mr. Moore's recollections are slighter, though
extremely engaging. Above all, with his trained
eye of a painter, he sketches for us another view
of Pater, one not quite so attractive. Mr. Moore
saw a very ugly man — "it was like looking at a
leaden man, an uncouth figure, badly moulded,
moulded out of lead, a large, uncouth head, the
head of a clergyman, . . . a large, overarching
skull, and small eyes; they always seemed afraid
of you, and they shifted quickly. There seemed
to be a want of candour in Pater's face, . . . an
abnormal fear of his listener and himself. There
was little hair on the great skull, and his skull
and his eyes reminded me a little of the French
poet Verlaine, a sort of domesticated Verlaine,
a Protestant Verlaine." His eyes were green-
gray, and in middle life he wore a brilliant apple-
green tie and the inevitable top-hat and frock
coat of an urban Englishman. In one of his
early essays Max Beerbohm thus describes Pater:
"a small, thick, rock-faced man, whose top-hat
and gloves of *bright* dog skin struck one of
the many discords in that little city of learning

307

and laughter. The serried bristles of his mustachio made for him a false-military air." Pater is said to have come of Dutch stock. Mr. Benson declares that it has not been proved. He had the amiable fancy that he may have had in his veins some of the blood of Jean Baptiste Pater, the painter. His father was born in New York. He went to England, and near London in 1839 Walter Horatio, his second son, was born. To The Child in the House and Emerald Uthwart, both "imaginary portraits," we may go for the early life of Pater, as Marius is the idealized record of his young manhood. When a child he was fond of playing Bishop, and the bent of his mind was churchly, further fostered by his sojourn at Canterbury. He matriculated at Oxford in 1858 as a commoner of Queen's College, where he was graduated after being coached by Jowett, who said to his pupil, "I think you have a mind that will come to great eminence." Years afterward the Master of Balliol seems to have changed his opinion, possibly urged thereto by the parody of Pater as Mr. Rose by Mr. Mallock in The New Republic. Jowett spoke of Pater as "the demoralizing moralizer," while Mr. Freeman could see naught in him but "the mere conjurer of words and phrases." Others have denounced his "pulpy magnificence of style," and Max Beerbohm declared that Pater wrote English as if it were a dead language; possibly an Irish echo of Pater's own assertion that English should be written as a learned language.

He became a Fellow of Brasenose, and Oxford
— with the exception of a few years spent in
London, and his regular annual summer visits
to Italy, France, and Germany, where he took
long walks and studied the churches and art
galleries — became his home. Contradictory legends still float in the air regarding his absorbed
demeanour, his extreme sociability, his companionable humour, his chilly manner, his charming
home, his barely furnished room, with the bowl of
dried rose leaves; his sympathies, antipathies,
nervousness, and baldness, and, like Baudelaire,
of his love of cats, and a host of mutually exclusive
qualities. Mr. Zangwill relates that he told Pater
he had discovered a pun in one of his essays.
Thereat, great embarrassment on Pater's part.
Symons, who knew him intimately, tells of his
reading the dictionary — that "pianoforte of
writers," as Mr. Walter Raleigh cleverly names it
—for the opposite reason that Gautier did, *i.e.*,
that he might learn what words to avoid. Another time Symons asked him the meaning of a
terrible sentence, Ruskinian in length and invo-
lution. Pater carefully scanned the page, and
after a few minutes said with a sigh of relief:
"Ah, I see the printer has omitted a dash." Yet,
with all this meticulous precision, Pater was a
man with an individual style, and not a mere
stylist. What he said was of more importance
than the saying of it.

The portraits of Pater are, so his friends declare, unlike him. He had irregular features,

309

and his jaw was prognathic; but there was great variety of expression, and the eyes, set deeply in the head, glowed with a jewelled fire when he was deeply aroused. In Mr. Greenslet's wholly admirable appreciation, there is a portrait executed by the unfortunate Simeon Solomon, and dated 1872. There is in Mosher's edition of the Guardian Essays a copy of Will Rothenstein's study, a characteristic piece of work, though Mr. Benson says it is not considered a resemblance. And I have a picture, a half-tone, from some magazine, the original evidently photographic, that shows a Pater much more powerful in expression than the others, and without a hint of the ambiguous that lurks in Rothenstein's drawing and Moore's pen portrait. Pater never married. Like Newman, he had a talent for friendship. As with Newman, Keble, that beautiful soul, made a deep impression on him, and, again like Newman, to use his own words, he went his way "like one on a secret errand."

And the Pater style! Matthew Arnold on a certain occasion advised Frederic Harrison to "flee Carlylese as the very devil," and doubtless would have given the same advice regarding Paterese. Pater is a dangerous guide for students. This theme of style, so admirably vivified in Mr. Walter Raleigh's monograph, was worn threadbare during the days when Pater was slowly producing one book every few years — he wrote five in twenty years, at the rate of an essay or two a year, thus matching Flaubert in his tormented production.

The principal accusation brought against the Pater method of work and the Pater style·is that it is lacking in spontaneity, in a familiar phrase, "it is not natural." But a "natural" style, so called, appears not more than a half dozen times in its full flowering during the course of a century. The French write all but faultless prose. To match Flaubert, Renan, or Anatole France, we must go to Ruskin, Pater, and Newman. When we say: "Let us write simple, straightforward English," we are setting a standard that has been reached of late years only by Thackeray, Newman, and few besides. There are as many victims of the "natural English" formula as there are of the artificial formula of a Pater or a Stevenson. The former write careless, flabby, colourless, undistinguished, lean, commercial English, and pass unnoticed in the vast whirlpool of universal mediocrity, where the *cliché* is king of the paragraph. The others, victims to a misguided ideal of "fine writing," are more easily detected.

Now, properly speaking, there is no such thing as a "natural" style. Even Newman confesses to laborious days, though he wrote with the idea uppermost, and with no thought of the style. Renan, perfect master, disliked the idea of teaching "style" — as if it could be taught! — yet he worked over his manuscripts. We all know the Flaubert case. With Pater one must not rush to the conclusion that because he produced slowly and with infinite pains, he was all artificiality. Prose for him was a fine art. He would no more

311

have used a phrase coined by another man than
he would have worn his hat. He embroidered
upon the canvas of his ideas the grave and lovely
phrases we envy and admire. Prose — "cette
ancienne et très jalouse chose," as it was called
by Stéphane Mallarmé — was for Pater at once
a pattern and a cadence, a picture and a song.
Never suggesting hybrid "poetic-prose," the great
stillness of his style — atmospheric, languorous,
sounding sweet undertones — is always in the
rhythm of prose. Speed is absent; the *tempo* is
usually lenten; brilliance is not pursued; but there
is a hieratic, almost episcopal, pomp and power.
The sentences uncoil their many-coloured lengths;
there are echoes, repercussions, tonal imagery,
and melodic evocation; there is clause within clause
that occasionally confuses; for compensation we
are given newly orchestrated harmonies, as
mordant, as salient, and as strange as some chords
in the music of Chopin, Debussy and Richard
Strauss. Sane it always is — simple seldom.
And, as Symons observes: "Under the soft
and musical phrases an inexorable logic hides
itself, sometimes only too well. Link is added
silently but faultlessly to link; the argument
marches, carrying you with it, while you fancy
you are only listening to the music with which
it keeps step." It is very personal, and while it
does not make melody for every ear, it is exquisitely
adapted to the idea it clothes. Read aloud Ruskin and then apply the same vocal test — Flaubert's procedure — to Pater, and the magnificence

312

of the older man will conquer your ear by storm; but Pater, like Newman, will make it captive in a persuasive snare more delicately varied, more subtle, and with modulations more enchanting. Never oratorical, in eloquence slightly muffled, his last manner hinted that he had sought for newer combinations. Of his prose we may say, employing his own words concerning another theme: "It is a beauty wrought from within, . . . the deposit, little cell by cell, of strange thoughts and fantastic reveries and exquisite passions."

The prose of Jeremy Taylor is more impassioned, Browne's richer, there are deeper organ tones in De Quincey's, Ruskin's excels in effects, rhythmic and sonorous; but the prose of Pater is subtler, more sinuous, more felicitous, and in its essence consummately intense. Morbid it sometimes is, and its rich polyphony palls if you are not in the mood; and in greater measure than the prose of the other masters, for the world is older and Pater was weary of life. But a suggestion of morbidity may be found in the writings of every great writer from Plato to Dante, from Shakespeare to Goethe; it is the faint spice of mortality that lends a stimulating if sharp perfume to all literatures. Beautiful art has been challenged as corrupting. There may be a grain of truth in the charge. But man cannot live by wisdom alone, so art was invented to console, disquiet, and arouse him. Whenever a poet appears he is straightway accused of tampering with the moral code; it is mediocrity's mode of adjusting

313

violent mental disproportions.   But persecution
never harmed a genuine talent, and the accusa-
tions against the art of Pater only provoked from
him such beautiful books as Imaginary Portraits,
Marius the Epicurean, and Plato and Platonism.
Therefore let us be grateful to the memory of his
enemies.

There is another Pater, a Pater far removed
from the one who wove such silken and coloured
phrases.   If he sometimes recalls Keats in the
rich texture of his prose, he can also suggest the
aridity of Herbert Spencer.   There are early essays
of his that are as cold, as logically adamant, and as
tortuous as sentences from the Synthetic Philosophy.   Pater was a metaphysician before he became an artist.   Luckily for us, his tendency to
bald theorising was subdued by the broad human-
ism of his temperament.   There are not many
"purple patches" in his prose, "purple" in the
De Quincey or Ruskin manner; no "fringes of
the north star" style, to use South's mocking expression.   He never wrote in sheer display.
For the boorish rhetoric and apish attitudes of
much modern drama he betrayed no sympathy.
His critical range is catholic.   Consider his essays
on Lamb, Coleridge, Wordsworth, Winckelmann,
setting aside those finely wrought masterpieces,
the studies of Da Vinci, Giorgione, and Botticelli.
As Mr. Benson puts it, Pater was not a modern
scientific or archæological critic, but the fact that
Morelli has proved the Concert of Giorgione not to
be by that master, or that Vinci is not all Pater

314

says he is, does not vitiate the essential values of his criticism.

Like Maurice Barrès, Pater was an egoist of the higher type; he seldom left the twilight of his *tour d'ivoire;* yet his work is human and concrete to the core. Nothing interested him so much as the human quality in art. This he ever sought to disengage. Pater was a deeply religious nature *au fond,* perhaps addicted a trifle to moral preciosity, and, as Mr. Greenslet says, a lyrical pantheist. His essay on Pascal, without plumbing the ethical depths as does Leslie Stephen's study of the same thinker, gives us a fair measure of his own religious feelings. A pagan with Anatole France in his worship of Greek art and literature, his profounder Northern temperament, a Spartan temperament, strove for spiritual things, for the vision of things behind the veil. The Paters had been Roman Catholic for many generations; his father was not, and he was raised in the Church of England. But the ritual of the older Church was for him a source of delight and consolation. Mr. Benson deserves unstinted praise for his denunciation of the pseudo-Paterians, the self-styled disciples, who, totally misinterpreting Pater's pure philosophy of life, translated the more ephemeral phases of his cyrenaicism into the grosser terms of a gaudy æsthetic. These defections pained the thinker, whose study of Plato had extorted praise from Jowett. He even withdrew the much-admired conclusion of The Renaissance because of the wilful miscon-

315

structions put upon it. He never achieved the ataraxia of his beloved master. And Oxford was grudging of her favour to him long after the world had acclaimed his genius. Sensitive he was, though Mr. Gosse denies the stories of his suffering from harsh criticism; but there were some forms of criticism that he could not over-look. Books like his Plato and Marius the Epicur-ean were adequate answers to detractors. Some-what cloistered in his attitude toward the normal world of work; too much the artist for art's sake, he may never trouble the greater currents of litera-ture; but he will always be a writer for writers, the critic whose vision pierces the shell of ap-pearances, the composer of a polyphonic prose-music that recalls the performance of harmonious adagio within the sonorous spaces of a Gothic cathedral, through the windows of which filters alien daylight. It was a favourite contention of his that all the arts constantly aspire toward the condition of music. This idea is the keynote of his poetic scheme, the keynote of Walter Pater, mystic and musician, who, like his own Marius, carried his life long "in his bosom across a crowded public place — his own soul."

IX

IBSEN

I

HENRIK IBSEN was the best-hated artist of the nineteenth century. The reason is simple: He was, himself, the arch-hater of his age. Yet, granting this, the Norwegian dramatist aroused in his contemporaries a wrath that would have been remarkable even if emanating from the fiery pit of politics; in the comparatively serene field of æsthetics such overwhelming attacks from the critics of nearly every European nation testified to the singular power displayed by this poet. Richard Wagner was not so abused; the theatre of his early operations was confined to Germany, the Tannhäuser fiasco in Paris a unique exception. Wagner, too, did everything that was possible to provoke antagonism. He scored his critics in speech and pamphlet. He gave back as hard names as he received. Ibsen never answered, either in print or by the mouth of friends, the outrageous allegations brought against him. Indeed, his disciples often darkened the issue by their unsolicited, uncritical championship.

3¹7

In Edouard Manet, the revolutionary Parisian painter and head of the so-called impressionist movement — himself not altogether deserving the appellation — we have an analogous case to Wagner's. Ridicule, calumny, vituperation, pursued him for many years. But Paris was the principal scene of his struggles; Paris mocked him, not all Europe. Even the indignation aroused by Nietzsche was a comparatively local affair. ·Wagner is the only man who approaches Ibsen in the massiveness of his martyrdom. Yet Wagner had consolations for his opponents. His music-drama, so rich in colour and rhythmic beauty, his romantic themes, his appeal to the eye, his friendship with Ludwig of Bavaria, at times placated his fiercest detractors. Manet painted one or two successes for the official Salon; Nietzsche's brilliant style and faculty for coining poetic images were acclaimed, his philosophy declared detestable. Yes, fine phrases may make fine psychologues. Robert Browning never felt the heavy hand of public opinion as did Ibsen. We must go back to the days of Byron and Shelley for an example of such uncontrollable and unanimous condemnation. But, again, Ibsen tops them all as victim of storms that blew from every quarter: Norway to Austria, England to Italy, Russia to America. There were no mitigating circumstances in his *lèse-majesté* against popular taste. No musical rhyme, scenic splendour, or rhythmic prose, acted as an emotional buffer between him and his audiences. His social

318

dramas were condemned as the sordid, heartless
productions of a mediocre poet, who wittingly
debased our moral currency. And as they did
not offer as bribes the amatory intrigue, the witty
dialogue, the sensual arabesques of the French
stage, or the stilted rhetoric and heroic postures
of the German, they were assailed from every
critical watch-tower in Europe. Ibsen was a
stranger, Ibsen was disdainfully silent, therefore Ibsen must be annihilated. Possibly if he
had, like Wagner, explained his dramas, we
should have had confusion thrice confounded.

The day after his death the entire civilised
world wrote of him as the great man he was: great
man, great artist, great moralist. And A Doll's
House only saw the light in 1879 — so potent
a creator of critical perspective is Death. There
were, naturally, many dissonant opinions in this
symphony of praise. Yet how different it all
read from the opinions of a decade ago. Ad-
verse criticism, especially in America, was vitiated
by the fact that Ibsen the dramatist was hardly
known here. Ibsen was eagerly read, but seldom played; and rarely played as he should be.
He is first the dramatist. His are not closet
dramas to be leisurely digested by lamp-light;
conceived for the theatre, actuality their key-note,
his characters are pale abstractions on the printed
page — not to mention the inevitable distortions
to be found in the closest translation. We are
all eager to tell what we think of him. But do
we know him? Do we know him as do the play-

319

goers of Berlin, or St. Petersburg, Copenhagen, Vienna, or Munich? And do we realise his technical prowess? In almost every city of Europe Ibsen is in the regular repertory. He is given at intervals with Shakespeare, Schiller, Dumas, Maeterlinck, Hauptmann, Grillparzer, Hervieu, Sudermann, and with the younger dramatists. That is the true test. Not the isolated divinity of a handful of worshippers, with an esoteric message, his plays are interpreted by skilled actors and not for the untrained if enthusiastic amateur. There is no longer Ibsenism on the Continent; Ibsen is recognised as the greatest dramatist since Racine and Molière. Cults claim him no more, and therefore the critical point of view at the time of his death had entirely shifted. His works are played in every European language and have been translated into the Japanese.

The mixed blood in the veins of Ibsen may account for his temperament; he was more Danish than Norwegian, and there were German and Scotch strains in his ancestry. Such obscure forces of heredity doubtless played a rôle in his career. Norwegian in his love of freedom, Danish in his artistic bent, his philosophic cast of mind was wholly Teutonic. Add to these a possible theologic prepossession derived from the Scotch, a dramatic technique in which Scribe and Sophocles are not absent, and we have to deal with a disquieting problem. Ibsen was a mystery to his friends and foes. Hence the avidity with which he is claimed by idealists, realists, socialists,

320

anarchists, symbolists, by evangelical folk, and by agnostics. There were in him many contradictory elements. Denounced as a pessimist, all his great plays have, notwithstanding, an unmistakable message of hope, from Brand to When We Dead Awake. An idealist he is, but one who has realised the futility of dreams; like all world-satirists, he castigates to purify. His realism is largely a matter of surfaces, and if we care to look we may find the symbol lodged in the most prosaic of his pieces. His anarchy consists in a firm adherence to the doctrine of individualism; Emerson and Thoreau are of his spiritual kin. In both there is the contempt for mob-rule, mob-opinion; for both the minority is the true rational unit; and with both there is a certain aloofness from mankind. Yet we do not denounce Emerson or Thoreau as enemies of the people. To be candid, Ibsen's belief in the rights of the individual is rather naïve and antiquated, belonging as it does to the tempestuous period of '48. Max Stirner was far in advance of the playwright in his political and menacing egoism; while Nietzsche, who loathed democracy, makes Ibsen's aristocracy timid by comparison.

Ibsen can hardly be called a philosophic anarch, for the body of doctrine, either political or moral, deducible from his plays is so perplexing by reason of its continual affirmation and negation, so blurred by the kaleidoscopic clash of character, that one can only fuse these mutually exclusive qualities by realising him as a dramatist

321

who has created a microcosmic world; in a word, we must look upon the man as a creator of dramatic character not as a theorist. And his characters have all the logical illogicality of life.

Several traits emerge from this welter of cross-purposes and action. Individualism is a leading motive from the first to the last play; a strong sense of moral responsibility — an oppressive sense, one is tempted to add — is blended with a curious flavour of Calvinism, in which are traces of predestination. A more singular equipment for a modern dramatist is barely conceivable. Soon we discover that Ibsen is playing with the antique dramatic counters under another name. Free-will and determinism — what are these but the very breath of classic tragedy! In one of his rare moments of expansion he said: "Many things and much upon which my later work has turned — the contradiction between endowment and desire, between capacity and will, at once the entire tragedy and comedy of mankind — may here be dimly discerned." Moral responsibility evaded is a favourite theme of his. No Furies of the Greek drama pursued their victims with such relentless vengeance as pursues the unhappy wretches of Ibsen. In Ghosts, the old scriptural wisdom concerning the sins of parents is vividly expounded, though the heredity doctrine is sadly overworked. As in other plays of his, there were false meanings read into the interpretation; the realism of Ghosts is negligible; the symbol looms

322

large in every scene. Search Ibsen throughout and it will be found that his subject-matter is fundamentally the same as that of all great masters of tragedy. It is his novel manner of presentation, his transposition of themes hitherto treated epically, to the narrow, unheroic scale of middle-class family life that blinded critics to his true significance. This tuning down of the heroic, this reversal of the old æsthetic order extorted bitter remonstrances. If we kill the ideal in art and life, what have we left? was the cry. But Ibsen attacks false as well as true ideals and does not always desert us after stripping us of our self-respect. A poet of doubt he is, who seldom attempts a solution; but he is also a puritan — a positivist puritan — and his scourgings are an equivalent for that *katharsis*, in the absence of which Aristotle denied the title of tragedy.

Consider, then, how Ibsen was misunderstood. Setting aside the historical and poetic works, we are confronted in the social plays by the average man and woman of every-day life. They live, as a rule, in mediocre circumstances; they are harried by the necessities of quotidian existence. Has this undistinguished *bourgeoisie* the potentialities of romance, of tragedy, of beauty? Wait, says Ibsen, and you will see your own soul, the souls of the man and woman who jostle you in the street, the same soul in palace or hovel, that orchestra of cerebral sensations, the human soul. And it is the truth he speaks. We follow with growing uneasiness his exposition of a soul. The

323

spectacle is not pleasing. In his own magical but charmless way the souls of his people are turned inside out during an evening. No monologues, no long speeches, no familiar machinery of the drama, are employed. But the miracle is there. You face yourself. Is it any wonder that public and critic alike waged war against this showman of souls, this new psychologist of the unflattering, this past master of disillusionment? For centuries poets, tragic and comic, satiric and lyric, have been exalting, teasing, mocking, and lulling mankind. When Aristophanes flayed his victims he sang a merry tune; Shakespeare, with Olympian amiability, portrayed saint and sinner alike to the accompaniment of a divine music. But Ibsen does not cajole, amuse, or bribe with either just or specious illusions. He is determined to tell the truth of our microcosmic baseness. The truth is his shibboleth. And when enounced its sound is not unlike the chanting of a *Nox Irae*. He lifted the ugly to heroic heights; the ignoble he analysed with the cold ardour of a moral biologist — the ignoble, that "sublime of the lower slopes," as Flaubert has it.

This psychological method was another rock of offence. Why transform the playhouse into a school of metaphysics? But Ibsen is not a metaphysician and his characters are never abstractions; instead, they are very lively humans. They offend those who believe the theatre to be a place of sentimentality or clowning; these same Ibsen men and women offend the lovers of Shakespeare

324

and the classics. We know they are real, yet we dislike them as we dislike animals trained to imitate humanity too closely. The simian gestures cause a feeling of repulsion in both cases; surely *we* are not of such stock! And we move away. So do we sometimes turn from the Ibsen stage when human souls are made to go through a series of sorrowful evolutions by their stern trainer. To what purpose such revelations? Is it art? Is not our ideal of a nobler humanity shaken?

Ibsen's report of the human soul as he sees it is his right, the immemorial right of priest, prophet, or artist. All our life is a huge lie if this right be denied; from the Preacher to Schopenhauer, from Æschylus to Molière, the man who reveals, in parable or as in a mirror, the soul of his fellow-being is a man who is a benefactor of his kind, if he be not a cynical spirit that denies. Ibsen is a satirist of a superior degree; he has the gift of creating a *Weltspiegel* in which we see the shape of our souls. He is never the cynic, though he has portrayed the cynic in his plays. He has too much moral earnestness to view the world merely as a vile jest. That he is an artist is acknowledged. And for the ideals dear to us which he so savagely attacks, he so clears the air about some old familiar, mist-haunted ideal of duty, that we wonder if we have hitherto mistaken its meaning.

From being denounced as a corrupter of youth, an anarch of letters, a debaser of current moral coin, we have learned to view him as a force ma-

325

king for righteousness, as a master of his craft,
and as a creator of a large gallery of remarkably
vivid human characters. We know now that
many modern dramatists have carried their pails
to this vast northern lake and from its pine-
hemmed and sombre waters have secretly drawn
sparkling inspiration.

The truth is that Ibsen can be no longer denied — we exclude the wilfully blind — by critic
or public. He is too big a man to be locked up
in a library as if he were full of vague forbidden
wickedness. When competently interpreted he
is never offensive; the scenes to which the critics refer as smacking of sex are mildness itself
compared to the doings of Sardou's lascivious
marionettes. In the theatrical sense his are not
sex plays, as are those of Dumas the younger.
He discusses woman as a social as well as a
psychical problem. Any picture of love is toler-
ated so it be frankly sentimental; but let Ibsen
mention the word sex and there is a call to arms
by the moral policemen of the drama. Thus,
by some critical hocus-pocus the world was led
for years to believe that this lofty thinker, moralist, and satirist concealed an immoral teacher.
It is an old trick of the enemy to place upon an
author's shoulders the doings and sayings of his
mimic people. Ibsen was fathered with all the
sins of his characters. Instead of being studied
from life, they were, so many averred, the result
of a morbid brain, the brain of a pessimist and a
hater of his kind.

326

We have seen that Ibsen offended by his disregard of academic dramatic attitudes. His personages are ordinary, yet like Browning's meanest soul they have a human side to show us. The inherent stuff of his plays is tragic; but the hero and heroine do not stamp, stalk, or spout blank verse; it is the tragedy of life without the sop of sentiment usually administered by second-rate poets. Missing the colour and decoration, the pretty music, and the eternal simper of the sensual, we naturally turn our back on such a writer. If he knows souls, he certainly does not understand the box-office. This for the negative side. On the positive, the apparent baldness of the narrative, the ugliness of his men and women, their utterance of ideas foreign to cramped, convention-ridden lives, mortify us immeasurably. The tale always ends badly or sadly. And when one of his characters begins to talk about the "joy of life," it is the gloom of life that is evoked. The women — and here is the shock to our masculine vanity — the women assert themselves too much, telling men that they are not what they believe themselves to be. Lastly, the form of the Ibsen play is compact with ideas and emotion. We usually don't go to the theatre to think or to feel. With Ibsen we must think, and think closely; we must feel — worse still, be thrilled to our marrow by the spectacle of our own spiritual skeletons. No marvellous music is there to heal the wounded nerves as in Tristan and Isolde; no prophylactic for the merciless

327

acid of the dissector. We either breathe a rarefied atmosphere in his Brand and in When We Dead Awake, or else, in the social drama, the air is so dense with the intensity of the closely wrought moods that we gasp as if in the chamber of a diving-bell. Human, all too human!

Protean in his mental and spiritual activities, a hater of shams — religious, political, and social shams — more symbolist than realist, in assent with Goethe that no material is unfit for poetic treatment, the substance of Ibsen's morality consists in his declaration that men to be free must first free themselves. Once, in addressing a group of Norwegian workmen, he told them that man must ennoble himself, he must *will* himself free; "to will is to have to will," as he says in Emperor and Galilean. Yet in Peer Gynt he declares "to be oneself is to slay oneself." Surely all this is not very radical. He wrote to Georg Brandes, that the State was the foe of the individual; therefore the State must go. But the revolution must be one of the spirit. Ibsen ever despised socialism, and after his mortification over the fiasco of the Paris Commune he had never a good word for that vain legend: Liberty, Equality, Fraternity. Brandes relates that while Ibsen wished — in one of his poems — to place a torpedo under the social ark, there was also a time when he longed to use the knout on the willing slaves of a despised social system.

Perhaps the main cause of Ibsen's offending is his irony. The world forgives much, irony

328

never, for irony is the ivory tower of the intellectual, the last refuge of the original. It is not the intellectual irony of Meredith, nor the playful irony of Anatole France, but a veiled corrosive irony that causes you to tread suspiciously every yard of his dramatic domain. The "second intention," the secondary dialogue, spoken of by Maeterlinck, in the Ibsen plays is very disconcerting to those who prefer their drama free from enigma. Otherwise his dialogue is a model for future dramatists. It is clarity itself and, closely woven, it has the characteristic accents of nature. Read, we feel its gripping logic; spoken by an actor, it tingles with vitality.

For the student there is a fascination in the cohesiveness of these dramas. Ibsen's mind was like a lens; it focussed the refracted, scattered, and broken lights of opinions and theories of his day upon the contracted space of his stage. In a fluid state the ideas that crystallised in his prose series are to be found in his earliest work; there is a remorseless fastening of link to link in the march-like movement of his plays. Their author seems to delight in battering down in Ghosts what he had preached in A Doll's House; The Enemy of the People exalted the individual man, though Ghosts taught that a certain kind of personal liberty is deadly; The Wild Duck, which follows, is another puzzle, for in it the misguided idealist is pilloried for destroying homes by his truth-telling, dangerous tongue; Rosmersholm follows with its portrayal of lonely souls; and

329

the danger of filling old bottles with the fermenting wines of new ideas is set forth; in The Lady from the Sea free-will, the will to love, is lauded, though Rebekka West and Rosmersholm perished because of their exercise of this same will; Hedda Gabler shows the converse of Ellida Wangel's "will to power." Hedda is a creature wholly alive and shocking. Ibsen stuns us again, for if it is healthy to be individual and to lead your own life, in neurasthenic Hedda's case it leads to a catastrophe which wrecks a household. This game of contradiction is continued in The Master-Builder, a most potent exposition of human motives. Solness is sick-brained because of his loveless egoism. Hilda Wangel, the "younger generation," a Hedda Gabler à rebours, that he so feared would come knocking at his door, awakens in him his dead dreams, arouses his slumbering self; curiously enough, if the ordinary standards of success be adduced, he goes to his destruction when he again climbs the dizzy spire. In John Gabriel Borkman the allegory is clearer. Sacrificing love to a base ambition, to "commercialism," Borkman at the close of his great and miserable life discovers that he has committed the one unpardonable offence: he has slain the love-life in the woman he loved, and for the sake of gold. So he is a failure, and, like Peer Gynt, he is ready for the Button-Moulder with his refuse-heap, who lies in wait for all cowardly and incomplete souls. The Epilogue returns to the mountains, the Ibsen

330

symbol of freedom, and there we learn for the last time that love is greater than art, that love is life. And the dead of life awake.

The immorality of these plays is so well concealed that only abnormal moralists detect it. It may be admitted that Ibsen, like Shakespeare, manifests a preference for the man who fails. What is new is the art with which this idea is developed. The Ibsen play begins where other plays end. The form is the "amplified catastrophe" of Sophocles. After marriage the curtain is rung up on the true drama of life, therefore marriage is a theme which constantly preoccupies this modern poet. He regards it from all sides, asking whether "by self-surrender, self-realisation may be achieved." His speech delivered once before a ladies' club at Christiania proves that he is not a champion of latter-day woman's rights. "The women will solve the question of mankind, but they must do so as mothers." Yet Nora Helmer, when she slammed the door of her doll's home, caused an echo in the heart of every intelligent woman in Christendom. It is not necessary now to ask whether a woman would, or should, desert her children; Nora's departure was only the symbol of her liberty, the gesture of a newly awakened individuality. Ibsen did not preach — as innocent persons of both sexes and all anti-Ibsenites believe — that woman should throw overboard her duties; this is an absurd construction. As well argue that the example of Othello must set jealous husbands smothering their wives. A

Doll's House enacted has caused no more evil than Othello. It was the plea for woman as a human being, neither more nor less than man, which the dramatist made. Our withers must have been well wrung, for it aroused a whirlwind of wrath, and henceforth the house-key became the symbol of feminine supremacy. Yet in his lovely drama of pity and resignation, Little Eyolf, the tenderest from his pen, the poet set up a counter-figure to Nora, demonstrating the duties parents owe their children.

Without exaggeration, he may be said to have discovered for the stage the modern woman. No longer the sleek cat of the drawing-room, or the bayadere of luxury, or the wild outlaw of society, the "emancipated" Ibsen woman is the sensible woman, the womanly woman, bearing a not remote resemblance to the old-fashioned woman, who calmly accepts her share of the burdens and responsibilities of life, single or wedded, though she insists on her rights as a human being, and without a touch of the heroic or the supra-sentimental. Ibsen should not be held responsible for the caricatures of womanhood evolved by his disciples. When a woman evades her responsibilities, when she is frivolous or evil, an exponent of the "life-lie" in matrimony, then Ibsen grimly paints her portrait, and we denounce him as cynical for telling the truth. And truth is seldom a welcome guest. But he knows that a fiddle can be mended and a bell not; and in placing his surgeon-like finger on the sorest spot of our social

33²

life, he sounds this bell, and when it rings cracked he coldly announces the fact. But his attitude toward marriage is not without its mystery. In Love's Comedy his hero and heroine part, fearing the inevitable shipwreck in the union of two poetic hearts without the necessary means of a prosaic subsistence. In the later plays, marriage for gain, for home, for anything but love, brings upon its victims the severest consequences; John Gabriel Borkman, Hedda, Dora, Mrs. Alving, Allmers, Rubek, are examples. The idea of man's cruelty to man or woman, or woman's cruelty to woman or man, lashes him into a fury. Then he becomes Ibsen the Berserker.

Therefore let us beware the pitfalls dug by some Ibsen exegetists; the genius of the dramatist is too vast and versatile to be pinned down to a single formula. If you believe that he is dangerous to young people, let it be admitted — but so are Thackeray, Balzac, and Hugo. So is any strong thinker. Ibsen is a powerful dissolvent for an imagination clogged by theories of life, low ideals, and the facile materialism that exalts the letter but slays the spirit. He is a foe to compromise, a hater of the half-way, the roundabout, the weak-willed, above all, a hater of the truckling politician — he is a very Torquemada to politicians. At the best there is ethical grandeur in his conceptions, and if the moral stress is unduly felt, if he tears asunder the veil of our beloved illusions and shows us as we are, it is because of his righteous indignation against the platitudinous hypocrisy

333

of modern life. His unvarying code is: "So to
conduct one's life as to realise oneself." Withal
an artist, not the evangelist of a new gospel, not
the social reformer, not the exponent of science
in the drama. These titles have been thrust
upon him by his overheated admirers. He never
posed as a prophet. He is poet, psychologist,
skald, dramatist, not always a soothsayer. The
artist in him preserved him from the fate of the
didactic Tolstoy. With the Russian he shares the
faculty of emptying souls. Ibsen, who vaguely
recalls Stendhal in his clear-eyed vision and dry
irony, is without a trace of the Frenchman's cynicism or dilettantism. Like all dramatists of the
first rank, the Norwegian has in him much of the
seer, yet he always avoided the pontifical tone; he
may be a sphinx, but he never plays the oracle.
His categorical imperative, however, "All or nothing," does not bear the strain of experience. Life
is simpler, is not to be lived at such an intolerable
tension. The very illusions he seeks to destroy
would be supplanted by others. Man exists because of his illusions. Without the "life-lie" he
would perish in the mire. His illusions are his
heritage from æons of ancestors. The classic view
considered man as the centre of the universe;
that position has been ruthlessly altered by science — we are now only tiny points of consciousness in unthinkable space. Isolated then, true
children of our inconsiderable planet, we have in
us traces of our predecessors. True, one may be
disheartened by the pictures of unheroic mean-

334

ness and petty corruption, the ill-disguised instincts of ape and tiger, in the prose plays, even to the extent of calling them — as did M. Melchior de Vogüé, Flaubert's Bouvard et Pécuchet — a grotesque Iliad of Nihilism. But we need not despair. If Ibsen seemed to say for a period, "Evil, be thou my good," his final words in the Epilogue are those of pity and peace: *Pax vobiscum!*

II

This old man with the head and ·hair of an electrified Schopenhauer and the torso of a giant, his temperament coinciding with his curt, imperious name, left behind him twenty-six plays, one or more in manuscript. A volume of very subjective poems concludes this long list; among the dramas are at least three of heroic proportion and length. Ibsen was born at Skien, Norway, 1828. His forebears were Danish, German, Scotch, and Norwegian. His father, a man of means, failed in business, and at the age of eight the little Henrik had to face poverty. His schooling was of the slightest. He was not much of a classical scholar and soon he was apprenticed to an apothecary at Grimstad, the very name of which evokes a vision of gloominess. He did not prove a success as a druggist, as he spent his spare time reading and caricaturing his neighbours. His verse-making was desultory, his accustomed mien an unhappy combination of Hamlet and Byron; his misanthropy at this period recalls that of the

335

young Schopenhauer. His favourite reading was
poetry and history, and he had a predilection for
sketching and conjuring tricks. It might be
pointed out that here in the raw were the aptitudes
of a future dramatist: poetry, pictures, illusion.
In the year 1850 Ibsen published his first drama,
derived from poring over Sallust and Cicero.
It was a creditable effort of youth, and to the
discerning it promised well for his literary future.
He was gifted, without doubt, and from the first
he sounded the tocsin of revolt. Pessimistic and
rebellious his poems were; he had tasted misery,
his home was an unhappy one — there was little
love in it for him — and his earliest memories were
clustered about the town jail, the hospital, and
the lunatic asylum. These images were no doubt
the cause of his bitter and desperate frame of
mind; grinding poverty, the poverty of a third-
rate provincial town in Norway, was the climax
of his misery. And then, too, the scenery, rugged
and noble, and the climate, depressing for months,
all had their effect upon his sensitive imagination.
From the start, certain conceptions of woman
took root in his mind and reappear in nearly all
his dramas. Catalina's wife, Aurelia, and the
vestal Furia, who are reincarnated in the Dagny
and Hjordis of his Vikings, reappear in A Doll's
House, Hedda Gabler, and at the last in When We
Dead Awake. One is the eternal womanly, the
others the destructive feminine principle, woman
the conqueror. As Catalina is a rebel against
circumstances, so are Maja and the sculptor in

336

the Epilogue of 1899. There is almost a half century of uninterrupted composition during which this group of men and women disport themselves. Brand, a poetic rather than an acting drama, is no exception; Brand and the Sheriff, Agnes and Gerda. These types are cunningly varied, their traits so concealed as to be recognised only after careful study. But the characteristics of each are alike. The monotony of this procedure is redeemed by the unity of conception—Ibsen is the reflective poet, the poet who conceives the idea and then clothes it, therein differing from Shakespeare and Goethe, to whom form and idea are simultaneously born.

In March, 1850, he went to Christiania and entered Heltberg's school as a preparation for the university. His studies were brief. He became involved in a boyish revolutionary outburst — in company with his life-long friend, the good-hearted Björnstjerne Björnson, who helped him many times — and while nothing serious occurred, it caused the young man to effervesce with literary plans and the new ideas of his times. The Warrior's Tomb, his second play, was accepted and actually performed at the Christiania theatre. The author gave up his university dreams and began to earn a rude living by his pen. He embarked in newspaper enterprises which failed. An extremist politically, he soon made a crop of enemies, the wisest crop a strong character can raise; but he often worked on an empty stomach in consequence. The metal of the man showed

337

from the first: endure defeat, but no compromise! He went to Bergen in 1851 and was appointed theatre poet at a small salary; this comprised a travelling stipend. Ibsen saw the Copenhagen and Dresden theatres with excellent results. His eyes were opened to the possibilities of his craft, and on his return he proved a zealous stage manager. He composed, in 1853, St. John's Night, which was played at his theatre, and in 1857 Fru Inger of Oesträtt was written. It is old-fashioned in form, but singularly life-like in characterization and fruitful in situations. The story is semi-historical. In the Lady Inger we see a foreshadowing of his strong, vengeful women. Olaf Liljekrans need not detain us. The Vikings (1858) is a sterling specimen of drama, in which legend and history are artfully blended. The Feast of Solhaug (1857) was very successful in its treatment of the saga, and is comparatively cheerful.

Ibsen left Bergen to take the position of director at the Norwegian Theatre, Christiania. He remained there until 1862, staging all manner of plays, from Shakespeare to Scribe. The value of these years was incalculable in his technical development. A poet born and by self-discipline developed, he was now master of a difficult art, an art that later he never lost, even when, weary of the conventional comedy of manners, he sought to spiritualize the form and give us the psychology of commonplace souls. It may be noted that, despite the violinist Ole Bull's generous support,

338

the new theatre endured only five years. More
than passing stress should be laid upon this forma-
tive period. His experience of these silent years
was bitter, but rich in spiritual recompense.
After some difficulty in securing a paltry pension
from his government, Ibsen was enabled to leave
Norway, which had become a charnel-house to
him since the Danish war with Germany, and with
his young wife he went to Rome. Thenceforth
his was a gypsy career. He lived in Rome, in
Dresden, in Munich, and again in Rome. He
spent his summers in the Austrian Tyrol, at Sor-
rento, and occasionally in his own land. His
was a self-imposed exile, and he did not return to
Christiania to reside permanently until an old, but
famous man. Silent, unsociable, a man of harsh
moods, he was to those who knew him an upright
character, an ideal husband and father. His
married life had no history, a sure sign of happiness, for he was well mated. Yet one feels that, despite his wealth, his renown, existence was for
him a *via dolorosa*. Ever the solitary dreamer,
he wrote a play about every two or three years,
and from the very beginning of his exile the effect in
Norway was like unto the explosion of a bomb-
shell. Not wasting time in answering his critics,
it was nevertheless remarked that each new piece
was a veiled reply to slanderous criticism.
Ghosts was absolutely intended as an answer to
the attacks upon A Doll's House; here is what
Nora would have become if she had been a dutiful
wife, declares Ibsen, in effect; and we see Mrs.

339

Alving in her motherly agonies. The counter-
blast to the criticism of Ghosts was An Enemy
of the People; Dr. Stockman is easily detected
as a partial portrait of Ibsen.

Georg Brandes, to whom the poet owes many
ideas as well as sound criticism, said that early in his
life a lyric Pegasus had been killed under Ibsen
This striking hint of his sacrifice is supplemented
by a letter in which he compared the education
of a poet to that of a dancing bear. The bear is
tied in a brewer's vat and a slow fire is built under
the vat; the wretched animal is then forced to
dance. Life forces the poet to dance by means
quite as painful; he dances and the tears roll
down his cheeks all the while. Ibsen forsook
poetry for prose and — the dividing line never to
be recrossed is clearly indicated between Emperor
and Galilean and The Pillars of Society — he
bestowed upon his country three specimens of
his poetic genius. As Italy fructified the genius
of Goethe, so it touched as with a glowing coal
the lips of the young Northman. Brand, a noble
epic, startled and horrified Norway. In Rome
Ibsen regained his equilibrium. He saw his country and countrymen more sanely, more steadily,
though there is a terrible fund of bitterness in this
dramatic poem. The local politics of Christiania no longer irritated him, and in the hot, beautiful South he dreamed of the North, of his beloved fiords and mountains, of ice and avalanche,
of troll and saga. Luckily for those who have not
mastered Norwegian, C. H. Herford's transla-

340

tion of Brand exists, and, while the translator deplores his sins of omission, it is a work — as are the English versions of the prose plays by William Archer — that gives one an excellent idea of the original. In Brand (1866) Ibsen is at his furthest extremity from compromise. This clergyman sacrifices his mother, his wife, his child, his own life, to a frosty ideal: "All or nothing." He is implacable in his ire against worldliness, in his contempt of churchmen that believe in half-way measures. He perishes on the heights as a voice proclaims, "He is the God of Love." Greatly imaginative, charged with spiritual spleen and wisdom, Brand at once placed Ibsen among the mighty.

He followed it with a new Odyssey of his soul, the amazing Peer Gynt (1867), in which his humour, hitherto a latent quality, his fantasy, bold invention, and the poetic evocation of the faithful, exquisite Solveig, are further testimony to his breadth of resource. Peer Gynt is all that Brand was not: whimsical, worldly, fantastic, weak-willed, not so vicious as perverse; he is very selfish, one who was to himself sufficient, therefore a failure. The will, if it frees, may also kill. It killed the soul of Peer. There are pages of unflagging humour, poetry, and observation; scene dissolves into scene; Peer travels over half the earth, is rich, is successful, is poor; and at the end meets the Button-Moulder, that ironical shadow who tells him what he has become. We hear the Boyg, the spirit of compromise, with its huge, deadly, coiling lengths, gruffly bid Peer to "go around." Facts of life are to be slunk about, never to be faced. Peer comes to harbour in the arms of his deserted Solveig. The resounding sarcasm, the ferociousness of the attack on all the idols of the national cavern, raised a storm in Norway that did not abate for years. Ibsen was again a target for the bolts of critical and public hatred. Peer Gynt is the Scandinavian Faust.

Having purged his soul of this perilous stuff, the poet, in 1873, finished his double drama Emperor and Galilean, not a success dramatically, but a strong, interesting work for the library, though it saw the footlights at Berlin, Leipsic, and Christiania. The apostate Emperor Julian is the protagonist. We discern Ibsen the mystic philosopher longing for his Third Kingdom.

After a silence of four years The Pillars of Society appeared. Like its predecessor in the same *genre*, The Young Men's League, it is a prose drama, a study of manners, and a scathing arraignment of civic dishonesty. All the rancour of its author against the bourgeois hypocrisy of his countrymen comes to the surface; as in The Young Men's League the vacillating nature of the shallow politician is laid bare. It seems a trifle banal now, though the canvas is large, the figures animated. One recalls Augier without his Gallic *esprit*, rather than the later Ibsen. A Doll's House was once a household word, as was Ghosts (1881). There is no need now to retell the story of either play. Ghosts, in particular, has an antique quality, the *dénouement* leaves us shivering. It may be set down as the strongest play of the nineteenth century, and also the most harrowing. Its intensity borders on the hallucinatory. We involuntarily recall the last act of Tristan and Isolde or the final movement of Tschaikowsky's Pathetic symphony. It is the shrill discord between the mediocre creatures involved and the ghastly punishment meted out to the innocent that agitates and depresses us. Here are human souls illuminated as if by a lightning flash; we long for the anticipated thunder. It does not sound. The drama ends in silence — one of those pauses (Ibsen employs the pause as does a musical composer) which leaves the spectator unstrung. The helpless sense of hovering about the edge of a bottomless gulf is engendered by this play. No man could have written it but Ibsen, and we hope that no man will ever attempt a parallel performance, for such art modulates across the borderland of the pathologic.

The Wild Duck (1884) followed An Enemy of the People (1882). It is the most puzzling of the prose dramas except The Master-Builder, for in it Ibsen deliberately mocks himself and his ideals. It is, nevertheless, a profoundly human and moving work. Gina Ekdal, the wholesome, sensible wife of Ekdal, the charlatan photographer — a *revenant* of Peer Gynt — has been called a feminine Sancho Panza. Gregers Werle, the meddlesome truth-teller; Relling — a sardonic incarnation of the author — who believes in feed-

343

ing humanity on the "life-lie" to maintain its courage; the tiny Hedwig, sweetest and freshest of Ibsen's girls — these form a memorable *ensemble*. And how the piece plays! Humour and pathos alternate, while the symbol is not so remote that an average audience need miss its meaning. The end is cruel. Ibsen is often cruel, with the passionless indifference of the serene Buddha. But he is ever logical. Nora must leave her husband's house — a "happy ending" would be ridiculous — and Hedwig must be sacrificed instead of the wild duck, or her fool of a father. There is a battalion of minor characters in the Ibsen plays who recall Dickens by their grotesque, sympathetic physiognomies. To deny this dramatist humour is to miss a third of his qualities. His is not the ventripotent humour of Rabelais or Cervantes; it seldom leaves us without the feeling that the poet is slyly laughing at us, not with us, though in the early comedies there are many broad and telling strokes.

Rosmersholm (1886) is a study of two temperaments. Rebekka West is another malevolent portrait in his gallery of dangerous and antipathetic women. She ruins Rosmersholm, ruins herself, because she does not discover this true self until too late. The play illustrates the extraordinary technique of the master. It seems to have been written backward; until the third act we are not aware that the peaceful home of the Rosmersholms is the battle-field of a malignant soul. The Lady from the Sea (1888) illustrates

344

the thesis that love must be free. The allegory is
rather strained and in performance the play lacks
poetic glamour. Hedda Gabler (1890) is a ·
masterpiece. A more selfish, vicious, cold nature
than Hedda's never stepped from the page of a
Russian novel — Becky Sharp and Madame
Marneffe are lovable persons in comparison.
She is not in the slightest degree like the stage
"adventuress," but is a magnificent example of
egoism magnificently delineated and is the true
sister in fiction of Julien Sorel. That she is dramatically worth the while is beside the question.
Her ending by a pistol shot is justice itself; alive
she fascinates as does some exotic reptile. She
is representative of her species, the loveless
woman, the petty hater, a Lady Macbeth reversed. Ibsen has studied her with the same
care and curiosity he bestowed upon the homely
Gina Ekdal.

His Master-Builder (1892) is the beginning
of the last cycle. A true interior drama, we enter
here into the region of the symbolical. With
Ibsen the symbol is always an image, never an abstraction, a state of sensibility, not a formula, and
the student may winnow many examples from
The Pretenders (1864), with its "kingship" idea, ·
to the Epilogue. Solness stands on the heights
only to perish, but in the full possession of his
soul. Hilda Wangel is one of the most perplexing characters to realise in the modern theatre.
She, with her cruelty and loveliness of perfect
youth, is the work of a sorcerer who holds us spell-

345

bound while the souls he has created by his black art slowly betray themselves. It may be said that all this is not the art of the normal theatre. Very true. It more nearly resembles a dramatic confessional with a hidden auditory bewitched into listening to secrets never suspected of the humanity that hedges us about in street or home. Ibsen is clairvoyant. He takes the most familiar material and holds it in the light of his imagination; straightway we see a new world, a northern dance of death, like the ferocious pictures of his fellow-countryman, the painter Edvard Munch.

Little Eyolf (1894) is fairly plain reading, with some fine overtones of suffering and self-abnegation. Its lesson is wholly satisfying. John Gabriel Borkman (1896), written at an age when most poets show declining power, is another monument to the vigour and genius of Ibsen. The story winds about the shattered career of a financier. There is a secondary plot, in which the parental curses come home to roost — the son, carefully reared to wipe away the stain from his father's name, prefers Paris and a rollicking life. The desolation under this roof-tree is almost epical: two sisters in deadly antagonism, a blasted man, the old wolf, whose footfalls in the chamber above become absolutely sinister as the play progresses, are made to face the hard logic of their misspent lives. The doctrine of compensation has never had such an exponent as Ibsen.

In the last of his published plays, When We

346

Dead Awake (1899), we find earlier and familiar
themes developed at moments with contrapuntal
mastery. Rubek, the sculptor, has aroused a
love that he never dared to face. He married the
wrong woman. His early dream, the inspiration
of his master work, he has lost. His art withers.
And when he meets his Irene, her mind is full of
wandering ghosts. To the heights, to the same
peaks that Brand climbed, they both must mount,
and there they are destroyed, as was Brand, by
an avalanche. Eros is the triumphant god of the
aged magician.

III

It must be apparent to those who have not
read or seen the Ibsen plays that, despite this
huddled and foreshortened account, they are in
essence quite different from what has been re-
ported of them. Idealistic, symbolistic, moral,
and ennobling, the Ibsen drama was so vilified
by malice and ignorance that its very name was
a portent of evil. Mad or wicked Ibsen is not.
His scheme of life and morals is often oblique
and paradoxical, his interpretation of truths so
elliptical that we are confused. But he is essentially sound. He believes in the moral continuity of the universe. His astounding energy is
a moral energy. Salvation by good works is his
burden. The chief thing is to be strong: your
faith. He despises the weak, not the strong sinner. His Supermen are the bankrupts of ro-

347

mantic heroism. His strong man is frequently
wrong-headed; but the weakling works the real
mischief. Never admit you are beaten. Begin
at the bottom twenty times, and when the top is
achieved die, or else look for loftier peaks to
climb. Ibsen exalts strength. His "ice-church"
is chilly; the lungs drink in with difficulty the
buffeting breezes on his heights; yet how bra-
cing, how inspiring, is this austere place of worship. Bad as is mankind, Ibsen, who was ever
in advance of his contemporaries, believed in its
possibility for betterment. Here the optimist
speaks. Brand's spiritual pride is his downfall;
nevertheless, Ibsen, an aristocratic thinker, believes that of pride one cannot have too much.
He recognised the selfish and hollow foundation
of all "humanitarian" movements. He is a
sign-post for the twentieth century when the
aristocratic of spirit must enter into combat with
the herd instinct of a depressing socialism. His
influence has been tremendous. His plays teem
with the general ideas of his century. His chief
value lies in the beauty of his art; his is the rare
case of the master-singer rounding a long life with
his master works. He brought to the theatre new
ideas; he changed forever the dramatic map of
Europe; he originated a new method of surprising life, capturing it and forcing it to give up a
moiety of its mystery for the uses of a difficult and
recondite art. He fashioned character anew. And
he pushed resolutely into the mist that surrounded
the human soul, his Diogenes lantern glimmering,

his brave, lonely heart undaunted by the silence and the solitude. His message? Who shall say? He asks questions, and, patterning after nature, he seldom answers them. When his ideas sicken and die — he asserted that the greatest truth outlives its usefulness in time, and it may not be denied that his drama is a dissolvent; already the early plays are in historical twilight and the woman question of his day is for us something quite different — his art will endure. Henrik Ibsen was a man of heroic fortitude. His plays are a bold and stimulating spectacle for the spirit. Should we ask more of a dramatic poet?

X

MAX STIRNER

I

In 1888 John Henry Mackay, the Scottish-German poet, while at the British Museum reading Lange's History of Materialism, encountered the name of Max Stirner and a brief criticism of his forgotten book, Der Einzige und sein Eigenthum (The Only One and His Property; in French translated L'Unique et sa Propriété, and in the first English translation more aptly and euphoniously entitled The Ego and His Own). His curiosity excited, Mackay, who is an anarchist, procured after some difficulty a copy of the work, and so greatly was he stirred that for ten years he gave himself up to the study of Stirner and his teachings, and after incredible painstaking published in 1898 the story of his life. (Max Stirner: Sein Leben und sein Werk: John Henry Mackay.) To Mackay's labours we owe all we know of a man who was as absolutely swallowed up by the years as if he had never existed. But some advanced spirits had read Stirner's book, the most revolutionary ever written, and had felt

350

its influence. Let us name two: Henrik Ibsen and Frederick Nietzsche. Though the name of Stirner is not quoted by Nietzsche, he nevertheless recommended Stirner to a favourite pupil of his, Professor Baumgartner at Basel University. This was in 1874.

One hot August afternoon in the year 1896 at Bayreuth, I was standing in the Marktplatz when a member of the Wagner Theatre pointed out to me a house opposite, at the corner of the Maximilianstrasse, and said: "Do you see that house with the double gables? A man was born there whose name will be green when Jean Paul and Richard Wagner are forgotten." It was too large a draught upon my credulity, so I asked the name. "Max Stirner," he replied. "The crazy Hegelian," I retorted. "You have read him, then?" "No; but you haven't read Nordau." It was true. All fire and flame at that time for Nietzsche, I did not realise that the poet and rhapsodist had forerunners. My friend sniffed at Nietzsche's name; Nietzsche for him was an aristocrat, not an Individualist — in reality, a lyric expounder of Bismarck's gospel of blood and iron. Wagner's adversary would, with Renan, place mankind under the yoke of a more exacting tyranny than Socialism, the tyranny of Culture, of the Superman. Ibsen, who had studied both Kierkegaard and Stirner — witness Brand and Peer Gynt — Ibsen was much nearer to the champion of the Ego than Nietzsche. Yet it is the dithyrambic author of Zarathustra who is responsible,

351

with Mackay, for the recrudescence of Stirner's teachings.

Nietzsche is the poet of the doctrine, Stirner its prophet, or, if you will, its philosopher. Later I secured the book, which had been reprinted in the cheap edition of Reclam (1882). It seemed colourless, or rather gray, set against the glory and gorgeous rhetoric of Nietzsche. I could not see then what I saw a decade later — that Nietzsche had used Stirner as a springboard, as a point of departure, and that the Individual had vastly different meanings to those diverse temperaments. But Stirner displayed the courage of an explorer in search of the north pole of the Ego.

The man whose theories would make a *tabula rasa* of civilisation, was born at Bayreuth, October 25, 1806, and died at Berlin June 25, 1856. His right name was Johann Caspar Schmidt, Max Stirner being a nickname bestowed upon him by his lively comrades in Berlin because of his very high and massive forehead. His father was a maker of wind instruments, who died six months after his son's birth. His mother remarried, and his stepfather proved a kind protector. Nothing of external importance occurred in the life of Max Stirner that might place him apart from his fellow-students. He was very industrious over his books at Bayreuth, and when he became a student at the Berlin University he attended the lectures regularly, preparing himself for a teacher's profession. He mastered the classics, modern philosophy, and modern lan-

352

guages. But he did not win a doctor's degree; just before examinations his mother became ill with a mental malady (a fact his critics have noted) and the son dutifully gave up everything so as to be near her. After her death he married a girl who died within a short time. Later, in 1843, his second wife was Marie Dähnhardt, a very "advanced" young woman, who came from Schwerin to Berlin to lead a "free" life. She met Stirner in the Hippel circle, at a Weinstube in the Friedrichstrasse, where radical young thinkers gathered: Bruno Bauer, Feuerbach, Karl Marx, Moses Hess, Jordan, Julius Faucher, and other stormy insurgents. She had, it is said, about 10,000 thalers. She was married with the ring wrenched from a witness's purse — her bridegroom had forgotten to provide one. He was not a practical man; if he had been he would hardly have written The Ego and His Own.

It was finished between the years 1843 and 1845; the latter date it was published. It created a stir, though the censor did not seriously interfere with it; its attacks on the prevailing government were veiled. In Germany rebellion on the psychic plane expresses itself in metaphysics; in Poland and Russia music is the safer medium. Feuerbach, Hess, and Szeliga answered Stirner's terrible arraignment of society, but men's thoughts were interested elsewhere, and with the revolt of 1848 Stirner was quite effaced. He had taught for five years in a fashionable school for young ladies; he had written for several periodicals, and trans-

353

lated extracts from the works of Say and Adam Smith.

After his book appeared, his relations with his wife became uneasy. Late in 1846 or early in 1847 she left him and went to London, where she supported herself by writing; later she inherited a small sum from a sister, visited Australia, married a labourer there, and became a washerwoman. In 1897 Mackay wrote to her in London, asking her for some facts in the life of her husband. She replied tartly that she was not willing to revive her past; that her husband had been too much of an egotist to keep friends, and was "very sly." This was all he could extort from the woman, who evidently had never understood her husband and execrated his memory, probably because her little fortune was swallowed up by their mutual improvidence. Another appeal only elicited the answer that "Mary Smith is preparing for death" — she had become a Roman Catholic. It is the irony of things in general that his book is dedicated to "My Sweetheart, Marie Dähnhardt."

Stirner, after being deserted, led a precarious existence. The old jolly crowd at Hippel's seldom saw him. He was in prison twice for debt — free Prussia — and often lacked bread. He, the exponent of Egoism, of philosophic anarchy, starved because of his pride. He was in all matters save his theories a moderate man, eating and drinking temperately, living frugally. Unassuming in manners, he could hold his own in debate — and Hippel's appears to have been a rude debating society — yet one who avoided life rather than mastered it. He was of medium height, ruddy, and his eyes deep-blue. His hands were white, slender, "aristocratic," writes Mackay. Certainly not the figure of a stalwart shatterer of conventions, not the ideal iconoclast; above all, without a touch of the melodrama of communistic anarchy, with its black flags, its propaganda by force, its idolatry of assassinations, bomb-throwing, killing of fat, harmless policemen, and its sentimental gabble about Fraternity. Stirner hated the word Equality; he knew it was a lie, knew that all men are born unequal, as no two grains of sand on earth ever are or ever will be alike. He was a solitary. And thus he died at the age of fifty. A few of his former companions heard of his neglected condition and buried him. Nearly a half century later Mackay, with the co-operation of Hans von Bülow, affixed a commemorative tablet on the house where he last lived, Phillipstrasse 19, Berlin, and alone Mackay placed a slab to mark his grave in the Sophienkirchhof.

It is to the poet of the Letzte Erkentniss, with its stirring line, "Doch bin ich mein," that I owe the above scanty details of the most thoroughgoing Nihilist who ever penned his disbelief in religion, humanity, society, the family. He rejects them all. We have no genuine portrait of this insurrectionist — he preferred personal insurrection to general revolution; the latter, he asserted, brought in its train either Socialism or a tyrant —

355

except a sketch hastily made by Friedrich Engels, the revolutionist, for Mackay. It is not reassuring. Stirner looks like an old-fashioned German and timid pedagogue, high coat-collar, spectacles, clean-shaven face, and all. This valiant enemy of the State, of socialism, was, perhaps, only brave on paper. But his icy, relentless, epigrammatic style is in the end more gripping than the spectacular, volcanic, whirling utterances of Nietzsche. Nietzsche lives in an ivory tower and is an aristocrat. Into Stirner's land all are welcome. That is, if men have the will to rebel, and if they despise the sentimentality of mob rule. The Ego and His Own is the most drastic. criticism of socialism thus far presented.

II

For those who love to think of the visible universe as a cosy corner of God's footstool, there is something bleak and terrifying in the isolated position of man since science has postulated him as an infinitesimal bubble on an unimportant planet. The soul shrinks as our conception of outer space widens. Thomas Hardy describes the sensation as "ghastly." There is said to be no purpose, no design in all the gleaming phantasmagoria revealed by the astronomer's glass; while on our globe we are a brother to lizards, bacteria furnish our motor force, and our brain is but a subtly fashioned mirror, composed of neuronic filaments, a sort of "dark room" in which is somehow pictured

356

the life without. Well, we admit, for the sake of the argument, that we banish God from the firmament, substituting a superior mechanism; we admit our descent from star-dust and apes, we know that we have no free will, because man, like the unicellular organisms, "gives to every stimulus without an inevitable response." That, of course, settles all moral obligations. But we had hoped, we of the old sentimental brigade, that all things being thus adjusted we could live with our fellow man in (comparative) peace, cheating him only in a legitimate business way, and loving our neighbour better than ourselves (in public). Ibsen had jostled our self-satisfaction sadly, but some obliging critic had discovered his formula — a pessimistic decadent — and with bare verbal bones we worried the old white-haired mastiff of Norway. Only a decadent! It is an easy word to speak and it means nothing. With Nietzsche the case was simpler. We couldn't read him because he was a madman; but he at least was an aristocrat who held the *bourgeois* in contempt, and he also held a brief for culture. Ah! when we are young we are altruists; as Thackeray says, "Youths go to balls; men go to dinners."

But along comes this dreadful Stirner, who cries out: Hypocrites all of you. You are not altruists, but selfish persons, who, self-illuded, believe yourselves to be disinterested. Be Egoists. Confess the truth in the secrecy of your mean, little souls. We are all Egotists. Be

357

Egoists. There is no truth but my truth. No world but my world. I am I. And then Stirner waves away God, State, society, the family, morals, mankind, leaving only the "hateful" Ego. The cosmos is frosty and inhuman, and old Mother Earth no longer offers us her bosom as a reclining-place. Stirner has so decreed it. We are suspended between heaven and earth, like Mahomet's coffin, hermetically sealed in Self. Instead of ".smiting the chord of self," we must reorchestrate the chord that it may give out richer music. (Perhaps the Higher Egoism which often leads to low selfishness.)

Nevertheless, there is an honesty in the words of Max Stirner. We are weary of the crying in the market-place, "Lo! Christ is risen," only to find an old nostrum tricked out in socialistic phrases; and fine phrases make fine feathers for these gentlemen who offer the millennium in one hand and perfect peace in the other. Stirner is the frankest thinker of his century. He does not soften his propositions, harsh ones for most of us, with promises, but pursues his thought with ferocious logic to its covert. There is no such hybrid with him as Christian Socialism, no dodging issues. He is a Teutonic Childe Roland who to the dark tower comes, but instead of blowing his horn — as Nietzsche did — he blows up the tower itself. Such an iconoclast has never before put pen to paper. He is so sincere in his scorn of all we hold dear that he is refreshing. Nietzsche's flashing epigrammatic blade often

358

snaps after it is fleshed; the grim, cruel Stirner, after he makes a jab at his opponent, twists the steel in the wound. Having no mercy for himself, he has no mercy for others. He is never a hypocrite. He erects no altars to known or unknown gods. Humanity, he says, has become the Moloch to-day to which everything is sacrificed. Humanity — that is, the State, perhaps, even the socialistic state (the most terrible yoke of all for the individual soul). This assumed love of humanity, this sacrifice of our own personality, are the blights of modern life. The Ego has too long been suppressed by ideas, sacred ideas of religion, state, family, law, morals. The conceptual question, "What is Man?" must be changed to "Who is Man?" I am the owner of my might, and I am so when I know myself as *unique*.

Stirner is not a communist — so long confounded with anarchs — he does not believe in force. That element came into the world with the advent of Bakounine and Russian nihilism. Stirner would replace society by groups; property would be held, money would be a circulating medium; the present compulsory system would be voluntary instead of involuntary. Unlike his great contemporary, Joseph Proudhon, Stirner is not a constructive philosopher. Indeed, he is no philosopher. A moralist (or immoralist), an *Ethiker*, his book is a defence of Egoism, of the submerged rights of the Ego, and in these piping times of peace and fraternal humbug, when every nation, every man embraces his neighbour preparatory to disembowelling him in commerce or war, Max Stirner's words are like a trumpet-blast. And many Jericho-built walls go down before these ringing tones. His doctrine is the Fourth Dimension of ethics. That his book will be more dangerous than a million bombs, if misapprehended, is no reason why it should not be read. Its author can no more be held responsible for its misreading than the orthodox faiths for their backsliders. Nietzsche has been wofully misunderstood; Nietzsche, the despiser of mob rule, has been acclaimed a very Attila — instead of which he is a culture-philosopher, one who insists that reform must be first spiritual. Individualism for him means only an end to culture. Stirner is not a metaphysician; he is too much realist. He is really a topsy-turvy Hegelian, a political pyrrhonist. His Ego is his Categorical Imperative. And if the Individual loses his value, what is his *raison d'être* for existence? What shall it profit a man if he gains the whole world but loses his own Ego? Make your value felt, cries Stirner.. The minority may occasionally err, but the majority is always in the wrong. Egoism must not be misinterpreted as petty selfishness or as an excuse to do wrong. Life will be ennobled and sweeter if we respect ourselves. "There is no sinner and no sinful egoism. . . . Do not call men sinful; and *they are not*." Freedom is not a goal. "Free — from what? Oh! what is there that cannot be shaken off? The yoke of serfdom, of sovereignty, of aristocracy and princes,

360

the dominion of the desires and passions; yes, even the dominion of one's own will, of self-will, for the completest self-denial is nothing but freedom — freedom, to wit, from self-determination, from one's own self." This has an ascetic tang, and indicates that to compass our complete Ego the road travelled will be as thorny as any saint's of old. Where does Woman come into this scheme? There is no Woman, only a human Ego. Humanity is a convenient fiction to harry the individualist. So, society, family are the clamps that compress the soul of woman. If woman is to be free she must first be an individual, an Ego. In America, to talk of female suffrage is to propound the paradox of the masters attacking their slaves; yet female suffrage might prove a good thing — it might demonstrate the *reductio ad absurdum* of the administration of the present ballot system.

Our wail over our neighbour's soul is simply the wail of a busybody. Mind your own business! is the pregnant device of the new Egoism. Puritanism is not morality, but a psychic disorder.

Stirner, in his way, teaches that the Kingdom of God is within you. That man will ever be sufficiently perfected to become his own master is a dreamer's dream. Yet let us dream it. At least by that road we make for righteousness. But let us drop all cant about brotherly love and self-sacrifice. Let us love ourselves (respect our Ego), that we may learn to respect our brother; self-sacrifice means doing something that we be-

361

lieve to be good for our souls, therefore *egotism*
—the higher *egotism*, withal *egotism*. As for
going to the people — the Russian phrase — let
the people forget themselves as a collective body,
tribe, or group, and each man and woman develop
his or her Ego. In Russia "going to the people"
may have been sincere — in America it is a trick
to catch, not souls, but votes.

"The time is not far distant when it will be
impossible for any proud, free, independent
spirit to call himself a socialist, since he would be
classed with those wretched toadies and worshippers of success who even now lie on their knees
before every workingman and lick his hands simply
because he is a workingman."

John Henry Mackay spoke these words in a
book of his. Did not Campanella, in an unforgettable sonnet, sing, "The people is a beast of
muddy brain that knows not its own strength.
. . . With its own hands it ties and gags itself"?

III

The Ego and His Own is divided into two
parts: first, The Man; second, I. Its motto
should be, "I find no sweeter fat than sticks to
my own bones." But Walt Whitman's pronouncement had not been made, and Stirner was
forced to fall back on Goethe — Goethe, the
grand Immoralist of his epoch, wise and wicked
Goethe, from whom flows all that is modern. "I
place my all on Nothing" ("Ich hab' Mein Sach'

362

auf Nichts gestellt," in the joyous poem Vanitas! Vanitatum Vanitas!) is Stirner's keynote to
his Egoistic symphony. The hateful I, as Pascal
called it, caused Zola, a solid egotist himself, to assert
that the English were the most egotistic of races
because their I in their tongue was but a single
letter, while the French employed two, and not
capitalised unless beginning a sentence. Stirner
must have admired the English, as his I was the
sole counter in his philosophy. His Ego and not
the family is the unit of the social life. In antique times, when men were really the young,
not the ancient, it was a world of reality. Men
enjoyed the material. With Christianity came
the rule of the spirit; ideas were become sacred,
with the concepts of God, Goodness, Sin, Salvation. After Rousseau and the French Revolution humanity was enthroned, and the State
became our oppressor. Our first enemies are
our parents, our educators. It follows, then,
that the only criterion of life is my Ego. Without my Ego I could not apprehend existence.
Altruism is a pretty disguise for egotism. No
one is or can be disinterested. He gives up one
thing for another because the other seems better,
nobler to him. Egotism! The ascetic renounces
the pleasures of life because in his eyes renunciation is nobler than enjoyment. Egotism again!
"You are to benefit yourself, and you are not to
seek your benefit," cries Stirner. Explain the
paradox! The one sure thing of life is the Ego.
Therefore, "I am not you, but I'll use you if you

363

are agreeable to me." Not to God, not to man, must be given the glory. "I'll keep the glory myself." What is Humanity but an abstraction? I am Humanity. Therefore the State is a monster that devours its children. It must not dictate to me. "The State and I are enemies." The State is a spook. A spook, too, is freedom. What is freedom? Who is free? The world belongs to all, but *all* are *I*. I alone am individual proprietor.

Property is conditioned by might. What I have is mine. "Whoever knows how to take, to defend, the thing, to him belongs property." Stirner would have held that property was not only nine but ten points of the law. This is Pragmatism with a vengeance. He repudiates all laws; repudiates competition, for persons are not the subject of competition, but "things" are; therefore if you are without "things" how can you compete? Persons are free, not "things." The world, therefore, is not "free." Socialism is but a further screwing up of the State machine to limit the individual. Socialism is a new god, a new abstraction to tyrannise over the Ego. And remember that Stirner is not speaking of the metaphysical Ego of Hegel, Fichte, Schelling, but of your I, my I, the political, the social I, the economic I of every man and woman. Stirner spun no metaphysical cobwebs. He reared no lofty cloud palaces. He did not bring from Asia its pessimism, as did Schopenhauer; nor deny reality, as did Berkeley. He was a foe to general

364

ideas. He was an implacable realist. Yet while he denies the existence of an Absolute, of a Deity, State, Categorical Imperative, he nevertheless had not shaken himself free from Hegelianism (he is Extreme Left as a Hegelian), for he erected his I as an Absolute, though only dealing with it in its relations to society. Now, nature abhors an absolute. Everything is relative. So we shall see presently that with Stirner, too, his I is not so independent as he imagines.

He says "crimes spring from fixed ideas." The Church, State, the Family, Morals, are fixed ideas. "Atheists are pious people." They reject one fiction only to cling to many old ones. Liberty for the people is not my liberty. Socrates was a fool in that he conceded to the Athenians the right to condemn him. Proudhon said (rather, Brisson before him), "Property is theft." Theft from whom? From society? But society is not the sole proprietor. Pauperism is the valuelessness of Me. The State and pauperism are the same. Communism, Socialism abolish private property and push us back into Collectivism. The individual is enslaved by the machinery of the State or by socialism. Your Ego is not free if you allow your vices or virtues to enslave it. The intellect has too long ruled, says Stirner; it is the will (not Schopenhauer's Will to Live, or Nietzsche's Will to Power, but the sum of our activity expressed by an act of volition; old-fashioned will, in a word) to exercise itself to the utmost. Nothing compulsory, all voluntary. Do what you will.

EGOISTS

Fay ce que vouldras, as Rabelais has it in his Abbey of Thélème. Not "Know thyself," but get the value out of yourself. Make your value felt. The poor are to blame for the rich. Our art to-day is the only art possible, and therefore real at the time. We are at every moment all we can be. There is no such thing as sin. It is an invention to keep imprisoned the will of our Ego. And as mankind is forced to believe theoretically in the evil of sin, yet commit it in its daily life, hypocrisy and crime are engendered. If the concept of sin had never been used as a club over the weak-minded, there would be no sinners — *i.e.,* wicked people. The individual is himself the world's history. The world is my picture. There is no other Ego but mine. Louis XIV. said, "*L'Etat, c'est moi*"; I say, "*l' Univers, c'est moi.*" John Stuart Mill wrote in his famous essay on liberty that "Society has now got the better of the individual."

Rousseau is to blame for the "Social Contract" and the "Equality" nonsense that has poisoned more than one nation's political ideas. The minority is always in the right, declared Ibsen, as opposed to Comte's "Submission is the base of perfection." "Liberty means responsibility. That is why most men dread it" (Bernard Shaw). "Nature does not seem to have made man for independence" (Vauvenargues). "What can give a man liberty? Will, his own will, and it gives power, which is better than liberty" (Turgenev). To have the will to be responsible for

366

one's self, advises Nietzsche. "I am what I am"
(Brand). "To thyself be sufficient" (Peer
Gynt). Both men failed, for their freedom kills.
To thine own self be true. God is within you.
Best of all is Lord Acton's dictum that "Liberty
is not a means to a higher political end. It is
of itself the highest political end." To will is
to have to will (Ibsen). My truth is the truth
(Stirner). Mortal has made the immortal, says
the Rig Veda: Nothing is greater than I (Bha
gavat Gita). I am that I am (the Avesta, also
Exodus). Taine wrote, "Nature is in reality a
tapestry of which we see the reverse side. This
is why we try to turn it." Hierarchy, oligarchy,
both forms submerge the Ego. J. S. Mill
demanded: "How can great minds be produced
in a country where the test of a great mind is agree-
ing in the opinions of small minds?" Bakounine in his fragmentary essay on God and the
State feared the domination of science quite as
much as an autocracy. "Politics is the madness
of the many for the gain of the few," Pope asserted.
Read Spinoza, The Citizen and the State (Tracta-
tus Theologico-Politicus). Or Oscar Wilde's
epigram: "Charity creates a multitude of sins."
"I am not poor enough to give alms," says Nietzsche. But Max Beerbohm has wittily said — and
his words contain as much wisdom as wit — that
"If he would have his ideas realised, the Socialist
must first kill the Snob."

Science tells us that our *I* is really a *We;* a
colony of cells, an orchestra of inherited instincts.

367

We have not even free will, or at least only in
a limited sense. We are an instrument played
upon by our heredity and our environment. The
cell, then, is the unit, not the Ego. Very well,
Stirner would exclaim (if he had lived after Darwin
and 1859), the cell is my cell, not yours! Away
with other cells! But such an autonomous gospel
is surely a phantasm. Stirner saw a ghost. He,
too, in his proud Individualism was an aristocrat.
No man may separate himself from the tradition
of his race unless to incur the penalty of a sterile
isolation. The solitary is the abnormal man.
Man is gregarious. Man is a political animal.
Even Stirner recognises that man is not man
without society.

In practice he would not have agreed with
Havelock Ellis that "all the art of living lies in
the fine mingling of letting go and holding on."
Stirner, sentimental, henpecked, myopic Berlin
professor, was too actively engaged in wholesale
criticism — that is, destruction of society, with
all its props and standards, its hidden selfishness
and heartlessness — to bother with theories of
reconstruction. His disciples have remedied the
omission. In the United States, for example,
Benjamin R. Tucker, a follower of Josiah War-
ren, teaches a practical and philosophical form
of Individualism. He is an Anarch who believes
in passive resistance. Stirner speaks, though
vaguely, of a Union of Egoists, a Verein, where all
would rule all, where man, through self-mastery,
would be his own master. ("In those days there

368

was no king in Israel; every man did that which was right in his own eyes.") Indeed, his notions as to Property and Money — "it will always be money" — sound suspiciously like those of our "captains of industry." Might conquers Right. He has brought to bear the most blazing light-rays upon the shifts and evasions of those who decry Egoism, who are what he calls "involuntary," not voluntary, egotists. Their motives are shown to the bone. Your Sir Willoughby Patternes are not real Egoists, but only half-hearted, selfish weaklings. The true egotist is the altruist, says Stirner; yet Leibnitz was right; so was Dr. Pangloss. This is the best of possible worlds. Any other is not conceivable for man, who is at the top of his zoological series. (Though Quinton has made the statement that birds followed the mammal.) We are all "spectres of the dust," and to live on an overcrowded planet we must follow the advice of the Boyg: "Go roundabout!" Compromise is the only sane attitude. The world is not, will never be, to the strong of arm or spirit, as Nietzsche believes. The race is to the mediocre. The survival of the fittest means survival of the weakest. Society shields and upholds the feeble. Mediocrity rules, let Carlyle or Nietzsche thunder to the contrary. It was the perception of these facts that drove Stirner to formulate his theories in The Ego and His Own. He was poor, a failure, and despised by his wife. He lived under a dull, brutal régime. The Individual was naught, the

369

State all. His book was his great revenge. It was the efflorescence of his Ego. It was his romance, his dream of an ideal world, his Platonic republic. Philosophy is more a matter of man's temperament than some suppose. And philosophers often live by opposites. Schopenhauer preached asceticism, but hardly led an ascetic life; Nietzsche's injunctions to become Immoralists and Supermen were but the buttressing up of a will diseased, by the needs of a man who suffered his life long from morbid sensibility. James Walker's suggestion that "We will not allow the world to wait for the Superman. We are the Supermen," is a convincing criticism of Nietzscheism. I am Unique. Never again will this aggregation of atoms stand on earth. Therefore I must be free. I will myself free. (It is spiritual liberty that only counts.) But my I must not be of the kind described by the madhouse doctor in Peer Gynt: "Each one shuts himself up in the barrel of self. In the self-fermentation he dives to the bottom; with the self-bung he seals it hermetically." The increased self-responsibility of life in an Egoist Union would prevent the world from ever entering into such ideal anarchy (an-arch, *i.e.*, without government). There is too much of renunciation in the absolute freedom of the will — that is its final, if paradoxical, implication — for mankind. Our Utopias are secretly based on Chance. Deny Chance in our existence and life would be without salt. Man is not a perfectible animal; not on this side of eternity.

37o

He fears the new and therefore clings to his old beliefs. To each his own chimera. He has not grown mentally or physically since the Sumerians — or a million years before the Sumerians. The squirrel in the revolving cage thinks it is progressing; Man is in a revolving cage. He goes round but he does not progress. Man is not a logical animal. He is governed by his emotions, his affective life. He lives by his illusions. His brains are an accident, possibly from overnutrition as De Gourmont has declared. To fancy him capable of existing in a community where all will be selfgoverned is a poet's vision. That way the millennium lies, or the High Noon of Nietzsche. And would the world be happier if it ever did attain this condition?

The English translation of The Ego and His Own, by Stephen T. Byington, is admirable; it is that of a philologist and a versatile scholar. Stirner's form is open to criticism. It is vermicular. His thought is sometimes confused; he sees so many sides of his theme, embroiders it with so many variations, that he repeats himself. He has neither the crystalline brilliance nor the poetic glamour of Nietzsche. But he left behind him a veritable breviary of destruction, a striking and dangerous book. It is dangerous in every sense of the word — to socialism, to politicians, to hypocrisy. It asserts the dignity of the Individual, not his debasement.

"Is it not the chief disgrace in the world not to be a unit; to be reckoned one character; not

371

to yield that peculiar fruit which each man was created to bear, but to be reckoned in the gross, in the hundred of thousands, of the party, of the section to which we belong, and our opinion predicted geographically as the North or the South?"

Herbert Spencer did not write these words, nor Max Stirner. Ralph Waldo Emerson wrote them.